RUMORS
OF MY DEMISE

RUMORS
OF MY DEMISE

EVAN DANDO
WITH JIM RULAND

GALLERY BOOKS
NEW YORK AMSTERDAM/ANTWERP LONDON
TORONTO SYDNEY/MELBOURNE NEW DELHI

G

Gallery Books
An Imprint of Simon & Schuster, LLC
1230 Avenue of the Americas
New York, NY 10020

For more than 100 years, Simon & Schuster has championed authors and the stories they create. By respecting the copyright of an author's intellectual property, you enable Simon & Schuster and the author to continue publishing exceptional books for years to come. We thank you for supporting the author's copyright by purchasing an authorized edition of this book.

No amount of this book may be reproduced or stored in any format, nor may it be uploaded to any website, database, language-learning model, or other repository, retrieval, or artificial intelligence system without express permission. All rights reserved. Inquiries may be directed to Simon & Schuster, 1230 Avenue of the Americas, New York, NY 10020 or permissions@simonandschuster.com.

Copyright © 2025 by Evan Dando

All rights reserved, including the right to reproduce this book or portions thereof in any form whatsoever. For information, address Gallery Books Subsidiary Rights Department, 1230 Avenue of the Americas, New York, NY 10020.

First Gallery Books hardcover edition October 2025

GALLERY BOOKS and colophon are registered trademarks of Simon & Schuster, LLC

Simon & Schuster strongly believes in freedom of expression and stands against censorship in all its forms. For more information, visit BooksBelong.com.

For information about special discounts for bulk purchases, please contact Simon & Schuster Special Sales at 1-866-506-1949 or business@simonandschuster.com.

The Simon & Schuster Speakers Bureau can bring authors to your live event. For more information or to book an event, contact the Simon & Schuster Speakers Bureau at 1-866-248-3049 or visit our website at www.simonspeakers.com.

Interior design by Kyle Kabel

Manufactured in the United States of America

10 9 8 7 6 5 4 3 2 1

Library of Congress Control Number is available.

ISBN 978-1-9821-7522-1
ISBN 978-1-9821-7524-5 (ebook)

For Antonia

If you don't skate the streets you might as well just go home.

—Sean Porter

PIECEMEAL SCURVY

I dropped my wallet in the hedges of Walgreens.

I'd come to Falmouth to go to the dentist. It was February 27, 2021. I'd moved to Martha's Vineyard in 2013. Those in the know don't go to the dentists on the island. After twenty years in New York City, the novelty of being a country mouse in the big city had worn off. For me, walking on the beach in the moonlight for a few minutes was more fulfilling than two years of New York City nightlife. Dorothy Gale and Ian MacKaye were right: there's no place like home. So where am I?

Martha's Vineyard has soul. There's something in the air out there. It's a singular place. Back in the seventies it was bursting with intellectuals. It was like a piece of Cambridge that had been chucked out to sea and floated away. Not to mention the sheer volume of children's book authors who lived and wrote there: Judy Blume, Roald Dahl, Jules Feiffer, Maurice Sendak, and Shel Silverstein.

It's a little bigger than Manhattan, but doesn't have a single stoplight, just a couple of flashers. During the summer the population swells from 20,000 people to 150,000. Every summer the number gets higher. The part-time residents used to keep a beater to drive around. An old Volkswagen or Jeep made it easy to observe the forty-five-mile-per-hour speed limit. They'd walk onto the ferry, take a cab to their faithful carriage, and they were set for the season. Now they bring their $250,000 cars over on the ferry.

There's no bridge to the Vineyard. You have to fly Cape Air or JetBlue or make your way to Woods Hole and initiate a relationship with the tough-loving Steamship Authority. I crashed at my friend and fellow musician Willy Mason's West Tisbury house for a while, and when I had to leave, he helped me find an old trailer at 237 State Road. Shrouded by yew trees, the trailer had low ceilings and particleboard walls that were decorated with the previous tenant's art. It had a heady, fulsome odor of black mold and wet dog. I was running out of options and hoped that good will, bad faith, hard drugs, scratch tickets, and the evil eye would sustain me.

As the years melted away, I knew I needed to do something different. I had come to the island to quit heroin, but I fell into my old habits. Martha's Vineyard is a tough place to be a junkie. Everybody knows you there. It was impractical and embarrassing. I swallowed my pride and became a miserable pariah. Most of my real friends retreated, hoping things would change. The rest got a kick out of watching me unravel. I was in horrible shape, losing teeth, and living off cheeseburgers—which I could barely chew—Marlboro Reds, purple Powerade (two for the price of one at Cumberland Farms), and a $200 daily drug budget.

I like the Vineyard during the off-season. Being a double Viking with Swedish and Norman blood on each side of my family, the cold never bothered me. The winters keep the bad people away. That's what Prince used to say about Minneapolis. That pandemic winter I went a little overboard. I sat around injecting dope, coke, and speed and smoking weed all day. I actually watched every episode of *Gilmore Girls* and I didn't even like it. Ditto *Gossip Girl*, but that one was more enjoyable.

I lose stuff all the time: phones, guitars, pencil sharpeners, gin and tonics, girlfriends, jewelry, bagels, tuners . . . You get the idea. I had all kinds of methods for keeping my wallet and me together, but when I arrived at the ferry parking lot on Palmer Avenue, it was missing. I'd had it when I checked out of the Inn on the Square that morning, so it disappeared somewhere along Main Street. I started freaking out because the wallet had my driver's license and a couple of debit cards, but I was really bumming when I remembered there was a photo of Keith Richards with Mick Jones of the Clash hanging by the pool in Ocho Rios that had been given to me by Keith's son, Marlon. I posted a message on Twitter asking people to keep an eye out for it. I'd recovered a wallet in Toronto that way and also got back a stolen 1967 country and western Gibson acoustic guitar, so I was feeling pretty good about the whole thing.

In a matter of minutes, a guy named Mike Ghelfi answered my SOS. He worked at the Walgreens on Main Street. He wrote that someone had found my wallet and turned it in at the store.

I went over to Walgreens and, sure enough, it was there, and nothing was missing. I was so grateful I played a few songs for Mike and the staff and endured the gruesome chore of autographing Lemonhead candy boxes with a smile on my face.

I hadn't planned on playing a set next to a rack of Utz potato chips at a Cape Cod Walgreens, but I was happy to do it. It was a way to say thank you. Mike recorded the performance and posted it on Twitter. By the time I got back to my trailer on the island, the video had been picked up by a few music websites. Most of the comments were positive. There were a few negative ones about me not wearing a mask, and the usual jokers who expressed their surprise that I was still alive.

The comments didn't bother me. What bothered me was how I looked, how I sounded. When I watched the video, I didn't see *me*. I didn't see Evan Dando the musician. I saw Evan Dando the heroin addict. I was trying very hard not to be that person. I didn't like that person.

That winter I decided I was done with heroin for good. That meant it was time to go. If I was going to finish writing my stories and composing my songs, I had to get off the island. I've been lost and found more times than I can count, but it was time to make a change.

MAGICAL THINKING

I never would have become a musician if my dad hadn't left the family. The Lemonheads wouldn't have happened if I hadn't flunked my freshman year of high school.

The Commonwealth School in Boston is a small, pricey private school that is painfully academic. As the story goes, I was at Singing Beach in Manchester-by-the-Sea, Massachusetts, with my mother and my sister, Holly, and my mother spotted a group of interesting-looking kids. She talked to them for a while and was so impressed that she asked them where they went to school. They said Commonwealth.

There was just one rule at Commonwealth: no roller-skating in the hallways. The founders didn't have anything against roller-skating—it was a way to say, "Do what you want, just don't be an asshole."

The school was started by Charles Merrill Jr., the son of the founder of Merrill Lynch. His brother was the Pulitzer Prize–winning poet James Merrill. The Merrills had tons of dough at their disposal and plenty of connections. They created a private school in Boston's Back Bay that championed alternative learning.

Commonwealth wasn't a private playground for rich kids. Over half the students were there on full scholarship. A big part of my high school education was being friends with people from all walks of life.

My parents could afford it, and it was right around the corner from our apartment building. That meant I was always late for school. The farther you are from where you want to be the more anxious you are to get there, but when you're close you think you've got it made. That's a lesson I've had to learn on more than one occasion.

Once a week at 10 a.m. we had chapel. It was an elective, but you'd have to be less than a half-wit not to go. People like Buckminster Fuller, Seamus Heaney, Yo-Yo Ma, Mark Sands, Joseph Brodsky, and Peter Cameron, to name a few, came and spoke at chapel. In 1994, I was asked to do one, and I brought my guitar and Australian musician Robyn St. Clare for emotional support. That was something I couldn't have imagined, and while I'm proud to have been asked, if the roles were reversed and I was one of the students, I would have skipped my own performance.

I loved Commonwealth. We were encouraged to use our imaginations, not to be too careful, to be aware of dogma, to become our true selves. We were reading Kafka's diary by the tenth grade. You could fall asleep in a closet, throw pottery, chew the fat with Rusty Crump (who called himself Crusty Rump) from the art department. One of our French teachers would yell, "Smoke pot!" as he passed me and the other Marlboro Red smokers gathered out in front of the school. And there were plenty of cute girls.

There was just one problem: I struggled with my homework, and by struggle, I mean I didn't do it. I liked my classes, had plenty of friends, and loved reading. As long as it was something I was interested in, I had sharp concentration skills. But I never did my homework, which was a problem.

I wanted to make my teachers happy and complete all my assignments on time. I just couldn't be bothered and that bothered me. Sometimes I'd set my alarm and get up at five in the morning so I could get something done before school, but I'd just stay in bed. Then, the next day, I'd start the process all over again, with that feeling of dread hanging over me that every kid knows. I'd miss deadline after deadline on papers about the Franco-Prussian War or William Faulkner's *The Wild Palms*. I still have nightmares about it.

At the end of the school year Principal Featherstone invited me, my mom, and my dad to his office. The principal indulged in the usual double-talk. "Evan, we think it's a mismatch. You'd be better off somewhere else." I felt like I was on trial, except I hadn't done anything—literally.

My mom didn't let the principal get too far along with his spiel. "He'll do it again," she said.

"Excuse me?" he asked.

"He'll repeat his freshman year. There's no rule against that, is there?"

"No, I suppose not," he said.

I could see the wheels turning in his head as he considered the question. Usually, when kids get kicked out of school, especially expensive private schools, the parents blame the school for failing the child, not the other way around. My mom knew me all too well—better than I knew myself.

"How does that sound, Ev? Do you want to come back to Commonwealth?" she asked, like she was the one calling the shots.

Before she married my dad, my mom was an art major at Alfred University, which is about ninety miles west of Ithaca, where my dad studied civil engineering and law at Cornell University. He was twenty-one and she was twenty-three when a mutual friend set them up on a date. The way my dad told the story, she chose him. She was glamorous and charismatic. She swept him off his feet. He didn't stand a chance. She had that effect on people.

I had to hand it to my mom: it was a brilliant idea. There was no school in the universe like Commonwealth. I have to thank her for understanding this and keeping me there. It was a magical place back then and the perfect school for me. If I hadn't repeated my freshman year, I wouldn't have been in Bible class with Ben Deily and Jesse Peretz—my future bandmates in the Lemonheads.

* * *

I made up my first melody, my mom tells me, when I was two years old. I was riding in the back seat of my parents' black VW Bug. My parents were both surfers and we were going to the beach. We were making one of those family trip audio tapes, and among the burps and giggles and putting the microphone out the window, I broke into this melody that was both wistful and operatic.

"Well," my mom said to my dad, "that was something."

My parents loved music. An old family fable was they got married because they had the same record collection. They loved soul, jazz, and funk, but especially the Kingston Trio, the Four Freshmen, and the Everly Brothers, which is a great foundation for listening to recorded music. A good place to start would be James Brown, Al Green, and Marvin Gaye. Then make your way through the rest of the Motown classics. Be sure to make detours when you have to, like Curtis Mayfield and the Impressions, the Meters, and Parliament, but don't miss Charles Wright and the Watts 103rd Street Rhythm Band. You can trace all of rock and roll back to Robert Johnson and Hank Williams via Little Richard.

RUMORS OF MY DEMISE

The first time I heard "Heatwave" by Martha & the Vandellas it grabbed me. Whoa! What is that? The background vocals, the drum sound. I was only five years old, but it pushed everything out of my head and took over my body. From that moment on I knew I wanted to make music.

I was always singing, tapping on stuff, and making sounds with my hands. I had a baby ring that I played with all the time. Everyone was happy when I lost that ring. I asked my mom for a drum set.

"Absolutely not." In my mother's book, noise annoyed.

From the day I was born until the summer of '76 we lived in a white house from the 1830s on a cute little hill with two linden trees in front on Western Avenue in Essex, Massachusetts. Not quite the suburbs, but not exactly rural, either. We lived next to a farm and had a barn in the backyard. Even with all that space, I couldn't talk her into buying a drum set. I had to make do with pots and pans.

I liked singing along to songs on the radio. When I was ten years old, me, my mom and dad, and my sister, Holly, went to a pizza place in the North End. I was singing along to Led Zeppelin when Holly said, "You think you're so cool just because you know the words."

I didn't see what the big deal was. We both liked Led Zeppelin. I just ignored her, which just made her more annoyed at me.

"Evan, I'll tell you one thing for sure," Holly said. "You'll never write a song and you'll never be in a band."

"You don't know that," I said.

"I do know, because you're not the kind of person who can do those things."

Challenge accepted.

My mom used to say that I had a better singing voice and that I was more musically inclined than my sister. It wasn't just my mom who thought so. I won the third-grade music award, where I played a snare drum and sang with a bunch of girls behind me. It was a James Taylor song. I also sang lead when we did *H.M.S. Pinafore*, "When I Was a Lad" by Gilbert and Sullivan. That was when I had the whole class behind me doing backflips. My classmate Grace Gardner used to make fun of me because I would sing in different octaves sometimes.

Holly was two years and seven months older than me, and three years ahead of me in school (four years after I had to repeat my freshman year). Because we were so close in age we had a bit of a sibling rivalry, and it started as soon as I showed up. A few months after I was born my parents asked Holly if she liked having a baby brother.

"I like him very much," she said, "but can we take him back now?"

Though obviously I never forgot that fateful day at the pizza place, Holly and I got along great. I was way smaller than her until a certain point, and we were both featherweights and could have a fair fight, which for a few months was a bit of an issue. One time, my sister picked me up by my shirt and pants and spun me round and round until I went flying headfirst into a big mahogany dresser.

Another early memory of a slightly violent event was one afternoon when she moved our cat, Gypsy, out of the way by throwing her off the bed. Because I loved Gypsy, any small indignity done to my cat could bring me to a rage.

Holly followed the rules, while I would get around them when I could. We were opposites in that way, but it wasn't just me and Holly. I knew from a very early age that I wasn't like other kids. I was super skinny, and my hair was long and blond—longer and prettier than some of the girls in my class. I never wanted to have a haircut. My mom made me trim it, but I insisted she not cut above a certain bone on top of my spine. I liked wearing weird clothes, like dashikis. I liked all of those things about myself, even though they made me stick out. Being different didn't bother me because, in my mind, I wasn't just different, I was exceptional. And I was *me*.

The rhyme from the story "The Gingerbread Man" exemplified that feeling. "Run, run, as fast as you can. You can't catch me. I'm the gingerbread man!" I recognized myself in those lines. No one could catch the gingerbread man because he was different. He was special, and so was I. I felt like I could get away with things that no one else could. I wanted it all and on my terms.

As I got older the notion that I was different grew into a belief in myself, a quiet confidence that expressed itself in different ways. For instance, I was never going to let myself end up in a horrible job or wear a suit like my dad. Not that I didn't work many mind-numbing, shit-stupid jobs on my way. I thought a person should love their work. No matter what kind of trouble I got myself into, I knew I would always be okay because you can't catch me, I'm a gingerbread man.

That became my mantra.

* * *

From a very young age, I liked doing things by myself. It was perfectly normal for me to go exploring for hours at a time. I loved being outdoors, whether it was cruising around on my skateboard, riding my orange bike with a silver sissy bar, or wandering around the woods. I used to take off on my own without any kind of supervision—like all the kids were allowed to do back then. I would wander off just to see how far I could go.

Early one summer morning at Alex Hodge's house on Apple Street, we packed a lunch box with grape juice, ginger ale, Oreos, and a compass. I'd stayed over at the Hodges's for a sleepover the night before, as Holly and I often did. After many bowls of sugary Quisp cereal, which I didn't get at home, Alex and I took to the woods. We walked for some time and came across a little natural amphitheater of boulders. We sat down, and after a few minutes it occurred to Alex we could swear and no one would be the wiser.

"Fuck, shit, piss!"

Maybe it was the latent Calvinism in the hearts of us New Englanders, but we decided we should accidentally get hurt for the swearing to be more meaningful. So we slid down the rocks, half hoping to slip or bang an elbow or something to earn and own our joyful, pissed-off swearing. A couple of bad falls later we tired of our game, but I don't remember us swearing again that day. We continued through the woods, and it wasn't long before we were lost.

We fumbled on, changing our minds about a road with power lines we thought might lead us somewhere, and by the time it started to get dark we could hear very distant shouting of our names. It was eerie, barely audible. Was it our imagination? We figured the folks back home would be wondering where we were by now. Despite all that, I wasn't the least bit scared. I may have been a little worried about being late for dinner, but I was completely at ease out there. I had to keep my cool, as Alex was a few years younger than me.

When we didn't come home Alex's mom started calling people. My dad rushed home from the office. He called the cops and they alerted the National Guard. He had a hundred people looking for us—an actual search party.

We got tired of wandering around the woods and decided to camp where it looked pretty comfortable. Should we put leaves on ourselves to make blankets? All kinds of ridiculous ideas were discussed. Alex had had enough, and I was becoming less suave as the minutes went by when, God bless his soul, a member of the search party came through the trees and we were rescued.

No one yelled at me as we were driving home. They were just relieved. Mrs. Holden, our babysitter, said just the right thing. She said the right thing always: "No sympathy."

* * *

I was nine years old when I went to my first rock concert. Heart was playing a free show and I went by myself. I'll never forget it because the show took place on the day we moved to Boston.

I wasn't thrilled about leaving Essex. I may have only been nine, but I was madly in love with a girl named Emily Getchel, and I was heartbroken when we moved. My dad didn't want to leave, either, but my mom was set on moving to Boston, and I think that tension put a strain on their relationship. Like a lot of things, you can look backward through the binoculars on this dynamic.

Our new address was 172 Beacon Street, Apartment #7, and was right on the Charles River. My dad was doing well at his law firm, and our 3,300-square-foot apartment took up the entire seventh floor of the building between Beacon Street and Back Street. We had five bedrooms, four bathrooms, and four fireplaces. It was huge by any standard, and my dad bought it for $45,000. The living room and my parents' bedroom were on the river side; my and Holly's rooms looked down onto the corner of Beacon and Clarendon Streets. This was a fantastic place to listen to horrific late-night car crashes because Clarendon was the highway exit. A hallway that ran from the back alley right to Beacon Street separated our bedrooms from the rest of the apartment, so Holly and I had lots of room to spread out and do our own thing.

While we were moving in, I heard a band playing at the Hatch Band Shell, which was directly across from our building. Amid all the hustle and bustle of moving our stuff into our new home, I snuck off to check out the concert.

Heart was up onstage rocking away. They sounded like a female Led Zeppelin. I don't recall a whole lot about the concert. It was early in the band's career, and they played "Barracuda."

The people in the audience made as big an impression on me as the band. I remember walking through the crowd with my skateboard. There were lots of bikers at the concert, which I'd never seen before. Who were all these guys in leather with motorcycles? There was a funny smell in the air, which I knew was weed. These tough-looking dudes and hard-looking women saw this long-haired boy walking around and smiled at me. I felt welcome there. I didn't know anything about anything, but I'd somehow stumbled into the world I would inhabit for the rest of my life.

The thing I remember most vividly about that day was that the music was extremely loud, a physical thing. It was a different kind of feeling than listening to records on my parents' stereo or WBCN on the radio, which was on all the time. I could feel this music hitting me. Live music through a big PA is an experience like no other. When I like a record by a band, I still have to see them live to know if I love them or not.

* * *

I was ten or eleven years old when I started playing guitar in earnest. When my father moved out, I sank into the Beatles songbook, with the dots where your fingers go. "Golden Slumbers" was the first song I learned. The first chord is Am7. Ring finger, second fret, fourth string. Index finger, first fret, second string. I enjoyed playing the guitar for its own sake, but I really loved singing songs, and the guitar would let me do that more completely. I learned guitar to accompany myself. It took a year before my left hand caught up to my right hand to become proficient.

My parents' divorce surprised and saddened me. Me not doing my homework was a direct result of my parents' messy split. I felt like they weren't holding up their end of the family contract, and when they divorced, all the rules went out the seventh-floor window and smashed on the pavement. If they weren't going to make an effort, then neither would I.

All through that difficult, lonely time, I kept busy learning songs from the Beatles book, and playing along to albums like the Rolling Stones' *Flowers* and *Hot Rocks*, Rod Stewart's *Every Picture Tells a Story*, and *Beatles for Sale*, which was one of my favorites and included the songs "I Don't Want to Spoil the Party," "Eight Days a Week," the cover of Buddy Holly's "Words of Love," and the life-affirming cover of Larry Williams's "Bad Boy."

My parents were good-looking people. My dad was handsome and athletic and looked like Lee Majors—the actor who played *The Six Million Dollar Man*. He had a wry sense of humor. We were very close, and through all our ups and downs we had this weird ESP going on between us where I could usually discern his presence in the sound of the telephone's ring when he called. I remember singing along to "One Way Out" by the Allman Brothers and my dad said, "Your voice sounds good, Griff!" My dad called me Griff, short for Griffith, which is my middle name. "Maybe you're the rocker of the family!"

You could say my dad is responsible for my career in music. Learning how to play gave me something to do and made me feel good at a time when I needed it.

EVAN DANDO

My friends Alex Star and George Bolucas turned me on to the Stooges, the Velvet Underground, and the Modern Lovers, among many other bands. The first record I bought myself was a weird bootleg that Kim Fowley put out on his label, Mohawk Records: *The Original Modern Lovers*. I learned about the Ramones from the Dogtown articles in *Skateboarder* magazine. Tony Alva, Stacy Peralta, et al., were my real heroes at the time, and the Dogtown crew's favorite band was the Ramones, and so I took their lead.

I loved music with a passion, but I wanted to be a writer. James Joyce and Dylan Thomas were above the skaters in my personal pantheon. I wrote my first short story when I was eleven years old. It was called "The Aqua Slide." It's about my friend Helen Hoar, a girl my age who was epileptic and died suddenly. In the story I describe a few scenes from our friendship: riding horses around and swimming in her family's pool. In the story I can see Helen at the top of the pool slide about to let herself go. The image haunted me in flashes, the surrender to what was about to happen being some kind of harbinger of her death.

We went on a family vacation the summer after third grade, and I read my mom's copy of *Papillon* on the beach in Portugal. It was the first long, bulky hardcover I read.

I loved to read: *The Phantom Tollbooth*, *James and the Giant Peach*, *Journey to the End of the Night*. Short stories by Fitzgerald, Hemingway, Guy de Maupassant. "A Mother's Tale" by James Agee, D. H. Lawrence, Tom and Thomas Wolfe, William S. Burroughs's *Junkie*, *The Ticket That Exploded*, and *Naked Lunch*.

At eleven I went on a serious Kurt Vonnegut and Carlos Castaneda jag. Looking at it now I can't see myself enjoying Vonnegut or Castaneda as much at any other age. I wonder what Kurt would make of that. I can't imagine he would have been anything but proud. Those books seem like they were written for eleven- to twelve-year-olds. When I picked up *Slaughterhouse-Five* recently, I didn't get as good a hit.

I was fourteen the first time I took LSD. I was hanging out with this kid who was in the jazz band with me. We'll call him James, and he played the drums. I'd bring my guitar over to his house in Brookline after school and we'd do drugs and play music in his basement.

His family lived in a mansion. James's parents were never around and there was usually a bunch of kids hanging out at his house. The kids were a bit older than me. James was a total pothead, but he was into other things as well, like cocaine, mushrooms, and LSD. The first time I took acid it was pretty cool for about four hours. My fingers in front of my face turned into bowing nuns in full habit. There was a lot of arsenic and speed in the stuff we took, and the last hours when I was at home unable to sleep were a little scary. There was no one to confide in without losing my skateboard privileges for a month.

I felt like there had to be more to this drug thing than that. Nevertheless, I kept doing it. I took a lot of questionable drugs with James, including angel dust by accident.

Once I got my hands on some liquid LSD, I had a different experience. That was the real deal. I finally had the kind of trip that resonated with the things I'd read about in books. I dropped acid the night of the jazz band's Christmas concert. I borrowed a friend's Les Paul guitar and did a ripping solo in "God Bless the Child."

I was eventually kicked out of the jazz band, but not because of drugs. My teacher realized I was playing everything by ear and that I didn't actually know anything about music. I was playing around on one of the school's jazz guitars when he interrupted me.

"Evan, play a major scale for me," he said.

I couldn't do it.

"Will you hand me the guitar, please?"

I thought he was going to show me what a major scale was, so I handed the guitar to him.

"That'll be all, Evan. You can go now."

I had a real passion for music and was invested in learning how to play to the best of my ability. Shouldn't that count for something?

I thought so. It's funny to me now, but at the time I couldn't really believe they kicked me out for such a petty reason. The teacher was right, of course; being in the jazz band required that you could read music and I couldn't, so I was out.

I was way too young to be doing coke and taking acid and hanging out with all these older kids in James's basement. I see fourteen-year-olds today and it doesn't seem possible that they are doing half the things I was doing when I was their age. But what do I know?

My friend Jesse Solomon and I performed "A Child's Christmas in Wales" for the school at lunch. Christmas break was a few days away. I read *as* Dylan Thomas, copying his whimsical Welsh-singing voice from the record. My effete pseudo-intellectual phase ended with a bang! The recital went over well with my teachers, I got a lot of laughs from my friends, and I was allowed to come back for another semester. I didn't know it yet, but my life as a Lemonhead was about to begin.

MAYBE YOU'D LIKE SOME BRAINS IN YOUR FACE?

One day, my friend Alex Star and I decided that jazz and classical were superior to rock and roll. I wanted to play jazz—I wanted to do a lot of things—but I couldn't play the guitar fast enough to fake it. I took a class to learn how to read and write music, but decided playing by ear with my tape recorder was good enough—like when I learned to snowboard but went back to skiing.

During the winter holiday break Ben Deily and Jesse Peretz took me to a punk rock show and it changed my life. I met Ben in Bible class. At Commonwealth all freshmen were required to read the Old Testament—not as a book of faith but as the most influential work of literature ever written. Ben and I hit it off when we realized we were both into wacked-out comedy records like the Firesign Theatre, *Beyond the Fringe*, and Steve Martin. Jesse was already in a band called the Drainpipes that played pool parties and school dances.

The first kid to go punk at Commonwealth was Patrick Amory. Patrick came from an old Boston family whose members had gone to Harvard every generation dating back to the 1600s. He dyed his hair red, donned black army boots, and wore a jacket with a patch that declared THINK FOR YOURSELF on the back. When Patrick turned punk, me and my friends were interested. Everyone was saying that punk was dead. We all fell in line championing the lost cause of punk.

It was 1984, and I was excited to be going to my first punk rock show at the Channel—the only big rock club in Boston that had all-ages matinee shows on the weekends. There were always some drunk skinheads with two-by-fours roaming around. The way to the club from South Street station was a concentration of graffiti, much of it sprayed by the bands themselves: KILSLUG, GANG GREEN, MISSION OF BURMA, JERRY'S KIDS, SSD. As we entered, a sign warned: NO SPIKES IN THE PIT. I'd clearly come into the hardcore world a little late. The party was almost over, but I didn't care.

The band that was playing that day was Flipper from San Francisco, and it was like nothing I'd ever seen or heard before. The Channel was *the* place. I saw Motörhead three times there and the Minutemen twice. It was a dark, cavernous space, covering three or four acres. Flipper was roaring away and kids were losing themselves in the music. Some kids I'd met on the way to the show brought a dead squirrel into the club and I saw it flying around the pit.

No one sounds like Flipper. Ted Falconi didn't look like a punk: he looked like Rambo up there on the stage in his army jacket. He played his guitar with such abandon it seemed as though he was making up the songs on the spot. His riffs were all over the place. Watching him play, I realized it was a well-formed and deliberate performance. It was all so messy and beautiful.

The next day, Flipper inspired me to pick up the cheap Japanese Epiphone electric guitar that my dad had bought for me. I started bashing away on it in a way that felt exciting and new. I realized I could mimic the sounds I'd heard at the Channel on my guitar. That was the day I started to listen to rock again.

RUMORS OF MY DEMISE

I had learned how to play the guitar by playing along to records. Same thing with singing. The first riff I learned as a kid was "Back Street Girl" from *Between the Buttons* by the Rolling Stones. The open A with the way-up-the-neck B-and-G-string melody line. It came naturally and easy. I was a sensitive eleven-year-old then, going through puberty without my dad around. Playing the guitar and singing comforted me immeasurably. Alex Star and I used to play "Run Run Run" and "There She Goes Again" by the Velvets, "Not Right" by the Stooges, "Looking for a Kiss" by the New York Dolls, "(I'm) Stranded" by the Saints, more Rolling Stones, and then it was all Minor Threat, Black Flag, Agent Orange, Government Issue, the Replacements, and Hüsker Dü, ad astra.

For our junior class project, Ben and I decided to record a couple of new songs he'd written. We could both sing and play the guitar a little bit and we'd taught ourselves how to play the drums. We wrote a song about a kid who killed himself during class. We recorded it after school in the Spanish classroom with John Lorch's black Yamaha drum kit on a Tascam 4-track. In any other school, "So I Fucked Up" would have gotten us in trouble. They did mention something about it sounding like someone falling down a very long staircase, but we had a blast!

I remember a few lyrics:

> Maybe you'd like some brains in your face
> Or splatters of blood on your leatherette briefcase
> Won't let me live my life at all
> But I don't need life so fuck you all

Ben and I were meeting more and more in the basement of his parents' house in Cambridge to record cover songs like "Lick It Up" by Kiss and the theme to the children's TV show *New Zoo Revue* with a full mosh breakdown. Jesse frequently joined our group down in Ben's basement. He got into punk rock because it was the opposite of cool (thus the coolest). He loved the idea of being in a punk band long after it had been declared dead. Jesse thought going punk in 1985 was the lamest thing you could possibly do, so he was all for it.

We started working on some songs and backed each other up on drums. If I wrote a song, Ben would play drums on it, and vice versa. Our songs were short. People thought our unpolished anti–show biz approach was refreshing. Kind souls. If we weren't playing in Ben's basement, we'd jam beneath the front stairs at Commonwealth.

The band name had become an enormous issue. We tried all kinds of angles. Alcohol: the Drunk Pigs, the Drunk Hogs, the Drunk Swine, Drink Drive Kill, Drunk Fuck and the Algae. Incredibly stupid: Yipes Stripes!, Stain X, the Mayan Artisans, 23" of Latex, Amerifucks. Nature: the Nebulae, Guppyhead, the Peg Legs, the Bad Fish, the Other Fish, the Liz Fish Experience. Food-homoerotic crossover: the Fried Chickens, the Citrus Fucks, Tender Vittles Fucks, Popcorn Fucks, the Candy Dicks, the Fruit Rolls, the Citrus Dicks, the Fucking Clocks, Ill Willy and the Tendershoots, the Ovalteenagers, the Piggy Popcorn Queers, and many others. If you need a band name, I'm sure that all of these are still available.

Finally, Jesse came up with an unbelievably and gratuitously offensive name that I'm not even going to register here, which we actually adopted—for about three minutes. Then, when we remembered this name might potentially be, like, limiting, we decided to go with the Whelps. Our new punk friends were horrified.

"You can't do that!"

"That's a terrible name!"

"You mean like little dogs? That's hackneyed!"

During summer break, Ben went on a trip to Brazil for a month or two. Jesse and I took advantage of his absence to change the name of the band. Our friends were right: the Whelps totally sucked. So we started again with the band names. A Commonwealth classmate, Ali Clark, whose father was dean of Harvard Law School, gave me a list of sixty names. Kids were calling me and Jesse on the phone, suggesting possibilities, and then hanging up. Our friend Ivan Kreilkamp got those calls, too, with someone yelling a word, usually an abstract noun, and then banging the phone into the receiver. It was Ivan who finally came up with the name Lemonheads. No definite article. He had a wrapper for Lemonhead candies tacked up on his bedroom wall and we went with it.

When Ben came back from Brazil, he was so pissed off that we'd tossed the name the Whelps and adopted Lemonheads without any input from him. He even threatened to quit, adding that "drummers are a dime a dozen." That was interesting. Ben knew damn well that drummers were actually quite hard to find in Boston. Also, he thought of himself at that time primarily as a drummer, not a singer-songwriter. On our first EP I'm listed as playing "guitar, drums, vocal," and Ben is "drums, guitar, vocal." Keep this incident in mind. Finding a good drummer would be the bane of the future Lemonheads.

Ben's family supposedly had something to do with the Tootsie Roll empire, which maybe explains why he didn't like our candy-themed name. In any case, the seeds of discontent were sown at a very early stage of the Lemonheads' development.

Jesse's dad, Marty, was the publisher of *The New Republic* and his mom was a serious artist and photographer. They had a lot of money, but they were great people, which is a rare combination. For someone who came from so much money, Jesse was one of the most well-adjusted people I'd ever met. He was compulsively creative, and it was fun to be around someone like that.

For a while our punk rock records were supplied by Tipper Gore. The Peretz family was friendly with the Gores, and Tipper had started up the Parents Music Resource Center, the group that succeeded in slapping Parental Advisory stickers on records with profane or provocative content. Tipper was always sending Marty Peretz supposedly offensive records and trying to get him to write about the PMRC in *The New Republic*.

Those records went directly into our collections. Thanks to Tipper's outrage, we were listening to the Dead Kennedys' *Frankenchrist* and other extreme examples of rock and roll that we might not have found on our own.

Although Ben's parents were wealthy, Jesse's parents were *really* wealthy, but also dyed-in-the-wool liberals. My dad became quite conservative, but he didn't start out that way. In the sixties he sang and played the guitar with his friends in college. Eventually, he gave up playing music to focus on his studies. I think he reached an understanding that if he was going to get into law school, he had to keep his nose to the grindstone.

My father fell into the Jerry Rubin yippie-to-yuppie "fiscally conservative" camp. In the eighties he stopped wearing his American flag T-shirt with a pot leaf in the middle. That said, conservatism wasn't part of my upbringing. My parents hung out with Cambridge intellectual types and hobnobbed with cool and interesting people, real heavyweights in arts and science and culture, which allowed me to meet people like Shel Silverstein and David Mamet. My parents encouraged us to do whatever we wanted to do in life.

* * *

"Why don't we make a record?" Jesse said.

We were on the verge of graduating from Commonwealth and we weren't sure what to do about the band. We wanted to play some shows that summer before we all went our separate ways to college in the fall, but we had no idea how to go about doing that. The Lemonheads was basically an after-school project.

We figured the best way to get a gig would be to make a 7-inch EP, which was what we could afford. With a lot of cheering on from Patrick Amory, we decided to put out a little record. We pooled our money and went to record it at a joint with an 8-track machine presided over by the exquisite Tom Hamilton from Cleveland.

We practiced every day at Jesse's house in a room that had a Rodin sculpture, a black figure in a fetal position, and, that summer only, a Rembrandt painting, which is so over the top that Jesse asked me not to write about it in this book. Also represented were Pissarros, Picassos, and a Paul Klee. You name it, they had it.

It wasn't all work and no play. One weekend Jesse's parents went out of town and he had a little party with about forty of our friends. People brought their own alcohol and weed. It was fairly mellow as high school parties go, but the next day, one of the art pieces was missing, the small black sculpture by Rodin. We woke up in the morning and there was literally just an empty pedestal where the sculpture should have been.

This was way more serious than any *Risky Business* situation. We tried to keep our cool. Jesse got busy looking around outside and finally found it in a garbage can a block away. Thanks, guys, very funny!

Meanwhile, the Lemonheads were ready to rock. Patrick helped us figure out the logistics of making a record. The day after we graduated from high school, we recorded five tracks with Tom Hamilton: "Glad

I Don't Know," "Mad," "I Like To," "So I Fucked Up . . . ," and a cover of "I Am a Rabbit" by Proud Scum from Auckland, New Zealand.

It took two days to make the record. We put four of the tracks on the 7-inch. I was miffed because my song "Mad" got left off. It was the first Lemonheads song I wrote, but Jesse said it was generic, and he was usually right. I still love that recording, and it came in handy later.

We had a blast in the studio and I think you can hear it on the record. My vocal style was pure plagiarism. On a given song I might pretend I was Joey Ramone, Richard Butler from the Psychedelic Furs, Paul Westerberg, or even Mick Jagger. Mostly I just screamed. I'll never forget hearing our songs played back to us when we were done. *Holy shit! This kinda sorta sounds like rock music!*

I think at that moment we realized we'd made something cool. We weren't a "real" band, and we knew it, but we sounded like one. More important, this was how all the bands we looked up to started out. The question as to whether we were a real band went out the window. Who the hell cares?

I came up with the title, *Laughing All the Way to the Cleaners*. It's basically laughing all the way to having no money, which seems appropriate because we were broke teenagers with zero expectations. We took the recordings, got them mastered, and had a thousand copies made at Rainbo Pressing.

It was time to start looking for gigs.

* * *

The first Lemonheads show, if you could call it that, was on Friday, July 18, 1986, in a basement in Central Square, Cambridge. The house on Green Street belonged to the guys in a punk-metal crossover band called Meltdown. The Meltdown House had the distinction of sitting squat in the middle of the worst-kept block in Cambridge, but it had the advantage of being indestructible. When the single-room occupancy next door was gutted in a five-alarm fire, the Meltdown House wasn't even touched. The concept of those parties was to cram as many people as possible into a very small basement, encourage everyone to get totally wasted, and then unleash the sounds of Meltdown at pain level. The band took its name from the Chernobyl disaster, which had happened a few months before. Our friend Corey "Loog" Brennan got us the gig. Corey was a disc jockey on WHRB, the student-run radio station at Harvard University and the lead guitarist of Meltdown.

We played the three original songs from the EP plus a bunch of covers. We did "I Wanna Be Your Boyfriend" by the Ramones, "I Think of Her" by the Forgotten Rebels from Canada, and "Ice" by the Screaming Tribesmen from Australia.

We'd been exposed to all kinds of punk rock on a show that aired on WHRB called *Record Hospital*. Patrick Amory was one of the DJs on the show and he helped organize an event in the spring of 1986 called the Punk Rock Orgy—168 consecutive hours of punk rock from every corner of the globe. We taped as much of the show as we could. We even skipped school to make sure we recorded it all. If we missed the show we'd trade tapes with our friends. We were obsessed with the Punk Rock Orgy.

Curtis Casella, another DJ at the station, wasn't a Harvard student, but he introduced WHRB's listeners to proto-punk bands beyond the Saints and Radio Birdman. He hipped us to the New Zealand comp *AK79*, which featured a bunch of bands from the Auckland punk scene in the seventies, including the Scavengers, Toy Love, Spelling Mistakes, and Proud Scum.

We got our punk rock education from Harvard by way of WHRB. We became friends with many of the disc jockeys, some of whom became important as the band expanded its following outside the Boston area.

Patrick Amory had enrolled at Harvard and worked at WHRB beginning in fall 1983, my junior year at Commonwealth. He continued to serve as our punk guru and unofficial adviser, along with fellow Commonwealth student George Bolucas. WHRB and other prominent local college stations are among the reasons why Boston and Cambridge went on to have such a big impact in the independent music scene in the late eighties and early nineties. With the rise of college radio as an industry force at the national level, it was some kind of epochal bonanza we were living through.

A few days after our mini-triumph, Jesse wrote a "press release" in an attempt to get some club dates:

> The Lemonheads are a rocking melodic punk trio from Boston and environs. All recently out of high school, the Lemonheads play a '77-style thunk that's well-documented on *Laughing All the Way to the Cleaners*, their forthcoming 7" EP on Patrick Amory's Angry Arms label. Their radio tape "Glad I Don't Know" has received massive play on WHRB and WMBR [the MIT station]. The Lemonheads have played Cambridge parties to enthusiastic crowds of over a hundred people.

People were stoked about our show at the Meltdown House, which led to the Lemonheads' first club gig the following month at the Rat in Kenmore Square in Boston, in August 1986. We gave a copy of *Laughing All the Way to the Cleaners* to our friends at the Harvard station and they kept playing our record and hyping the show. This had a huge impact because when the Lemonheads hit the stage at the Rat, we had three hundred people in the audience. That's crazy for a Tuesday night in August.

Holly was finishing up at Trinity College in Hartford, Connecticut, and couldn't make it, but my mom went. She wouldn't have missed it for the world. The night of the show she had a big dinner party at the apartment and brought a bunch of her friends to the Rat, including Ben Zander, the conductor of the Boston Philharmonic Orchestra—and he liked it. You won't find a bigger fan of the Lemonheads than my mom.

About twenty of our former classmates from Commonwealth came out to support us. So did a bunch of locals from the music scene, like Chris Brokaw of Come; Billy Ruane, the promoter at T.T. the Bear's Place in Cambridge; Corey from Meltdown; and all the people from WHRB. We'd been to lots of shows at the Rat with much smaller crowds.

I loved being onstage and thought we played well. I wasn't nervous and didn't find it difficult at all. It was a little bit like the first time I had sex: effortlessly fun. When I was fifteen, I lost my virginity to a classmate. We were dancing at a party and she came up to me and started banging her butt against mine. Then she asked if I wanted to fuck her. We found an empty bedroom, and one thing led to another.

We gave traveling punk bands that played in Boston and Cambridge a tape of our music, and the next time they came to town they invited us to play a show together. Not only did we get a lot of gigs that way, but we met all the people who booked shows at the clubs in town.

Everyone was supportive of each other. Nobody had a "career." We worked hard, put up flyers, and went to a ton of shows. Some might say there was a lot of cronyism involved, and there definitely was, but the DJs at WHRB put a lot of work into promoting us on the show *Record Hospital*. We were loyal listeners, and they appreciated our support.

The Lemonheads had its ups and downs. Our second club gig was much more subdued. We played a Nu Muzik night at T.T. the Bear's Place with a band that was also playing its second show ever: the Pixies. I'll never forget that show. The first couple of times we saw them play, there would be thirty people in the audience. We must have seen them ten times before they got famous. They seemed fully formed and ready to take the world by storm even though they were using little tiny guitar amps set on chairs.

Word was starting to get out about the Lemonheads. Ben had a van, and we spray-painted *The Lemonheads* on the side so that people would get to know the name. We circulated tapes of our EP all summer, and *Laughing All the Way to the Cleaners* finally came out in August. We put the sleeves together at Jesse's parents' house. We were the proud owners of one thousand Lemonheads records. Now what?

We met and became friends with the guys in Gang Green, a hard-partying punk band that started in the suburb of Braintree and moved to Boston. Their first single, "Sold Out," was the first release by Taang!—a local independent punk label started by WHRB DJ Curtis Casella. Curtis introduced us to Gang Green. The legend goes, Curtis signed them after listening to their tape in his car in the parking lot of the Channel while waiting for Bad Brains to show up. If Bad Brains had been on time, Curtis might not have started his label, but Bad Brains were never on time.

We met Chris Doherty of Gang Green at a show with Jerry's Kids and Society System Decontrol (SSD) at the Paradise in 1984.

RUMORS OF MY DEMISE

It was billed as "the Last Hardcore Show." Springa, the singer of SSD, announced from the stage, "We started hardcore here and we're ending it here tonight!" Before the show I met Springa at McDonald's. Me and my friend John were snorting Excedrin off the table in the middle of the restaurant, trying to be cool. Springa just shook his head. "Kids, get some real drugs."

We got to know SSD and all the bands. The Taang! bands used to hang out at Curtis's house, dubbed "the Taang! House," in Auburndale, west of Boston. Curtis suggested we put our EP in with the press kit for the new Gang Green album, *Another Wasted Night*. That was *the* turning point of us becoming something.

One of the places that sold our record was Newbury Comics, a legendary independent record and comic book store on Newbury Street, with a second location in Harvard Square. The Newbury Comics people were huge supporters of Boston punk and indie music. They had this place in the store where they displayed the top twenty singles. Every week they'd rearrange the singles display to reflect the popularity rankings. I used to go to the store just to look at it, and it was a thrill to see our record move up the charts. I don't remember how high we got—but we went through all one thousand copies in a matter of months.

We knew that certain punk bands like Black Flag put out their own records. We stood out from the pack—not because we were any good, but because we had a record. We also had our fair share of bad shows. The thing about Ben and I switching from drums to guitar all night messed with my muscle memory. It was a real hassle. Sharing a vintage Gibson SG meant constant tuning problems.

The best thing that happened to our little record was it getting reviewed by *Spin* magazine. The *Spin* review was a direct result of being included in Taang!'s official mailing to a variety of punk-friendly publications. *Spin* plucked it out of the pile and covered it, and not only did they review it, they liked it. *Spin* wasn't the only publication to show us some love. We got a lot of coverage from that Taang! mailing, including a review in the punk zine *Maximum Rocknroll*.

All this love from the press led to some incredible gigs. The Angry Samoans were huge for us. When they came to town, we brought them a cake. Our friend Andrew Hendrickson frosted a cake that expertly reproduced the cover of the Samoans' *Inside My Brain* EP. We brought it to their hotel and gave them a tape of *Laughing All the Way to the Cleaners*. The following year they invited us to open three shows for them on the East Coast, including a gig at the legendary Anthrax club in Norwalk, Connecticut. That was our first big out-of-town show.

All in all it was a successful summer. We'd made a record, heard our songs on the radio, and played with bands we loved. Not a bad start!

WALKING AFTER MIDNIGHT

I don't remember the first time I walked in my sleep.

When I was a kid, I had a vivid imagination. I'd wake up before everyone else at about five or six in the morning and bury my head in my pillow. I'd think about something and then I could see it. My eyes were closed, but I remember one time really testing it, thinking, *I want to see a big billfish coming out of the water*, or a dolphin or a butterfly or a fire hydrant, and I could see it plain as day. I don't know how I knew what all these things actually looked like.

When I went to sleep, I would often see fish swimming around the room in the dark, and I'd walk around looking at them in wonderment. People think of sleepwalking as being stuck halfway between sleeping and dreaming, but for me it was always both. I was always dreaming while I was sleepwalking, but my body thought it was awake. This made the dreams so much more intense because I was moving around inside them. That could be frightening for those who encountered me in my dreams.

Sleepwalking was such a big part of my childhood that it felt like a constant presence. At first, I limited my sleepwalking to my bedroom. Some nights I could tell it was coming. When I drifted off, the wallpaper would start to jiggle, almost like I was having a seizure. But those nights were rare. The sleepwalking usually came without warning. When I got a little older and could walk around a little easier, I started to leave my room and roam around the rest of the house. Some nights I would even go outside.

Then there was the screaming. Because my dreams were so intense and felt so real, they quickly became terrifying. When they turned into nightmares, which they almost always did, I would start screaming and freak out everybody in the house.

Sometimes I'd back myself into a corner in my bedroom with nowhere else to go and start crying out for help. Sometimes I'd knock things over in the kitchen or fumble around the bathroom or stand outside my parents' bedroom. Sometimes I'd go through the front door and take off running down the street.

It got to be a real problem. I don't have any children, but I don't think you ever get used to waking up to the sound of your kid screaming their head off in the middle of the night. You have to try to do something to make it stop. My mom or dad would get up and gently reassure me while guiding me back to bed.

"Everything's okay," they'd say. "It's just a dream, Ev. Go back to bed."

My dad tried to be calm about it, but the sleepwalking freaked him out. A friend of my parents named Jon Chiampa was more sympathetic. "You have an imagination that's as big as an elephant," he told me. "Elephants are a little out of control sometimes, but once you tame your imagination and set it in the right direction, you'll be ready to move mountains with your mind." He told me I was lucky to have such a powerful gift.

I tried to teach myself to control my sleepwalking. I would push my ankles underneath the bed frame to keep myself in place. I would pray not to sleepwalk, but I would often end up screaming bloody murder or hiding in a corner until I woke up embarrassed as fuck. On some occasions it felt like someone was chasing me or a ton of dirt was about to fall on me and I had to run away.

Al Kahn, my therapist in high school, called them night terrors and explained they were quite common. He warned me that trying to control them could have negative consequences. He told me the story of a patient of his who had a similar condition that she called "the Composers." While falling asleep she would hear beautiful music, music that had never been written before, and in time it got really scary for her, like it would go from Dvořák to Napalm Death or something.

"You have to be careful in those twilight times, Evan."

The worst times were when I left the house. Those were the nights I'd wake up running down the street or cowering behind some bushes, terrified that something was after me. It wasn't a thing like a person or a monster. It didn't have a face. But my instinct was always the same: run.

"Ssshhh," my parents would say. "It's just a dream."

But it wasn't *just a dream*. If it was *just a dream* I wouldn't wake up screaming. No one listens to you when you're a kid. You have no voice. Sometimes the only way to make your presence felt is to scream your brains out in the middle of the night, and even then they'll tell you that what your feeling isn't real. *It's just a dream.*

It's no fun waking up naked or in your boxer shorts hiding behind a tree and realizing the door is locked and you're stuck outside for the night.

My sleepwalking was the main reason I kept to myself as a kid. If I went over to a friend's house for a sleepover, my parents would have to explain the situation to the parents. "Evan walks around at night." Kids were usually cool with my sleepwalking—until it happened, and then I wouldn't be invited back for a while. We'd lie there in the dark, waiting for the werewolf to emerge.

* * *

Right before they split up, my parents said, "You're gonna stay over at the Walshes' house this weekend."

I hadn't asked to spend the weekend with my friend, but I didn't think anything of it until my dad picked me up on Sunday and he was oddly quiet during the drive home. I knew something was wrong when we got back to our apartment and he didn't get out of the car.

"Ev, I'm not going upstairs."

I was so confused. Why wouldn't he come upstairs? Where else would he go?

"Why?" I asked.

"I'm moving out."

I couldn't understand why he waited so long to tell me he was leaving. We could have had a conversation about it on the way home. We'd even stopped by McDonald's to eat. He could have given me the bad news over a Quarter Pounder with Cheese, large fries, and a Coke.

I didn't say anything. I just went completely blank while I tried to process what he was telling me. What did it mean? Were my parents getting divorced? Where would Holly and I live?

My dad didn't have any answers for me. He just dropped me off and drove away.

I didn't see him again for almost a year.

My mom found out my dad was having an affair with a secretary named Margie. She went to his office to leave him a note and found all kinds of incriminating evidence, including photos from a trip he took with Margie to Washington, DC, and an eight ball of cocaine. My mom didn't handle it well. She brought the evidence home with her and made a big production out of showing me and my sister the drugs before flushing them down the toilet. She told us all about the affair. I was too young to understand, but she treated us like we were adults. I wasn't ready.

She also went through the apartment and threw a bunch of my dad's stuff out of our seventh-floor window. Holly and I were under the impression that my parents were working things out, but that was either a lie or wishful thinking.

My mom took a photo of Margie and put it above the fridge. Every day she stuck a pin in it. Country club voodoo. My dad's affair with Margie was more than a fling and he ended up marrying her. My dad loved Margie and she loved him. They started a new life together in the house he bought on Martha's Vineyard.

Margie and my mom were total opposites. My mom was independent, progressive, and a proponent of the women's liberation movement. She was into the arts, but she wasn't a bohemian. She didn't drink or do drugs.

Margie had a more traditional view of gender roles. I guess that was the kind of woman my dad wanted, but I didn't understand how he could just leave us. The divorce was difficult for all of us, but it hit me especially hard. It changed my whole life. Holly and I didn't see my dad for a long time, which was baffling and strange. It didn't feel like my parents had split up, it felt like I'd been abandoned, like he didn't love us anymore.

It would be easy to say I became more impulsive after my parents split up, that I became more disruptive and more difficult to control, but I don't think that's true. I was always a bit of a problem child. The only difference was now there was less supervision.

In some ways, my parents getting divorced was the first normal thing to happen to me. I never had a cast or braces—not even a retainer. At least one thing about my life was average now. With my parents splitting up, I fit in with the rest of the kids at school whose parents had divorced.

After my dad left, I found it a lot harder to care about things that weren't that important to me, like school. Why bother even trying? What was the point? School felt like a competition set up to produce winners and losers. I just wanted to opt out of the whole thing.

I felt cut off from the rest of the family. Holly slept in my mom's room for a while, and I was left all alone at the other end of the apartment with my night terrors. While my mom and my sister bonded and became allies, I was left to myself, alone in my room, just me and my night-light. I felt like I'd been abandoned not just by my dad but by everyone. Deep down I started to feel as though I was responsible for what happened to our family. I got it into my head that my dad left because he was sick of dealing with a disturbed child. If I was "normal," he would have stayed.

I think my dad was so ashamed of what he did that he couldn't love me outwardly. He must have known how much that hurt me.

*   *   *

Sleepwalking is in my blood. My father was a sleepwalker and so was my grandfather on my mother's side. I got it from both sides of the family—like my Viking heritage. My father's sleepwalking was pretty mild. My mom told me the night they moved into the house in Essex, my dad got up out of bed and leaned against the bedroom wall.

"I can fix this," he said. "I can fix this."

My grandfather had it bad. I never met him, but he was a crazy drunk with severe somnambulist issues. The two do not go well together. My grandfather's favorite bar happened to be long and thin. He would go to the middle of the bar, start causing trouble, and when the cops came to get him, he would duck them and run out of the bar. He was fast. Once he even got into a cop car to escape the scene and drove to a cliff that was near his house, pushed the cop car over the side, and walked home. It wasn't unusual for him to come out of a blackout miles from his house in Scarsdale, New York, with no memory of how he got there. One time he woke up in a hotel room all the way out in California with a bunch of money stashed in his shoe.

My grandfather was a handsome guy, but he had a lot of issues. He was in and out of jails and institutions his whole life. My grandmother couldn't handle him and got tired of his shenanigans. They split up when my mom was just two years old. My grandmother remarried right away. My mom would say, "Where's Daddy?" and my grandmother denied that my grandfather had ever existed. She passed off her new husband as my mother's father! Even though my mom was only two, she never forgot who her real father was. She could still spell her real last name: *Mattern*. My grandmother didn't fess up about my mother's real father until my mom was thirty.

* * *

As I grew into my body I started to get more attention from girls. I've always preferred hanging out with girls rather than boys—even when I was very young. When I lived in Essex, I was an early girl chaser at my elementary school, Shore Country Day. I had a girlfriend when I was five years old. Her name was Anna Lee Hill and her family owned Hills department store. They let us run around the store and do whatever we wanted.

Then when I was in the second grade, I had a mad, passionate make-out session with my best friend's older sister. Her name was Molly Dearborn and she was in sixth grade. In the morning, we were sitting on the couch watching cartoons and she put her arm around me. I'm not going to lie: it was the best day of my life.

When I was a freshman at Commonwealth (the first time) there was a girl I had a crush on named Rachel. She was a dark-haired dancer and had the most beautiful smile. She was in the eleventh grade. She invited me to a party and we fooled around. It was the oldest story in the book: I loved her, but she didn't love me back.

I didn't suffer for long. The following year I started dating another girl, Jane, a classmate at Commonwealth. She was smart, liked cool music, and happened to be exceptionally cute. We were boyfriend and girlfriend all through the rest of high school. Senior year, she told me she'd applied and been accepted to Vassar. We probably should have ended the relationship then, but we continued to see each other, though not exclusively. Women could tell just by looking at me that I wasn't innocent anymore. Or maybe it was the way I looked at them.

Flirting with girls always helped me feel normal. I was never anxious or nervous around them. I was usually deep in my thoughts, and being around girls coaxed me out of my shell. That was never a problem for me. I think having a sister is a big plus when it comes to understanding women and having relationships with them.

* * *

RUMORS OF MY DEMISE

My dad bought a house on Martha's Vineyard in 1978 for $75,000. It was a good time to buy on the island. His plot was once part of a farm owned by the Whitings—one of the island's more prosperous families. In 1980 my dad and Margie got married and Margie became my stepmother. Their house was in West Tisbury, which is in the middle of Martha's Vineyard.

In the old days the early settlers avoided the coasts. Back then the ocean was something to respect and fear. They weren't swimming in the surf or working on their tans in those days. The most desirable property was inland, where the prosperous settlers established farms and built big elaborate Victorian homes that could withstand the storms that ravaged the island. As a result, the waterfront wasn't overdeveloped. The settlers worked the fields and built up the interior. Those old townships are loaded with history, and they each have their own church and their own town hall. Perhaps I'm old-fashioned, but in my opinion the Whiting farm is the best part of the island.

When I was fourteen years old, Holly and I spent the summer there for the first time. My first night in the house, I had a sleepwalking episode. I left the guest bedroom yelling, "Fuck you, Lou! Fuck you, Lou!"

"Who's Lou?" my dad asked.

"Holly's friend, Lou Ferrigno!"

In my dream, I thought Holly was friends with the Incredible Hulk and that he'd done her wrong. I went back to sleep and my dad told me about it the next morning.

That summer I worked as a stock boy at Alley's General Store during the day and chased girls 24-7. It was the beginning of a great phase in my life. At least I was getting to meet the real Jeff Dando. My sister cleaned and painted houses, and one miserable summer made donuts. At 5 a.m. I'd say, "Time to make the donuts!" She loved to sleep, and I don't think her baking career lasted the whole season. We hung out with other kids we knew on the island: Margie's niece and nephew, the kids whose parents owned the gas station, and friends from Commonwealth who had homes on the island—but not the tourists. We never hung out with the tourists. Our dad's house was next to a barn and adjacent to the local cemetery. A trifecta of teenage trouble, which I took complete advantage of.

The best part of being a teenager on Martha's Vineyard was when my dad and stepmother weren't around. His law firm kept him busy with long hours and lots of work, so he and Margie would stay in Boston during the week and return to the island on weekends.

The house was big and Holly and I each had our own room upstairs. Holly found our uncle's copy of *Paranoid* by Black Sabbath with marijuana crumbs still in the gatefold. The cover was so worn it looked like hundreds of joints had been rolled on it. *Paranoid* became the soundtrack for the summer.

Paranoid is a great record. There's something so satisfying about the repetition of the riffs. Black Sabbath is the heaviest band of all time. I loved that Black Sabbath didn't seem to take themselves too seriously. They weren't afraid to make fun of themselves, like on "War Pigs" when they speed up the tape at the end of the song. We'd lose ourselves in the music. Then when the weekend rolled around, we'd snap out of our stupor and try to clean up the house before my dad and stepmom came home.

Our favorite place to hang out was the old cemetery with tombstones that dated back to the 1600s. There are some old bones down there and it's definitely haunted. Whenever I hear Television's "Marquee Moon," I think of that old graveyard in West Tisbury.

We also spent time at the old barn at the end of our driveway. The barn wasn't always a barn. It began its life as a church built in 1790 that was converted sometime in the twentieth century.

It was a working barn with an actual loft, where the local farmers sometimes let us help them make hay while the sun shined. The hayloft was the perfect spot for a romantic encounter. If I had a girl over, that's where I'd bring her. Who doesn't love a good roll in the hay?

During my senior year of high school, we had a party at my dad's house. I was with my high school girlfriend Jane, but I snuck out of the house and went to the barn with this other girl. Of course, Jane figured out what was going on. Where else would I be? She broke up with me, but the next morning we drove back to Boston together. Our shirts said it all: Her shirt was white with yellow horizontal stripes. Mine was yellow with vertical black stripes. We laughed about it and ended up getting back together.

The barn was old and falling apart and could be dangerous. One time I was running around like a chicken minus its head and landed a little hard and my foot went through the hayloft floor. I'm lucky I didn't fall through the floor and snap my neck. I pulled my foot out of the hole, brushed myself off, and hammered the floorboards back into place. Because things were always falling apart, that was the protocol at the barn: you break it, you fix it.

Whenever I'm back on the island I visit the barn. The owner told me I could come anytime I want. The smell of the hay, the sound of my feet clomping up the wooden stairs, the way the light filters through the old walls brings back memories of my childhood. It's exactly like I remember it, like entering a time warp.

* * *

After barely graduating from high school, I somehow got into college. It just goes to show how good Commonwealth's reputation was that someone like me was admitted. Because of its academic rigor and reputation, the underlying assumption was its students would go on to a college or university. It was the next expected thing, and many of my classmates viewed their freshman year of college as the thirteenth grade. We were in Boston after all, home to Harvard, MIT, BU, and dozens of other highly respected schools. All my friends were going to college—even the punks. Jesse got into Harvard. Ben was going to Brandeis.

My parents also encouraged me to go to school. They put a high value on education; after the divorce, it was one of the few things they agreed on. Going to college was so ingrained in my upbringing that I never stopped to consider if it was right for me. I just sent off my applications like everyone else and hoped for the best.

I didn't get into any of the highly touted schools in Boston or even Massachusetts, but Skidmore, a private liberal arts college near Saratoga Springs in New York, took a chance on me. So when fall came around, I packed all my stuff into a white 1983 Chevy Cavalier station wagon that my dad gave me and drove off. The Chevy had a manual five-speed transmission. My dad said, "Griff, it's yours for as long as you can keep it running." Just like Thomas Jefferson said to America.

I loved that car. I called it Sheila. I put three stickers on it: I LOVE COUNTRY MUSIC, HAVE GUN WILL SHOOT, and MY WIFE YES! MY DOG MAYBE! MY GUN NEVER!

I was excited about being out on my own, but the thrill was short-lived. After Boston, Skidmore felt small and dull. Saratoga Springs is where Don McLean wrote "American Pie." Other than that, Skidmore didn't have a lot going for it. There wasn't much of a music scene in Saratoga Springs. I had two roommates in my dorm room and one of them was the nephew of the keyboard player in Lipps, Inc., the group that had the hit "Funkytown." My roommate brought the actual keyboard used in that song with him and it was in our room. I got along with my dorm mates just fine. They weren't the problem; I was.

They had tons of rules at Skidmore. (No roller-skating in the hallways wasn't one of them.) In the cafeteria you had to use a tray and I don't like using trays. I've never been a big eater. I just want to grab my food and go.

There was one pretty girl on the entire campus. Her name was Christina and I met her in one of my classes. We hung out for a little bit, but since I hardly ever went to class I didn't see her all that often.

My dad sent me dividend checks from Coca-Cola stock bought with money I made from being in a TV commercial as a child. A couple hundred here, a couple hundred there. I didn't buy books, I bought drugs. Vassar was only two hours away, so I spent a lot of time driving down to Poughkeepsie to hang out with Jane, some old friends from Commonwealth, and a few new ones that I made, including the drummer from the DC punk band Faith. Although I didn't give Skidmore much of a chance, Vassar seemed like a much cooler place to be.

I was also driving my Chevy back to Boston just about every weekend to play gigs with my bandmates. Whenever the Lemonheads had a show, that became my priority, even on short notice. I was young and dumb and thought I could drive ninety miles an hour on the highway without any consequences, so I got a lot of speeding tickets. The cops would pull me over and I'd plead my case.

"Officer, we're opening for Kilslug at the Rat tonight!"

"The State of New York doesn't care about your gig."

He had a point.

I didn't pay the tickets. Why would I? They were from the State of New York. I think in the back of my mind I knew that I would be heading back to Boston before too long. Also in the back of my mind, I knew those tickets would come to haunt me some day. So those unpaid tickets turned into warrants, but I didn't care. I'd officially run afoul of the law for the first time, but it wouldn't be the last.

College clearly wasn't for me.

Considering everything I had going on, it's probably not a surprise that I didn't make it through my first semester of college. When I dropped out I had a 0.32 grade point average: four F's and a D–. I've shared that little detail with countless reporters over the years.

After Commonwealth, going to college seemed like a step in the wrong direction. Skidmore felt like I was taking five steps back. That's not a knock on the school, it's more a reflection of how good my experience at Commonwealth had been. I felt like sleepy little Skidmore couldn't compete. My classmates regressed to being kids again. All they wanted to do was fuck around at college for four years. I wasn't interested in that. College is supposed to give you the tools to succeed in whatever you choose to do. Commonwealth had already done that for me. I was on the path to what I wanted to do with my life, which was to make music. Plus, I had spent five years at Commonwealth.

The only class I didn't fail at Skidmore was acting. I did the old Dylan Thomas routine in my acting class by pulling a performance out of my ass at the last minute to get a passing grade. In this case I channeled Billie Holiday's version of "Gloomy Sunday."

I wasn't at Skidmore long enough to declare a major. My college days were just that—a handful of days, fewer than a hundred. I don't think my teachers even knew my name. I went to college because I didn't know what else to do. I figured I owed it to myself to give it a shot and see if I liked it, but I didn't, so I left.

I didn't fail out of Skidmore—I resigned before the end of the semester. I packed up all my stuff, left a letter under the dean's door, and drove home in a snowstorm. It was all very dramatic in a Holden Caulfield kind of way, but that letter of resignation saved my dad from having to pay for another semester of college, which impressed and delighted him.

My dad wasn't mad that I quit. He took the news well. He never tried to push me in a different direction. His attitude was "You know what's best for you." He was very cut-and-dry about that sort of thing. His view of the Lemonheads was surprisingly positive. He wasn't going to fund my punk rock adventure, but he encouraged me to go for it.

"Do your thing, Griff," he told me, "but you aren't getting another penny from me."

That was the deal, which I totally respected. He'd always told me and Holly that he would pay for college and after that we were on our own.

My parents always supported what I wanted to do with my life. Although my mom was a bit distressed that she could no longer brag about me being a college student, she didn't lay a heavy trip on me. The only bummer about leaving college was it meant the beginning of the end of my relationship with Jane. When I stopped visiting her at Vassar she started fooling around with other guys, which I couldn't be too mad about, since I was doing the same thing and had cheated on her all through high school.

Jesse said, "Evan, you don't need to go to college. You'll be fine without it."

He was right. Jesse had a fresh perspective and with me he had a hunch. It helped that the Lemonheads were starting to happen. Toward the end of '86 we were invited to play on WERS's *Metrowave*, a live radio show out of Emerson College, next door to my mom's apartment. *Laughing All the Way to the Cleaners* was getting played on college radio stations around the country.

We closed out the year with a bang by opening up for the Ramones at Brandeis University. Ben had a friend who somehow got us on the bill. The band seemed pretty bored with the whole routine. We sat backstage and got drunk and excited and nervous. The Ramones didn't seem at all nervous or excited, but they were drunk. What a sight: Marky, Dee Dee, Johnny, and Joey, all in the Ramones uniform, coming at us down the carpeted hallway. They were so cool.

Playing with the Ramones and hearing our songs on the radio pointed toward the feasibility of taking the Lemonheads into the future. We knew what we were—a ramshackle punk rock party band that no one, including ourselves, took very seriously—but we also knew how rare it was for bands to get so lucky.

The mainstream music industry was slowly starting to change: post-punk bands were getting more popular and some of them were getting signed by majors. We couldn't have been in a better place at a better time. I'll tell you that for free.

YOU SHOULD TRY IT SOMETIME

After I dropped out of college, I briefly moved into my mom's apartment on Beacon Street, but I didn't really live there. I did a bit of couch surfing. Sometimes I'd stay with Curtis or Jane or even my dad. After Holly graduated from Trinity she moved to New York City. My mom was all alone in that big apartment and didn't mind me hanging around while I got settled. She told me I could stay as long as I had a job, so I immediately started looking for work.

I took a big social demotion and got a gig at the Country Club in Brookline. That's what it was called—the Country Club—and it was one of the oldest in the country. The job came with all the ugliness that one associates with a private club in the eighties. The Country Club was totally restricted and weird and I'm glad there's no possibility of me ever being a member.

A friend worked in the tennis club. He was looking to move on to something else, so I was able to slide into his position. My duties included answering the phone, booking court times, and rolling the clay courts. I was basically a racket boy. I wasn't allowed to use the facilities, so I didn't get to work on my tennis game. If you're thinking it was a situation like *Caddyshack* where I was flirting with rich old ladies or that I had a Mrs. Robinson experience at the club, I'm sorry to disappoint you. If anything, I think I was looked down upon because I didn't come from a super-wealthy family. I actually needed the money.

I worked for a lady named Louise, who had me running around doing all kinds of menial tasks for rich old white people. It was a terrible job, and I hated it, but I worked there for a surprisingly long time, like eight or nine months.

After the success of *Laughing All the Way to the Cleaners*, Curtis wanted the Lemonheads to make a full-length album for Taang! He was eager to do something right away, but we'd all gone off to college. We managed to record a few songs here and there, but with Ben at Brandeis and me at Skidmore it was hard to get us all together. That changed in the spring of 1987. I dropped out and Ben transferred to Harvard. With all of us back in town again, we went to work on our first album.

While Ben was at Brandeis he met a kid named Doug Trachten. He lived in the same dorm as Ben and they got to be friends. We hated his goth rattail, but what could we say? The rest of us were ardently sweater rock. Doug was a bit more demonstrative with his punk rock attire. He was also into crime, and I don't mean the San Francisco band. I think he had a couple of run-ins with the police and had crossed some dangerous people, but that's his story to tell.

As we wrote more songs and extended our set, switching instruments all the time became more challenging. Ben lobbied for Doug to be our designated drummer so that he and I could focus on singing and playing guitar. I had mixed feelings about that. I liked playing both instruments, but I was up for the change because it was hard going back and forth between the drums and the guitar.

RUMORS OF MY DEMISE

Our shows got easier after Doug started playing with the Lemonheads, but some of our friends were down on Doug at first. They liked our music-by-nonmusicians thing, switching instruments after every song, crashing into each other onstage, getting into arguments, etc.

After Ben transferred to Harvard, he moved back to the house that he'd grown up in on Gray Street off Linnaean in North Cambridge. At some point the house had been split into apartments, and Ben rented a small unit from his parents on the left-hand side. Ben's family let the band build a soundproof rehearsal space in a room in their basement, but you had to go through his parents' house to get there, which wasn't an ideal situation.

The Lemonheads entered a prolific phase. We would sit around Jesse's place on Brattle Street or in Ben's kitchen and write many songs together. The group dynamic was saved for throwaway songs. I gotta be honest. Ben and I were already too precious and craft-conscious to write our real songs that way. We wrote those by ourselves. Our main objective during these sessions was to finish the song. Just finish it. Some of this, a little of that, a few more of those, and we're done. It felt amazing when it came together that way.

"3-9-4" was a song that Ben brought in. He'd written the riffs on his own and it had a tricky ending. Toward the end of the song he'd be yelling, "Do you understand how it ends now?" like a conductor, or a hopped-up gym teacher, because we couldn't get it right. It became the lyric.

The first Lemonheads record marked the beginning of my obsession with Charlie Manson. When I look back on my influences, the things that have stayed with me the longest are Black Sabbath and Charlie. Black Sabbath doesn't need an endorsement from me, but every time I listen to Sabbath it's like I'm hearing them for the first time. So much extreme music begins with Black Sabbath.

My relationship with Charlie was a bit more complicated. I was fascinated not by what he had done, which was terrible, but by the things he said and the way he expressed himself. It's not that I was a secret satanist headbanger. I was never into the occult or anything like that. The conservatism of the eighties sent a lot of kids my age searching for inspiration from countercultural heroes out of the recent past. Some of my friends obsessed over the poetry of Jim Morrison. Others got into the gonzo journalism of Hunter S. Thompson. Many of my peers looked up to Allen Ginsberg, Jack Kerouac, or William S. Burroughs, the big three of the beat generation. I read all those books, too, but Charlie inspired me as a songwriter. I admit I was a bit of a weirdo, but my sister had something to do with it.

Holly passed along a copy of *The Family* by Ed Sanders. She plucked it off the bookshelf in the family room. My dad was a big fan of Sanders's work in the Fugs and owned several of his books, including *Tales of Beatnik Glory*. After I tore through *The Family*, I read Vincent Bugliosi's *Helter Skelter*, which isn't as good as *The Family* in my opinion. I read both books by the time I was eleven.

A few years ago, Holly and I went back to Essex to check out our old house. We climbed to the upper level of the barn, where we found an old medicine cabinet, and inside the cabinet was a mirror on which Holly had scrawled, *NIXON IS A PIG* in red lipstick. She wrote that in 1971 when she was seven years old.

We were a couple of precocious kids, but Charlie got his hooks into us at a very early age. Images of an army of LSD-crazed assassins creepy-crawling around the Hollywood Hills and driving around Death Valley in stolen dune buggies were irresistible to us. It didn't seem like something that could happen in real life, like a cartoon fever dream out of California.

I wasn't the only one who felt this way. In the eighties, Charlie inspired lots of alternative artists. People like Raymond Pettibon, Henry Rollins, Lydia Lunch, and the members of Sonic Youth all fell under Charlie's spell. The Lemonheads song "Sneakyville" is a direct reference to an interview Charlie gave in the prison in Vacaville, California, where he was transferred for medical reasons while serving a lengthy sentence. In the interview, Charlie says something about "everything is sneaky up around Sneakyville," which is emblematic of the kind of things that would pop out of Charlie's mouth.

The opening of "Sneakyville" is chaotic and weird, but the song is full of Charlie's jargon, like "I am God. You are God. We are God," which was fun to scream into a microphone. People always ask me if there's an LSD connection to the song, which I suppose there is. LSD is always in the mix when it comes to Charlie, but those lyrics get to the core of Charlie's worldview and represent the unique way he had of expressing himself.

"Hate Your Friends" is about some of our classmates at Commonwealth who were constantly turning on each other. Best friends today, bitter enemies tomorrow.

> You got problems you can't solve
> It's enough to make you start to hate your friends.
> You go to a show and they stare at your face.
> Don't you know? You hate your friends.

We recorded *Hate Your Friends* with Tom again. He worked with a bunch of Taang! bands. We recorded seven new tracks with Doug on drums and put them all together on side 1. The songs on side 2 were recorded way earlier, but there's something about it I love. Wuss-core, but with balls. "Hate Your Friends" kicks off with

Ben on drums. After that comes one of my favorite songs I ever wrote, "Don't Tell Yourself." I wasn't always so proud of it until Jeff Conolly of DMZ, the Lyres, etc., told me at the bar at the Middle East Cafe in 1992 that it was his favorite of my songs.

It took us a long time to find a photo that went with the title of the record. Jesse's mom was a photographer and we used one of her shots from the mid-sixties on the cover. The two children with toy guns are Jesse's older brother and sister. It's the best of all the Lemonheads' album covers. You can see us sitting on the stairs to our practice space in Ben's basement on the back of the *Hate Your Friends* LP.

* * *

I heard about the Blake Babies from my mom. I didn't know the singer, Juliana Hatfield, but my mom knew her mom, who told my mom, who told me: "Go see the Blake Babies."

My mom actually went to see them before I did. Juliana's mom worked at *The Boston Globe* and she invited my mom to see them play at the Rat, so she went. After the show, Juliana gave my mom a flyer.

"Would you give this to Evan?"

"I sure will!" my mom said.

Her band was playing at this café/art gallery in Boston called She's Leaving Home and Ben and I went to check them out. I was instantly smitten. We didn't know it at the time, but the feeling was mutual. The Blake Babies had attended the Lemonheads' first club show at the Rat and they were fans from the start.

The Blake Babies was a trio that formed while John Strohm, the guitar player in the white oxford shirt, was attending Berklee College of Music in Boston. That's how he met Juliana in the first place. Freda Love was the drummer. She'd never gone to Berklee, but had a badge that read FASTEST GUITAR PLAYER AT BERKLEE. They played appealingly trashy pop.

Around the same time we were putting out *Hate Your Friends*, they were working on a record called *Nicely, Nicely*. John and Freda saw Allen Ginsberg at the Sanders Theatre on the Harvard campus, where he had just performed. They stood in line and asked him to give them the name for their band. He simply said, "Blake Babies."

Juliana lived with her bandmates in an apartment over by Symphony Hall that was known as the Condo Pad. She was a serious girl who didn't have time for fun. The rest of us were high out of our minds most of the time, and she had to put up with us bringing random people over.

The Blake Babies knew what they were doing. They could read music and understood music theory. John and Freda were from Indiana and John had been in punk bands all through high school, including the band Killing Children. We knew all the same songs and bonded over our mutual love of the Zero Boys.

John was listening to the Lemonheads' first live set on WERS when we launched into "Livin' in the '80s" off of the Zero Boys' *Vicious Circle* LP. His estimation of us went up, I think it's safe to say. Freda was friendly and outgoing, and even though she was relatively new to the instrument, she had excellent instincts as a drummer and played with a great deal of verve. What I loved the most about the Blake Babies was they were all about the band. They had no backup plan. All they cared about was making music.

One afternoon I was jamming on John's guitar during a break in their band practice and John jumped on Freda's drum kit. We started ripping through all the old Minor Threat songs we loved so much. I had no idea John knew how to play the drums and he was incredible—much better than Doug. That gave me an idea.

"How'd you like to join the Lemonheads?" I asked.

John was down—as long as it didn't interfere with his duties in the Blake Babies. Then it was a matter of convincing Ben and Jesse to ditch Doug, which required a bit of duplicity. I'd given John a tape of *Hate Your Friends*, so he had all the songs down cold before the record even came out. I brought him to a rehearsal that I'd set up and conveniently forgot to invite Doug.

"Where's Doug?" my bandmates asked.

"I don't know," I said, "but since John's here . . ."

Ben and Jesse figured out what I was up to right away, but once they heard John play, it was a done deal. John was a super-fun guy to hang out with, and Doug's tenure in the Lemonheads came to an end. He took it pretty well, all things considered. I think he knew he was the odd man out in our little crew. Doug eventually became a Buddhist monk.

One of John's first shows with the band was the *Hate Your Friends* record release party during a Sunday matinee at an event sponsored by WHRB at T.T. the Bear's Place. The Lemonheads never felt tighter. Having a musician of John's caliber in the band brought out the best in all of us and inspired us to be better. We felt like a gang now.

John is in the video we recorded for the song "Second Chance," even though he doesn't play on the record. The video tells a story of missed connections and lost love with a young woman roaming around a bus station looking for . . . something. We never met the actress in the video. The concert footage is from a show we played at the Rat. I'm only in the video for a few seconds, but I'm proudly representing Boston hardcore with an SSD T-shirt. We were stoked when MTV played it on *120 Minutes* at the end of the year, but I still hated rock videos.

We hit the road in the summer of '87. When it came to planning the tour, we did everything ourselves. Jesse was our de facto manager, and he took care of all our band business, from booking shows to dealing with Taang! He was good at handling the details that no one else wanted to deal with. Jesse was smart, savvy, and had great taste. It also didn't hurt that he had a lot of connections. He was our first—and in my opinion—best manager.

The Lemonheads teamed up with a band called the Offbeats that had a record out with Relativity Records. We planned a joint tour.

I don't remember what happened to the Lemonheads' van, but it's in a video we made with our Super 8 cameras in high school for the song "A Circle of One." The van languished behind the offices at the Taang! House in Auburndale. If you can find the house, maybe you will see it parked there. For the tour we used a Peugeot station wagon that belonged to Jesse's mom. We didn't bring most of our gear along because we shared with the Offbeats and borrowed equipment when we needed to.

As the date of our departure loomed, I got more excited about the tour. The night before we left, Jane spent the night with me at my mom's apartment on Beacon Street. I was only going to be gone for a few weeks, but she would have been cool if it was longer. Jane wasn't clingy like a lot of people are in young relationships. We continued to see each other even though we were living in different cities. She had her own life to live and was always super supportive of the Lemonheads.

In the middle of the night, I jumped out of bed and ran out of my bedroom and down the long hallway, breaking all the mirrors as I passed. I grabbed a fire poker from the fireplace in the living room and started waving it around at an invisible assailant.

"Come back to bed, Evan," Jane said as she took the fire poker away from me. "There's no one here. There's nothing you have to worry about."

As I came to my senses, Jane coaxed me back to my bedroom—she had been through this many times—but I had trouble getting back to sleep. I couldn't get the look on her face out of my mind: a mixture of confusion and sadness and fear. Ben, Jesse, and John all knew about my night terrors, which had a tendency to flare up when I spent the night at someone else's house. I realized that with all the time we'd be spending together, they were going to get a front-row seat to the Evan Dando freak show. I hadn't even left home yet and the Lemonheads' tour was already off to a shaky start.

*   *   *

Our first gig of the tour was in the Offbeats' hometown of Cleveland, where we played with a band called Starvation Army. Cheetah Chrome of the Dead Boys, Les Black of the Pink Holes, and John from Death of Samantha, three of Ohio's greatest punk bands, showed up. There were a lot of legends in the house that night.

That summer we drove all over the Midwest, but we couldn't get away from Suzanne Vega's hit "Luka." That song was everywhere. During a long drive from Charleston, West Virginia, to Cedars Lounge in Youngstown, Ohio, we heard it so many times that we learned the song. We played a version of "Luka" that night at our gig at Cedars as a joke and people went bonkers over it. Thus began the Summer of Luka and the Lemonheads' complicated relationship with cover songs.

The Lemonheads played some memorable shows on that tour that weren't particularly well-attended. We played a show in Chicago that Jim Ellison of Material Issue booked at a place called Batteries Not Included. Our show at the Uptown in Minneapolis was better attended and the Pagans came to the gig. Toward the end of the set, we noticed they were there. I was sweaty and tired and wanted to hear some real rock and roll. We'd played with the Pagans in Boston a few months prior to the tour. We loved those guys and asked them to play our encore. They were totally up for it. The Pagans jazzed up the crowd with songs like "Six and Change" and "Street Where Nobody Lives." (If you don't know the Pagans, you should go listen to "What's This Shit Called Love" right now.)

In Indiana we broke off from the Offbeats for a bit and went to stay at John's dad's house in Bloomington. John's friends got us a basement show at this disgusting party house with a lot of feral cats they called the Litterbox. The guys who lived there turned a bathroom into one giant litter box they never cleaned. They just slapped a cat door on the bathroom door and locked it from the inside, giving the cats free rein. During the packed, sweaty show, a guy took off all his clothes and danced like a maniac inches away from us. We played every song we could think of and then "Louie Louie."

By this time, a lot of people hated the Lemonheads—especially anyone who had been into the Boston punk scene for more than three months. One of the first real critics to write about us, at least on the national level, was Gerard Cosloy, who would go on to found Matador Records with Patrick Amory, in his fanzine, *Conflict*. But it was in the fanzine *Incite!* where WHRB DJ Tim Alborn, founder of Harriet Records and now a history professor in New York City, unleashed our first really negative critique. It had to do with our release party. While we were playing "So I Fucked Up," my mom's friend Ben Zander, the conductor of the Boston Philharmonic, chatted him up. This destroyed what little street credibility we had. Jesse didn't help much, either, with stage patter like "I'd like to thank my mom for buying me a drink." Alborn went home and wrote his review, comparing our band to Little League baseball as it is played in Boston's wealthier suburbs. There was a lot more of that type of bullshit to come.

So, what was it precisely that people hated about the Lemonheads? Maybe it was the idea that we formed the band at a ritzy private school, and that our parents were wealthy and well-connected, which to tell the truth, they were. Maybe it was the openly derivative material. Or the fact that we were barely out of high school, with boyish good looks. Or the snowballing success. Or some combination of the above.

Like us or not, the Lemonheads were big enough by mid-August 1987 to hit the road on what we called the Fucked Forever '87 Tour or, alternately, the Crank the A/C, Push the LP, and Drink the Iced Tea Tour. Jesse's mom provided us with her Peugeot again, and Ben kept a diary.

Getting popular was the last thing in the world we thought would happen. We were a punk rock band in the mid-eighties. No one thought we were commercially viable. There was no path to success and we were okay with that because we were getting sick of it, too.

We were playing stripped-down rock and roll at a time when hair metal and synth pop ruled the airwaves. We were just a bunch of guys from New England rocking out in sweaters and having fun. All we wanted was a place to play, food to eat, and enough gas to get us to the next show. We slept on floors and lived out of the station wagon and that kept us in the black. Plus, we all had jobs and had saved up a little money to take with us on the road. They weren't the easiest days, but they were some of the best nights of my life. Our whole attitude was *We're gonna do something stupid and pointless because we like doing it.* We were doing something that most people would never understand. It wasn't cool and never would be and that was just fine with us.

Aside from the incident the night before the previous tour, my sleepwalking wasn't too bad. There were a couple of times I bolted awake in the middle of the night. As the nightmare faded away, I'd become aware of Ben or Jesse or John staring at me like I was some kind of lunatic, and then I'd go back to bed. Sometimes we'd talk about it the next day, but most of the time we didn't. Why would we? We got along great, but we were a bunch of immature kids, frightened of our feelings. How do you tell someone what's on your mind when you don't know yourself?

SLOW LEARNERS

After the tour, I moved into Ben's place in Porter Square in the fall of 1987. Rent was $200 a month. It was a small one-bedroom apartment and there wasn't much room for me. We set up a partition in the living room so that I'd have some space to call my own. I slept on the pullout couch and that worked for a while, but I didn't have any privacy, and I eventually moved into the closet. I felt safer in there for some reason, which was weird because I'd decorated the walls with pictures of Charlie. It probably wasn't such a great idea to go to sleep with Charlie every night because I was sleepwalking more than ever and girls hated it.

I don't know what I was thinking. Curtis furnished us with all kinds of Manson-related things. He had videotapes of all the Manson interviews. We used to watch them all the time, along with the Oscar-nominated documentary of Manson made in 1973 by Robert Hendrickson. Curtis even had the infamous tape that Henry Rollins made by smuggling a Walkman into one of his regular visits to Charlie's cell. It starts with Charlie saying menacingly, "This is an SST recording studio."

Holly and I would visit each other. Back then you could fly on Eastern Airlines between New York and Boston for thirty bucks. She was in grad school studying to be a social worker and living on Front Street in the Seaport with a writer named Rob Bingham. I'd go see her there and she would come visit us in Cambridge. One time she spent the night and woke up just as I was shuffling out the front door. She chased me down and brought me back inside.

I entered a climbing phase in my sleepwalking. I climbed out windows, crawled along ledges, and clambered over railings. My night terrors were becoming more terrifying, but I wasn't a kid anymore. I was past the monsters-in-the-closet phase, and I was putting myself in real peril with my nocturnal rambling. Ben was so freaked out by my sleepwalking that he locked himself in his room at night, and I can't say I blame him.

It was getting harder to explain my nightmares away when they kept happening. I think my bandmates thought I had something wrong with me, like a house with bad wiring. I was convinced my nightmares *meant* something. I refused to believe they were "just dreams." I thought there was something real lurking at the edge of my consciousness that I couldn't see, but what?

Things were getting weird at Ben's house. We were experimenting with all kinds of drugs. Hippie drugs are only fun if you're okay with yourself before you get high. Let's say we weren't. We knew what we needed: the White Lady, aka cocaine hydrochloride, and her boy smack. We were in an experimental mood: Thanksgiving E, Christmas acid, and Memorial Day mushrooms. We brought unusual instruments into the practice room, like synthesizers and twelve-string guitars. It was a time of hiccups, snowstorms, setbacks, Valium, Demerol, and video stores.

"Let's get together and finish this song!"

"Yeah, and let's record it before it morphs into something soft and boring."

There are only so many times I can rehearse a song with the band before it gets soggy. I hadn't learned my lesson yet. Practice is for practical assholes who don't understand reality. I mean, there's a time and a place for it, but I'd rather spend the time working up new material.

This was right before we recorded the only real stinker of the Lemonheads' catalog, *Creator*. We stopped practicing for three weeks before the *Creator* sessions. The songs were similar to what we'd done on *Hate Your Friends*, but our methods were changing. Ben was writing most of the songs, which meant he was doing most of the singing as well. I felt like my role in the band was diminishing, but it was a chicken-and-egg situation. Did I feel this way because I wasn't writing songs or was I not writing songs because of the way I felt?

For our generation of guitar rock, J Mascis of Dinosaur Jr. had raised the bar in his lazy, violent, and beautiful manner. By the time we started making *Creator*, it was J's world. We just played around in it. He woke me up to the possibilities of pop music, which are, and don't let anyone tell you different, endless.

Our obsession with Charlie was at its peak. I say "our," but I was the one driving the Charlie bus. We had a bong emblazoned with one of Charlie's cryptic slogans: "I'll never say never to always." We thought we were so clever. There's clever and there's smart, but they aren't the same thing, are they?

I sing on "Your Home Is Where You're Happy," which was one of Charlie's songs from the infamous album *Lie: The Love and Terror Cult*, which was released while he was on trial for murder. A lot of people were into Charlie because of the shock value, but I think he actually wrote some decent songs. "Home Is Where You're Happy" was one of his best. I wanted to show people that he had some chops as a songwriter.

I recorded the song on a water-damaged guitar that was barely playable. It was a nice classical guitar, but was difficult to play. I had to work to coax the notes out, but I liked the challenge. The damaged guitar seemed like a fitting instrument for one of Charlie's songs.

We weren't the first band to cover Charlie Manson. I think Redd Kross was the first to do it with a cover of "Cease to Exist" on their album *Born Innocent* in 1982. Of course, the Beach Boys did a modified version of "Cease to Exist" under the title "Never Learn Not to Love" way back in 1968. Even though Charlie wrote "Cease to Exist," he wasn't credited on the record. That contributed to some ill feelings between Charlie and the Beach Boys. It's trippy to think that in the span of a few months, Manson went from being a trendy, hip musician who'd written a song on a Beach Boys record to a murderer.

When Guns N' Roses covered "Look at Your Game, Girl" it created an uproar. The band caught a lot of shit for it, Axl in particular, because the song appeared as a hidden track on *The Spaghetti Incident?*, an album of cover songs that had influenced the band. David Geffen, the head of the record label, publicly reprimanded the band for selecting one of Charlie's songs and the media kept the story going for weeks. We'd released Manson's "Your Home Is Where You're Happy" without incident.

We were becoming more interested in hip-hop than Axl "Janis Joplin" Rose trying to get through a Manson song. It all started with Public Enemy's *It Takes a Nation of Millions to Hold Us Back*. We went down to the record store on the day N.W.A's "Gangsta Gangsta" came out. We got white-label, unmarked DJ copies of the single by Eric B. & Rakim. Boogie Down Productions was huge for us.

Ben contributed eight of the songs in the recording session that led to the *Creator* LP. They ranged from the moody rocker "Burying Ground" to the acoustic-damaged "Postcard," which was to the Lemonheads what "Beth" was to Kiss, and I am quite sure had a lot to do with Green Day's "Good Riddance (Time of Your Life)." I managed to cough up just three original numbers. There was "Clang Bang Clang," "Out," and "Die Right Now," plus the cover of Charlie's "Your Home Is Where You're Happy." I also added some audio samples of the incarcerated Manson, which had just found their way to the Taang! office. A jokey version of Kiss's "Plaster Caster" rounded out the LP.

My song "Die Right Now" almost died a few times before we committed it to tape. It's Charles Manson mixed up with Black Sabbath. Even though it makes direct references to both, it still manages to sound like a Hüsker Dü song. The lyrics take a cue from Charlie: "If you're willing to die right now you can live forever."

I also stole a line from Black Sabbath's "N.I.B." When I was in high school there were all these rumors about what N.I.B. stood for: Noodles in Borneo? Nativity in black, perhaps?

People say we were glorifying Charlie, but that wasn't it at all.

Ultimately, Manson exposed the hypocrisy of the news media, which was already on its way to becoming an offshoot of the entertainment industry. For years and years Charlie was the subject of books and movies. News teams pointed their cameras at him and broadcast his image and words via newspapers and television. They couldn't get enough of the spectacle and turned him into a bona fide celebrity. He was a famous person who had all kinds of associations with other famous people—some benign, some horrifying—but if you expressed an interest in the man and actually considered what he had to say, then *you* were the one who was glorifying a murderer. Fair play.

I think it's fair to say, no one really knew what to make of this record. On the LP liner, Ben was thanking "Emily Dickinson for a stolen stanza," while I was paying homage to the Charles Manson songbook. It was obvious that Ben and I had gone in different directions.

* * *

That's not a photo of Andy Warhol on the cover of our second album. The platinum hair, the box of Cheerios, and the title of the record create a tableau that screams "Warhol," but it's not him.

The guy on the cover of *Creator* is none other than Ivan Kreilkamp. After the somewhat controversial cover of *Hate Your Friends*, we wanted to do something stupid and we succeeded. Our friend Ivan had named the band. We thought, "Let's put him on the cover!"

The Warhol comparison, though inevitable, was unintentional. So *Creator* is our foray into pop art. Jesse took the photo. Although Ben and I wrote most of the original material on those early Lemonheads records, Jesse was our secret weapon in the art department. As I've said, we were big fans of Hüsker Dü and we loved the way Bob Mould, Grant Hart, and Greg Norton managed every aspect of the band. They wrote their own songs *and* played cool covers *and* designed their own albums. Jesse's artistic eye informed the visual style of our first three records.

While Ben and Jesse were at school, I was hanging out with the Blake Babies. Both John and I turned twenty-one that March, which meant we weren't limited to all-ages punk ragers anymore. We could go to all the shows we wanted at the Channel and the Rat in Boston and T.T. the Bear's Place and the Middle East in Cambridge.

At the end of the semester, we hit the road again and we had the strangest setup for that tour. We borrowed this weird trailer from a friend of Jesse's mother that was like an artist's studio on wheels, and it had a big picture window so she could paint landscapes from inside the trailer. We called it the Art Truck. Unfortunately, the Art Truck couldn't go over fifty miles per hour and had terrible ventilation, which made for some long, miserable drives.

We had no problem getting shows, and for the first time we had something like a tour manager, a guy named Marc Alghini, a disc jockey at Emerson College WERS. He was the first person to play the Blake Babies on the radio and was a big fan of the Lemonheads. He pieced together the Create Your Friends Tour to promote *Creator*.

Hüsker Dü were a lot of Boston's bands template for best band ever, which was wild because every time we saw them, they were a different band, playing new songs that hadn't been recorded yet. Hüsker Dü was constantly evolving, always striving to outdo themselves. We found that inspiring, but that inspiration played out in different ways. Some of us drew from the way their music sounded; some were inspired by their approach to making it.

By 1988, Hüsker Dü had broken up, so we asked Grant Hart to play with us at our gig in Minneapolis, and he accepted, which was nice of him to do. It didn't seem real that a songwriter who'd had such an influence on us would be willing to play with the Lemonheads.

His set was just him and his guitar, that's it. I thought that was the bravest thing, going onstage without a band to back him up. He was working on a solo album for SST Records that would come out the following year, so he played a lot of material off of that. Of course, we asked him to play our favorite Hüsker Dü songs that he'd written, and he obliged. He sang "Pink Turns to Blue" and other songs, but we couldn't get him to sing "Diane."

After the gig, we got into some cheap wine we'd bought at a truck stop as a joke. Grant told us all these stories about his days before, during, and after Hüsker Dü, and we hung on every word. His feelings about the dissolution of his old band were still pretty raw. He didn't have any advice for us or pass on any words of wisdom, but he didn't judge us or look down on us, either. He treated us like peers, not kids. He was trying something new and so were we.

Late that night, we talked Grant into coming with us to play our next show in Chicago. He had his boyfriend with him, which seemed radical to us at the time, and they traveled with us in the Art Truck. They pretended to be asleep, but it was kind of close quarters, so everyone could tell what they were up to under the blankets. We wanted to make it up to Grant in Minneapolis, but our show in Chicago at a club called Dreamerz wasn't much better. Sadly, only about fifty people showed up.

The next day we said goodbye to Grant and took him to the airport. There's some great footage of Grant and the Art Truck in the video for "A Circle of One," directed by Carl MacNeil. No live performances, just a bunch of kids goofing off in front of the camera, which was still kind of a novelty back then.

While we were crossing the country in the Art Truck we tried to pick up the local college stations on the radio. Our songs occasionally charted in *College Music Journal* and we were hoping to hear the Lemonheads on the radio, but we didn't have any luck.

Like all tours, the *Creator* tour had its ups and down. A bunch of shows fell through in the Southeast and we spent about a week in Chapel Hill, North Carolina—where John's brother lived—with nothing to do. During an interview with the college radio station at UNC, we told the audience we were stuck in Chapel Hill and we would play anywhere for free. We got a call from a guy at a frat house, who invited us to come over, so we did. It was a pretty fun show, and afterward Mac McCaughan and Laura Ballance, who would go on to form Superchunk, invited us to open for their band Wwax the following night. In the blink of an eye, we went from playing a frat party for free beer to performing at the indie music mecca Cat's Cradle.

We got some big gigs that were important for us on that tour, but none bigger than our show at the Cabaret Metro in Chicago with hometown heroes Naked Raygun. Because we were so well-connected in Boston, sometimes bands that we'd shared a bill with back home would return the favor on the road—even if we had nothing to do with putting on the gig. We'd played with Naked Raygun at T.T. the Bear's Place the previous September, so the band put us on the bill with them when we came to Chicago. It was easily one of the biggest shows we'd done up to that point. The show was sold out and there must have been more than twelve hundred people in the house. That was huge for us and it's a night I'll never forget.

I don't know why Naked Raygun helped us out like that, but they did. When I think of all the places we played, and how young we were and how little money we had during that tour, there's just no way we could have done it without people looking out for us and lending a helping hand along the way.

The Lemonheads weren't completely helpless. One thing we used to do on the road was make our own T-shirts. We had enough of our own art supplies to be able to roll up to a coffee shop and make a few shirts in the Art Truck that we'd sell at the show that night. It was a great way to kill time on the road. Like so many other aspects of the band, Jesse was the mastermind of our T-shirt operation. He could organize stuff like that and it would turn out really cool. I wish I had one of those T-shirts now.

*   *   *

While we took some parts of being in a band very seriously—the way the records looked and sounded, for example—other parts we didn't take seriously at all. People didn't come to see the Lemonheads because we were talented musicians who wrote great songs. They came to see a bunch of guys getting drunk and playing loud and fast. Part of the appeal of the Lemonheads was that it could all fall apart at a moment's notice. So it irked me that some of my songs weren't considered "good enough" for the records. In the context of our live shows, what did that even mean?

Ben and Jesse were starting their junior years at Harvard and were waking up to the realization that they needed to get serious about their studies—or at least more serious than they had been. Maybe they had that epiphany that my dad had at Cornell back in the sixties. As for me, I got a gig waiting tables, which I liked because the money was decent and I was good at it—sometimes. As a waiter, I was consistently inconsistent, but I had fun with it. It was the perfect situation for a musician: I had a car, my rent was cheap, and I was paid in cash. I was never interested in clothes or fashion or things like that, so I had plenty of extra money for drugs and alcohol.

Although I was still heavily invested in the local music scene, I was starting to have mixed feelings about my band. We were all into what we were doing when we were into it, but none of us thought the band had any kind of long-term future. Ben and Jesse weren't your typical punk rockers. They were Harvard guys doing Harvard things. Ben was deep into his studies of Irish literature. In addition to working at the radio station, Jesse had ambitions as a filmmaker. One of his good friends was the cellist Yo-Yo Ma. I was starting to get the sense that the Lemonheads, or even playing music, wasn't a big priority for my bandmates.

I think at that particular moment in time music meant more to me than it did to Ben or Jesse. We were all white boys with wealthy parents, but there were varying degrees of privilege in the band. I was a dropout, waiting tables, whilst Ben and Jesse were enrolled in the most prestigious school in the country. They had plenty of options. They were figuring things out, but I already knew what I wanted to do. I always knew that things were going to change with the band—it was just a matter of when—and I was getting the feeling that it was time for me to move on. After all, I was in a punk band with two Harvard guys. What's wrong with me?

The final meltdown came onstage at a packed Cambridge club. I was so frustrated with the whole palaver I used the "Sweet Child O' Mine" riff as my guitar solo for every song that night—even the ones that didn't have solos. It was obvious to me, and by the end of the night to most everyone else in the audience, that things had come to a head. We'd had two ripe years in the sun, with an EP and a couple of legit albums to show for it. We decided enough was enough—for about three months that is.

I started spending more time hanging out with the Blake Babies. It was more comfortable at the Condo Pad than the closet at Ben's place, but it was more than that. Juliana and I had become friends, then more than friends. For very different reasons, neither one of us was willing to commit to taking it further than that. Although things were kind of messy between us—she wrote a lot of songs about me—we eventually came to an understanding that we were better suited as friends than romantic partners.

I drifted away from the Lemonheads and became the Blake Babies' new bass player. John had already quit the Lemonheads so he could focus on his own band, which made it that much easier for me to follow him.

It seemed like I meshed better with Juliana, John, and Freda than I did with my own band. I'd only ever been in the Lemonheads. There was so much creativity in the Boston indie music scene and I wanted to be part of it. Juliana wasn't a dropout like me; she was a serious musician who knew her stuff. In that way we were total opposites.

My method, if you could even call it a method, was completely haphazard. Whenever I'd write a song, I'd start with the guitar parts and flounder around with the vocals. But Juliana could make the pieces of a song fit together in seemingly no time at all. While I was groping in the dark, Juliana could articulate why something wasn't working.

"Evan, you idiot," she'd say, "that's the wrong key for your voice!"

Juliana was hard on me, but she knew her shit. John taught me a few things about the guitar. He knew all these cool chords and showed me new places to put my hands. The Blake Babies opened my eyes to so many things. It wasn't just the music that Juliana, John, and Freda exposed me to, but the idea that we could do anything we wanted. We didn't have to be so strict about our approach. While the Lemonheads' style of play was loose, the type of music we played was actually quite rigid. I realized there was more to being in a band than rehashing punk formats. (At the only Blake Babies show that was filmed with me in the lineup, I'm wearing a Flipper T-shirt.)

RUMORS OF MY DEMISE

I remember taking acid and listening to a bunch of Sonic Youth records at the Condo Pad with John. That experience recalibrated my musical thinking. Whatever punk was, it wasn't loose or free anymore. It had become strict and dogmatic in some cases, and I started to rebel against it. I didn't want to write copies of Minor Threat songs.

With the Blake Babies, I realized I could make music that was whatever I wanted it to be. I didn't have to follow a particular path or limit myself to a certain sound or style of music. There were no rules, so why not use that freedom?

The more I got to know the Blake Babies, the more the scene expanded from the narrow confines of post-punk into something bigger and more interesting. I played bass on the Blake Babies' second album, *Slow Learner*, and the band already had enough material for a third record, which it was shopping around.

When I joined the band, we shared a practice space with the Pixies. If we got there early, we could sit on the floor and watch the Pixies play. Afterward we'd say to each other:

"Oh my fucking god!"

Life wasn't supposed to be this good—and it wasn't—but they were. We felt privileged to see them because Boston didn't seem like the kind of scene that created superstars. The Pixies were almost too good.

People think of Boston in the late eighties as this explosion of incredible bands, and it was, but not everyone realized it at the time. I went to so many amazing shows that were not completely full. I saw Dinosaur Jr. play at Green St. Station in Jamaica Plain with the Screaming Trees and there were maybe forty people there. The bands played two shows, and I had to work that night so I went to the matinee. I brought my mom with me to the gig. I gave her some earplugs, but she took them out halfway through the set because she wanted to get the full experience. Afterward we met J Mascis, the guitar player and creative force behind Dinosaur Jr. I think he was impressed my mom stayed for the entire performance; it was so punishingly loud. To this day my mom blames her tinnitus on that show, but doesn't regret it.

It's been said before, but it's worth repeating: the late eighties and early nineties were an incredible time for new music in Boston. There were so many great bands. I know I'm not the only one who felt there was something in that dirty water—just like the song by the Standells.

Maybe it was acid.

*   *   *

The Lemonheads were essentially a part-time band. Because Ben and Jesse were full-time students, we could only tour in the summer, which is the worst time to tour because it's hot and uncomfortable and there're no people around who want to go to gigs. Kids may be out of school, but for part of the summer they're away on vacation with their families or working summer jobs, and all the college towns are deserted. I wanted to be a full-time musician.

The Blake Babies had worked out a deal with Mammoth Records in North Carolina for its third album. That fall we put together a short tour. We hooked up a U-Haul trailer to Sheila—my Chevy station wagon—and headed south so we could play some gigs on our way to sign the contract. The Blake Babies ended up recording that album, *Earwig*, at Fort Apache in Boston. The record was produced by Gary Smith, who was very important in the Boston indie rock sound. Fort Apache was *the* place to go. The sound was so good that a lot of bands kept going there even after they got signed because it was cheaper than going all the way to LA.

While we were recording at Fort Apache I bumped into J Mascis again. We were recording *Earwig* during the day, and Dinosaur Jr. was recording *Bug* at night. I was there when they recorded "Don't." J has a reputation for being a quiet person who lets his guitar do his talking for him. He is those things, but he's also a lot of fun. For instance, he loves to ski.

I was wearing a triple threat goose down jacket that still had lift ticket tags on the zipper from my last ski trip. My mom and dad were avid skiers and after the divorce I'd do a lot of those outdoor activities with my mom: surfing, skiing. We used to go up to Cannon Mountain in New Hampshire and take the lift to the top and let all the people get off and go ahead of us. We'd wait until it was clear so that we had the whole mountain to ourselves. Another time we were skiing Mount Washington and this huge rainbow came over the mountain. My mom and I just looked at each other because there was nothing to say.

"You like to ski?" J asked.

"Yeah, man!" I said. "I love it."

"You want to come up to Stowe and ski?"

"That's very un–J Mascis of you," I didn't really say, but thought, "and yes, I will!"

As unlikely as it sounds, I went up to Vermont and went skiing with J. I think that's when he decided we'd be friends.

*   *   *

The Blake Babies never got the big break that took them to the next level, but we played some memorable shows, and we had some great times together. We didn't rock out as heavily as the Lemonheads, but the songs were more complicated and had a more sophisticated sound. If being a member of the Lemonheads was like a college education for me, then joining the Blake Babies was like going to graduate school. Playing with Juliana, John, and Freda was some of the most fun I've had in a band, and that experience put me on the path I wanted to follow as a singer and a songwriter.

NEW WAVE COVER BAND

The Lemonheads had our first big reunion show in February 1989, kind of hilarious considering how early it was in the band's career and how it had been only about six months since our summer tour the previous year. The show was at Axis on Lansdowne Street in Boston. I got Volcano Suns, which was Peter Prescott of Mission of Burma's band, to open for us. Mission of Burma set the bar for indie rock. There would be no Sonic Youth or Dinosaur Jr. without them. Volcano Suns had a bunch of records on the label Homestead before moving to SST and we were excited they agreed to play with us.

I asked GobbleHoof to open the show. GobbleHoof was J Mascis's band with Charlie Nakajima, the singer from Deep Wound. Charlie didn't sing much, per se. He had a spoken word kind of delivery. J, of course, played drums.

Getting GobbleHoof was a real score for us, but I wasn't sure if J would actually show up. When I asked him he said, "We might make it."

With J, that can mean all kinds of things, and I wanted to let him know that I was promoting the gig. It was our first show back and kind of a big deal for us and we were putting them on the ticket.

"Can I put you in *The Phoenix*?"

"We might come," he said.

"Okay, see you there!"

"Maybe."

But J showed up, GobbleHoof played a killer show, and the Lemonheads were officially back.

Sort of.

*   *   *

Of the two professions, rock and roll and waiting tables, which one would you say is the more dangerous? In my view, it's the latter: you gotta look out for the restaurant manager and serve people for hours. It's a stressful and boring job, but you walk out the door with hundreds of dollars in your pocket. What is one to do with all that cash? Drugs!

I was working at a restaurant called the Back Bay Bistro. It was close to my mom's apartment on Beacon Street. My favorite part of the job was writing the specials of the day before the lunch shift in fluorescent crayon on the backlit sandwich board in front of the restaurant. I would sneak *666*, Black Sabbath logos, and *Free Tex Watson* into the graphic design. I kept filling the board with satanic messages, so I eventually lost that privilege.

By the time I started waiting tables at the Back Bay Bistro, I'd tried heroin a couple of times. While on a smoke break, I heard a guy on a pay phone begging someone to let him be four dollars short on what I imagined was a drug deal. I walked up to him, handed him the four bucks, plus another sixty, and told him to get me some, too.

RUMORS OF MY DEMISE

This guy was a Vietnam vet named Carl and he lived directly across the street from my mom's building in a one-room apartment on the ground floor. Carl was cool and he was straight with me all through our short relationship. One day on the way to see my mom, I clocked him limping up the alley with two hookers. I had to see what this was all about. He had been shot in the leg, but didn't really care because he'd made off with an ounce of uncut cocaine hydrochloride. We had a great deal of fun doing smack and coke and making elaborate ice cream sundaes until late at night. That was the last time I saw Carl.

The first few times I got high on my own I was very careful. I knew that heroin could make you forget to breathe and die.

I only did a little bit and then I put it away. I took it slow because I didn't want to fuck up, because I liked it. Heroin was different than other drugs I'd tried. It gave me a real comfortable feeling. I was a moody guy, and I never knew how I was gonna feel or what situations would weird me out. Heroin was something I could do that would guarantee me feeling good for about six to twelve hours. I was sad and angry, putting out fires in the only way I saw possible.

On the nights I dabbled in heroin I fell into a deep and dreamless sleep. No night terrors. No sleepwalking. Instead, I'd wake up feeling rested and content, which was no small thing. I didn't think I was doing anything exceptional. All I wanted was to feel normal, and heroin delivered. Other drugs, like alcohol, weed, and cocaine, took me further from myself. Heroin locked me into a comfortable place. It seemed like everyone dabbled in it from time to time, but not everyone sought it out to the degree that I would.

* * *

Although the Lemonheads had more or less broken up while I was playing with the Blake Babies, we were popular on college radio and occasionally received offers to play. When we got the offer to tour Europe in the summer of '89, we said, "Fuck it. Let's do it!"

The offer solved another problem. Curtis wanted us to make another Lemonheads record and was considering putting one together with various odds and ends we'd recorded, which none of us was too thrilled about. What if we wrote some songs, put out a new record that used some of Curtis's filler, and went to Europe?

I'd fallen in love with Europe the first time I went to France with my mom and Holly. My parents were some of the most enthusiastic surfers in New England. Surfing is really bad there, but once the sport gets in your blood you gotta keep doing it. Through surfing they met the de Rosnays: Joël and Stella, and their kids. They were living in Nahant and Joël was teaching at MIT. We got along like a house on fire and they invited us to spend the summer with them at their château near Biarritz.

Biarritz in 1976 was a magical place. Just stunningly beautiful. The beaches were full of topless women. To my nine-year-old self it felt like I'd been dropped into the pages of *Playboy* and *Surfer* magazines combined. We went to the beach every day that summer. I taught myself how to surf on a long black board with a pink hammer and sickle. I spent so much time swimming and surfing, I didn't take a bath all summer, until right before we got on the plane to go home.

I had my eye on the de Rosnays's daughter, Tatiana. Even though she was quite a bit older than me, like six or seven years, I thought she was the prettiest girl I'd ever seen. I had a crush on her. It was all quite magical, and the disco roared.

My parents were well-off, but we weren't rich, and neither of them came from money. They were on the verge of splitting up.

Things were about to get ugly, but my memories of that first summer in Biarritz are really something.

We didn't return the following summer because of my parents' divorce, but my mom took us back the next year and for a third time two years after that. The quality of the hazelnut ice cream cones never wavered.

When I was seventeen, Tatiana was visiting Boston and she came to stay with us. Holly was away at school, so Tatiana slept in her room. I can't remember if she snuck into my room or if I snuck into hers, but somehow, we ended up in the same bed. I'd been smitten with her for so long that I didn't think twice about fooling around with her even though I was still dating Jane at the time. Tatiana was an enthusiastic and imaginative lover, and it all felt wonderfully subversive in my sister's bed. It was a dream come true for me, but she wasn't too happy when she figured out I had a girlfriend. She gave me a copy of William Faulkner's *Light in August* in which she wrote down some words of wisdom for me. I had to rip out the pages because they were too incriminating and I didn't want Jane to find them, but she eventually did. Tatiana went on to write a series of bestselling novels in France and she's way more famous than I'll ever be. I'm pretty sure she wrote about me in one of her books and now she's in mine.

*   *   *

Before I joined the Blake Babies, the Lemonheads performed at the WBCN Rock 'n' Roll Rumble at the Paradise. The contest was important, but also kind of cheesy. A lot of the bands that won it never went on to do anything else, and the contest had a bad track record. Doing well in the competition could help your career, but winning it all was seen as a curse. The trick was to win your night and advance to the finals, but fall short of winning the whole thing. In other words, we didn't want to win, but we didn't want to lose, either. That was a perfect scenario for the Lemonheads.

The Replacements were sorta what we wanted to be. They were a loud, drunken mess of a band that played lots of covers and didn't take itself too seriously. They'd just go out there, get drunk, and fuck shit up. We wanted to make our presence known. The night of the Rock 'n' Roll Rumble I wore one of my friend's girlfriend's tie dyed dresses.

The Paradise was packed, and back then it held about eight hundred people. Our show was borderline out of control, but we gave it our best shot and won our night. I can't remember who we were up against, but we made it to the finals. We didn't win the whole thing. Neither did our friends in Bullet Lavolta. The winner that year was a slick heavy metal band called Heretix.

The consolation prize was free studio time that allowed us to record our third album for Taang! First, we had to come up with some music.

"Mallo Cup" was an old song I couldn't think of a name for that we recorded for the new album. I probably should have called it "Mara" after this girl. I would skate over to her house in the middle of the night and look up at her bedroom window. It's basically a song about longing. A desolate, three-in-the-morning, skateboarding-around-town type of song with some pretty lyrics:

> I never will forget
> I ain't remembered yet
> Like mackerel in a net
> I forget to forget

A Mallo Cup is chocolate infused with coconut and stuffed with a marshmallow filling. I called the song "Mallo Cup." It's an ode to young love. In the end, I'm glad I called the song "Mallo Cup." I developed a taste for them, and fans give them to me from time to time.

"A Circle of One" was another one of mine. One of my favorite songs I'd written so far, it's about the absurdity of doing things over and over again without knowing why, and the futility of knowing you only have yourself to blame when things don't work out the way you want them to. It's a simple song lyrically—my explanation has more words than the lyrics—that's a little on the quiet side. Curtis wasn't a fan. Sonically, it was too R.E.M. for him.

"What is this?" he asked. "Where's the guitar?"

Curtis didn't want us to put such a mellow song on our new record, but he thought our cover of Suzanne Vega's "Luka" was the best thing he'd ever heard. He was there the first time we played it in Youngstown, Ohio, and he lobbied hard to include it on the new record.

We'd actually recorded "Luka" for *Creator*, which we didn't want to do, but by the time we were putting together *Lick*, our third record, we were ready to sell out. I felt if we were going to do the records there ought to be a reason, and a trip to Europe was good enough for me. Getting paid for your music isn't selling out. We were never this fringy, obscure band with a weird sound that would have to drastically change in order to become more commercial. We weren't one of those bands that was so difficult that it would never go platinum. We were a rock and roll band and we weren't afraid of success.

We didn't have much in the way of new material and no real direction as a whole. We'd only recorded five new songs for *Lick*;

the rest were bits and pieces we'd recorded over the last few years. In addition to "Luka," we covered "Strange" as the New York Dolls and slapped on our versions of "I Am a Rabbit" and "Glad I Don't Know." Another song we'd had lying around was "Ever," which we had recorded during our second recording session. Then there was "Sad Girl" and a cover of Big Star's "Mod Lang," which we'd recorded with Doug for the 1987 compilation *Crawling from Within*.

Crawling from Within wasn't the only comp we contributed to. In '87 or '88 we were invited to be on *Flipside Vinyl Fanzine Number Three* after the LA punk zine reviewed our record. *Flipside* put "Hate Your Friends" on the compilation with some pretty big bands like the 7 Seconds and the Circle Jerks.

One of my favorite songs on *Lick* is "Mad," which is the song that got cut from *Laughing All the Way to the Cleaners* after Jesse didn't like it, calling it generic. It's spy-punk with lots of tension. You can hear me screaming my headphones off at the end. I probably didn't stick up for myself as much as I should have in those days.

Lick is a kitchen-sink kind of record, more a of compilation than a studio album. We eventually got enough songs together to call it an LP. It had only been eight months since we'd put out *Creator*. The funny thing was people loved *Lick* and it was our most popular record by a fairly significant margin. Curtis issued "Luka" as a proper single and it blew up, generating interest in *Lick*. We also did a video for "Luka" that has Holly in it, displaying what she'd learned in her African dance class. Years later, when I ran into Suzanne Vega at Bubby's on North Moore Street in New York City, she told me she really liked our version.

* * *

RUMORS OF MY DEMISE

After recording *Lick*, it became obvious that Ben was considering life beyond the Lemonheads. His passion for Irish literature prompted him to make plans to go to Ireland to attend a Yeats conference. This conflicted with our club tour of northern Europe in June. He couldn't do both, and it seemed like he took a long time to make up his mind. Personally, I think he was sick of rock and roll. Ben wanted a break—from school and the band—so he followed his heart and went to Ireland.

John had returned to playing with the Blake Babies full-time, so I went back to playing drums in the Lemonheads. I had been playing a lot of drums back then, they were my favorite instrument. I had a blast banging away on my kit during rehearsals. Then, after Ben left, I had to return to the front. They say you get more trim out there. We asked Corey from Meltdown to play guitar with me and Jesse. He was playing in Bullet Lavolta, who played its first shows with the Lemonheads at T.T. the Bear's Place. We invited Bullet Lavolta to open for us on our European tour. It was all hectic and confusing, and we still needed a drummer.

We got this goth guy named Mark Newman, who called himself Budola, to go on tour with us. We called him Johnny Bravo. We didn't know him very well. For the longest time we didn't even know his real name. He had long hair that he dyed black and was very quiet and reserved, and usually wore a T-shirt that said FROZEN HUMANS. He wasn't the best fit for the Lemonheads, but he was good enough, so we gave Mark a shot.

Some musicians love touring; others hate it. I'm definitely one of the former. Some people don't like the pressure of rushing around so you can play in a completely new setting only to break your gear down and do it all over again the next day. For me, touring was the point. If you really want to know what a band is all about, you have to see them play live.

I was twenty-two years old and I was hungry. I had a fair sense of what I *didn't* want to do: I didn't want to commute to work in an office every day. Being in a band ensures that won't happen. I registered for the draft at sixteen, but never registered to vote so I could avoid jury duty. It was all very simple and it worked out, but you know what? I think I should have voted.

We played with so many great bands and made so many important connections. For instance, we played an incredible show with All at City Gardens in Trenton, New Jersey, where I got to meet Bill Stevenson and Karl Alvarez of the Descendents. When I met Bill, he had just taken a shit in a plastic cup. They would go on to play a crucial role in the Lemonheads' story—all because of Randy Ellis and his grimy punk rock bar in Trenton. When we played Philadelphia, my Philly cousins on my father's side came out to the show, and in Kansas City my stepmom's relatives did the same. In Washington, DC, Jesse's dad's cronies had a blast with the Lemonheads.

As before, on this tour, I didn't want to make that big of a deal about my night terrors. Sometimes my behavior was benign. One night one of my bandmates heard a noise in the kitchen and found me spreading my blanket out on the table like I was making my bed. Sometimes I'd mutter things in my sleep, and sometimes I'd scream.

Usually, I dealt with it by drinking too much and getting high. Drinking whiskey before going to bed was a bad idea, but it was years before I figured that out. I don't advise self-medicating. I'd use speed and cocaine to try to stay awake for as long as possible, and then I'd use alcohol and weed to come down. If there was something stronger available to help me achieve either of those ends, even better. I'm talking to you, Xanax and Valium. The best sleep came after taking a shot of heroin. To know I was going to get a guaranteed good time was worth a lot to me. If there was something that stopped you from waking up in the middle of the night and screaming your head off, would you take it?

I had a prescription for Valium for a while, but it stopped working and I had to take more and more. Or it was the other way around. You've heard of the law of diminishing returns? I used it recreationally until I realized it was mostly effective for a toothy shot of coke or speed. Opiates help you go to sleep. They can also help you drop your face in your carbonara.

* * *

Early in the tour we stayed in a convent school that had been converted into an upscale hippie commune in Nijmegen, one of the oldest cities in the Netherlands. The space was called De Refter and had been divided into *chambrettes*—little cubicles with four walls, a door, a bed, and a sink, but no ceiling. We each had our own *chambrette* to chill in, which was great because we never had any privacy on the road.

Touring made my sleepwalking worse. I was constantly going to sleep in unfamiliar places. The bed in the *chambrette* was small, so I had to sleep at an angle, which wasn't ideal, and I had myself turned around the wrong way . . . maybe something happened to me in my crib when I was a baby with a Fisher-Price mobile. Anything too claustrophobic can be a problem, which would have been nice to know before I moved into Ben's closet or stuffed myself into crowded vans.

I didn't think the setup in Holland would be an issue because the *chambrettes* didn't have a ceilings. Lying in bed, I could look all the way up to the roof of the church. I'd slept in worse places.

I don't know what happened, but in the middle of the night, I climbed up and over the eight-foot-high partition and into the next *chambrette*. Luckily, there was no one sleeping there. I woke up in a space that was similar to but different from the one I'd gone to sleep in and all my stuff was gone. As usual, I came out of it pretty quickly and was able to piece together what had happened when I went back to my *chambrette* and the door was locked, but all my stuff was inside. It was a disorienting experience.

Thankfully, it didn't happen again on that particular tour, and the times I woke up in a strange bed were for reasons unrelated to my sleepwalking.

The tour had its ups and down. We played about a dozen dates in Germany and Austria. After our one show in Switzerland, Mark went home with a girl without telling anyone. The next morning, we drove through the streets of some town calling out his name, which we didn't know. We called out "Bedola, behold-a." We had a last-minute opportunity to play that night with Living Colour in front of like three thousand people in Ghent, but we couldn't get to the gig on time. Pissed off, we then headed to the UK for shows in Wales and London.

I'll never forget that first show at the Fulham Greyhound. There was a huge crowd waiting for us outside the venue and they had our name in lights at Piccadilly Circus. We knew people had heard of us because *Lick* was available in the UK on World Service and had been selling well, but that first show was *insane*.

Unbeknownst to us, the Lemonheads had a hit on its hands. "Luka" was charting in the United States—a first for us. The single was doing well in the UK, too. *Melody Maker* named "Luka" the Single of the Week and compared it to Hüsker Dü's cover of the Byrds' "Eight Miles High" and Dinosaur Jr.'s reimagining of the Cure's "Just Like

Heaven." That was music to our ears—or it would have been had we known about it. We were out on the road and overseas phone calls were expensive. So it was a nice surprise when the news finally caught up to us at the end of the tour in London.

That was the first time we sensed the Lemonheads were capable of achieving some kind of notoriety. It wasn't because we thought we were any good, because we knew that we weren't. We were completely dysfunctional. We were dysfunctional when we started out and we stayed dysfunctional for years and years. We had so many bad shows in a scene that was loaded with talent. I don't think anyone who saw us in the eighties would say, "Now, there's a band that's going places." People didn't like us because we were good; they liked us because we were a fucking mess.

But things were happening in our little circle of friends. One by one our favorite bands started to get signed—and not just in Boston. Indie bands across the country were selling more records and playing in front of bigger crowds. Suddenly it didn't seem that far-fetched that we might do those things—people came to our shows and had a good time.

The rising popularity of college rock at the end of the eighties helped me keep things in perspective. It wasn't a matter of being good or bad, but ready. I was in the right place at the right time.

THE JELL-O FUND

At the end of the eighties, the Lemonheads were ready to make a move. With all the radio play "Luka" was getting, it was only a matter of time before the major labels started taking notice. Some were more serious than others, but after chatting with a few A&R reps it quickly became apparent that Atlantic Records was the most interested.

We didn't have any hang-ups about signing with a major label. It had a momentum of its own. My father used to say I was a spectator of my own life.

It was hard for me to know how to feel about the future of the Lemonheads because the band was in more disarray than usual. Corey left to focus on his PhD and we reverted to trio status. Jesse was gearing up for his final year at Harvard and was appropriately distracted. Also, neither of us were crazy about our drummer. As for Ben, he was still mad at everyone. After he heard that the majors were considering signing us, he threatened legal action if the Lemonheads signed with a major. I suppose that as a founding member and songwriter (and he wrote more songs than I did), he had an emotional stake in the band, but it was his decision to leave. As for me, I just wanted to make music and travel the world, and signing with a label that would pay us to do that seemed like the best way to make that happen.

The Lemonheads signed with Gold Mountain Entertainment, an artist management company that handled all the big bands in the early nineties, including the Beastie Boys, Sonic Youth, Nirvana, and Hole. We got hooked up with Gold Mountain through Richard Grabel, a lawyer who used to write for music magazines and came highly recommended by Sonic Youth. We liked him because he was able to get creative control for his artists. We could give him anything and they would have to put it out.

While Richard took a legal scalpel to the fifty-seven-page contract from Atlantic, I found myself back in Boston, living at home and totally broke. Success had redecorated our lives, but left the foundation cracked. After the European tour, I went back to waiting tables for a while at a place called Harvest, a cool, fancy restaurant that I particularly liked in Harvard Square. Harvest was kind of famous in Cambridge. That's where I met Tiffany.

Tiffany was the chief baker at Harvest, and she showed me the ropes when I was the new guy. We started hanging out after work and became close friends and pot smokers, and then briefly became more than friends. Tiffany liked to flirt with me at work by calling me Tarzan. She was into dumpster diving, and was always on the lookout for furniture and other things that people threw away, especially at the end of the semester, when college students were clearing out their apartments. She had a knack for finding the most amazing stuff, like beautiful old lamps or carpets that were practically new. She showed me her favorite treasure-hunting spots around Cambridge.

I've always been fascinated with the way objects can stand in for certain feelings and emotions, but Tiffany helped me bring this idea into focus. She wasn't content to wait for the things she wanted in her life; she sought them out, and in her own way gave them a new kind of life.

Tiffany was always telling me about her brother, David, a writer who occasionally performed his stories on the radio. She used to read me his letters to her, and they were very funny. She was certain that he would be a big deal some day and she was right. Her brother is David Sedaris.

Our relationship unraveled when I left Harvest. There was a party I wanted to go to in New York and I couldn't get someone to cover my shift, so I quit. That was the last job I ever had that wasn't related to music.

Tiffany was the kind of smart and quick-witted person that made Cambridge such an interesting place to be. We stopped hanging out after I quit, and we lost track of each other. Very sadly, Tiffany took her own life many years down the road.

* * *

One of the perks to signing with a major label was getting access to artists I loved, and I finally saw Ozzy at the Orpheum in 1989. I was hanging around backstage when I spotted Ozzy Osbourne. Ozzy was gracious enough to let me corner him and grill him about some song lyrics. The song in question was "Cornucopia" from Black Sabbath's *Vol. 4*. I recited a section of the lyrics for him, and he thought about it for a long time. Finally, after I wondered if he'd forgotten the question, he said, "Yeah, that's going back a ways."

I'll always love Ozzy. The show and talking to him made my night. Now you can look up lyrics on the internet, but in the eighties, song lyrics were the subject of intense debate. That was especially true with Black Sabbath, who didn't include lyric sheets in their albums. Ozzy was funny and endearing and he always made time for his fans.

At the end of 1989, I went to stay with Luisa Reichenheim and her family for Christmas in Frohnau, a suburb of Berlin. I'd met her when we came through Germany the previous summer. It was a wild, raucous time. The Berlin Wall was coming down. I got a hammer and knocked five pieces off the wall. Easiest Christmas shopping ever. We spent the holidays together partying at all the clubs, and on New Year's Eve we went to see Television Personalities, an English psychedelic pop band that Luisa was into and had turned me on to. We went to see them at the Ecstasy Club, and I jammed some Jonathan Richman tunes with them onstage. The leader of the band, singer-songwriter Dan Treacy, wrote a song about me called "Evan Doesn't Ring Me Anymore." It's on *I Was a Mod Before You Was a Mod*, which came out in 1994.

I came back to New York to sign the deal with Atlantic. The Lemonheads got $100,000. Twenty grand was divided up among the band members, another $20,000 went into the band fund for expenses, and $60,000 was allocated for making the record. When he heard the news that we'd signed, J Mascis said to me, "Evan, you should spend fifty thousand dollars on a new Corvette and ten thousand on the record."

"I don't get it?" I asked.

"So you can blow off the cops," he said. J had a wonderful take on things.

It's the biggest cliché in the world to sign a deal with a major record label and blow the advance like a rock star. It's not the sex and drugs that get you into financial peril—at least not right away—but impulsive purchases like sports cars and expensive jewelry, dumb things. When the checks finally cleared and the Lemonheads were officially signed to Atlantic Records, I was determined to blow my share of the advance, and I still wanted to have some fun. So I decided to break into my childhood piggy bank—the Jell-O fund.

When I was seven, I was in a television commercial for Jell-O. The whole thing was my mom's idea. She was a mode, and she got the entire family involved. Me, Holly, and my dad were all in the commercial, but my mom was the only one with a speaking part. It was kind of a big deal for our family because we were all going to be on TV.

This wasn't my first acting gig. I did a photo shoot for a sweater catalog a couple years before that. That was also my mom's idea. At first, I was grumpy about it and didn't want to do the shoot, but once they put me under the bright lights I totally enjoyed it. It turns out I liked being doted on by the people in makeup and wardrobe and I enjoyed being the center of attention.

"I've created a monster," my mom said.

My photo was also on the box with my sister and fake mom and dad for a board game that no one bought called Hot Potato. I remember they taped my hair back to make it look shorter. The Jell-O commercial was the peak of my career as a child actor, but I was only allowed to watch a half hour of TV a night, so I never saw it. My classmates saw it and teased me about it every day when I came into school.

The commercial was shot in the middle of summer, and it was incredibly hot, like ninety degrees. Because it had a holiday theme, they had me wrapped up in a parka and a scarf. The fake snow was made of cellophane.

When I watch the clip, it's always a trip to hear the narrator refer to my mom as "Mrs. Susan Dando of Boston." I walk in from the cold, bundled up in my thick winter clothes, and my mom and sister rush over to peel them off me before I pass out from heatstroke. Then my mom starts this whole spiel about how she always uses her mother's recipes when preparing Jell-O for her family, a total lie. We were not Jell-O eaters in the Dando household. In fact, we didn't even have ketchup in the house.

My mom was the star of the shoot and she sounds like a TV housewife from the fifties. I always associated Jell-O as a cool dessert you eat on a hot day. Who eats Jell-O at Christmas?

One of the strangest parts of the commercial is when my mom demonstrates how to prepare the traditional holiday Jell-O salad that's supposedly been in our family for generations.

"Pour some Jell-O brand gelatin into a mold and chill until it thickens," she says, sounding like she's on Xanax. "Then arrange nuts in any pattern you like, pressing them *in* like this."

The camera zooms in on a bright red ring of semisolid goop, real disgusting gore, as my mom sinks almonds into it with her fingers. The way they're arranged in a circle reminds me of a package of birth control pills.

After the commercial aired, the company sent us a shitload of free Jell-O. We had boxes and boxes and boxes of the stuff. We never got to the bottom of it. I can tell you that my mom did not use the Jell-O to give her salads a holiday look. Jell-O is mostly sugar, and I would eat it right out of the box when I got bored. When we moved to Boston a few years later, the Jell-O was old and expired but my mom brought it with us because she never threw anything away.

My mom made twenty grand from the commercial. Me, my sister, and my dad all got $5,000 each. My dad was shrewd about this sort of thing. He invested the money so that it accrued over the years. I may have added to it with other modeling gigs here and there, but my dad knew what he was doing when it came to investments and the money grew to a sizable amount.

I called it the Jell-O fund.

I had a few lyrics to finish for the album, so I checked into the Ritz-Carlton in Boston for two weeks, thinking it would help me concentrate. My Boston friends didn't approve. They would come over to party with me—eightball of coke, some weed, and some heroin every other day—and say, "Why are you doing this at the Ritz? Why don't you just get a motel?"

I guess they had a point, but even Ben came over to party. That was nice to see him again. I was thinking, *What would the Sex Pistols do? Would they stay at a motel or at the Ritz?* I thought they would have stayed at the Ritz. I am impressionable, over the top, and I was, even back then.

A few years later, I wrote a song about the whole experience called "The Jello Fund." There are no lyrics. It's basically two minutes of me noodling around on the piano. It was sheer numbers, I had to get 80 percent of the publishing.

* * *

The Lemonheads toured the West Coast with Mudhoney. We co-headlined with them, alternating nights in the top slot. Mudhoney was scorching live, and we kicked off the tour in San Francisco at the Kennel Club, which is now the Independent. We had played on our own the night before in Spokane. Mark quit the first day of the Mudhoney dates and we had to scramble to find a new drummer. We actually had tryouts at the Kennel Club all day for that night's show.

What happened was I scored some meth in Spokane, we took it, and he freaked out the next day. He quit the band and went home. We talked him into coming back out on tour with us, but things were never the same.

We kept stumbling like drunks in the dark after Mark returned. LA, our next stop, is a tough place to play and we struggled. LA crowds are somewhat jaded because they've seen it all before. Every time I play LA I feel like the audience is physically present, but mentally there's still glass between me and them, they're still in their cars. We had to go on after Mudhoney and they totally smoked us.

We've had our fair share of shows where the Lemonheads just died onstage. It happens sometimes, and the only thing you can do is carry on, doing your best, and hope the crowd comes around, because sometimes they do. It was hard when we were just starting out. When things went wrong or didn't come together the way we wanted them to, we had no idea how to fix it. I'd break a string, or some gear would come unplugged. We came to understand that those things are part of show business. The best solution for a bad show is to just keep going. Put it behind you and eventually you'll have a great night and the rest of the tour will fall into place.

One fact that confused me about those West Coast shows was my bandmates didn't even like Mudhoney. I loved them, and I became friends with the drummer, Dan Peters. I thought Mudhoney was onto something big. Why couldn't my bandmates see this was the future of rock and roll? Like Blue Cheer and the Stooges?

When I look back on my career and think about all the incredible bands we played with, it's amazing to me we were almost always the headliner or co-headliner. For whatever reason, the Lemonheads were rarely the supporting act. We were offered a spot with Neil Young once, but we were already on tour and had to turn it down.

We were kicking ourselves for weeks over that missed opportunity. It was going to take a lot of love to fix the way things were going.

I think being the headliner helped us. Our band didn't mix well with other bands. We were playing with Living Colour, because that was the sorta thing that was big back then, and they correctly pronounced us bad vibes. It shaped our outlook on things, because we never had that awful experience of opening for really big bands. We played with a lot of bands that would get big.

The Lemonheads were dysfunctional enough. We didn't need any outside help in that department. Our vibe was too weird and unpredictable for us to be someone else's warm-up band. We were in our own world.

The Lemonheads were a lot of things, but we weren't dull. We embraced spontaneity, kept things loose. I never wanted to wake up in the morning knowing that I was going to play the same songs in the same order that I played them the night before. But many mornings, I did wake up and do that. What's the point of that?

The Lemonheads have always been somewhat unpredictable. For better or worse, we've always found a way to keep things interesting.

RIDE WITH ME

Getting signed to a major label messed with my head in unexpected ways. Immediately after I signed my name to the contract, I met a girl named Kendra at a bar in New York City. Things got serious enough that we moved in together. We lived in a little one-room apartment on St. Botolph Street near the South End in Boston. The place was tiny. There was a big beautiful tree out in front of our apartment building that Kendra called the Groove Tree. We didn't stay there for long, and we moved to a bigger place on Newbury Street.

I liked Kendra, and now that I was going to be a major label recording artist, I thought I should settle down. I seriously considered asking her to marry me. I'd never thought of the Lemonheads, or even music, in terms of a career. Because the contract was a four-record deal, I started thinking about the future in new ways. I was willing to give marriage a try even though we spent most of our time together, drinking, taking drugs, and staying out late. I don't think either of us was ready to grow up.

The Lemonheads had plenty of unfinished business after our West Coast tour. The first thing we had to do was find a drummer—our sixth (if you count me and Ben as one and two). We needed someone who could handle the rigors of touring. We heard David Ryan was good, so we brought him in. I knew him as Dave Donut because he worked at the donut shop above the old Mission of Burma practice space in Kenmore Square, where we used to rehearse. As soon as he started playing, we knew we had our man.

Prior to signing with Atlantic, we committed to putting out a single with Roughneck Recording Company in the UK. As soon as Atlantic got wind of the project, they wanted to release it in the States. I'd gone back to a song that I'd written when I was hanging out with the Blake Babies called "Ride with Me." I played it for Holly's best friend, Rob Bingham.

Rob asked me, "Have you been listening to Gram Parsons or something?"

"Who's that?" I asked.

"Check this out."

Rob laid it down for me and explained Gram Parsons's role in bringing country and rock together through a lens of spirituality and drugs. Apparently, I was a Gram Parsons fan before I even knew his music.

Rob gave me Gram's first two solo records as well as *The Gilded Palace of Sin* by the Flying Burrito Brothers. Intrigued by the comparison to my song, I became obsessed with him. I loved the way Parsons used his voice. To this day, I study his relaxed delivery.

But my interest in Parsons went even deeper than that. I'd always been a fan of the Rolling Stones. Holly had all the old records. She loved the band and turned me on to them at an early age. The Rolling Stones and Flying Burrito Brothers played together at Altamont, where Gram heard "Wild Horses" for the first time. The band gave him permission to put his version of the song on *Burrito Deluxe*. That album came out a year before the Rolling Stones released its own version of "Wild Horses" on *Sticky Fingers*.

Parsons's tragic death by overdose in the California desert at the age of twenty-six struck a chord with me. I was still experimenting with heroin, chipping, but relatively clean and hadn't had any major scares. I had a tendency to romanticize heroin, especially when it came to Charlie Parker and Keith Richards, who I'd idolized for as long as I could remember. On more than ten occasions I've made the pilgrimage out to the Joshua Tree Inn, where Gram Parsons overdosed, and have stayed in the room where he died—room 8. A lot of people say he actually died in room 9, but I stayed in 8.

"Ride with Me" came out of an experience I had on the road. I went to visit my dad where he was living in Isla Maria in the Florida Keys. It was his sabbatical from his law firm. I drove Sheila from Boston to Key West in one straight shot.

I felt good about the trip. Fishing was the one thing my father and I could do together and feel completely at ease. After I got home safe, I decided to write a tongue-in-cheek song about my journey. There's a lot of Manson-speak in there, but there's something real, too.

> You're my girl, don't you show it
> To know you know is to know it
> When you can't trust yourself
> Baby, trust someone else

The "Ride with Me" single was released in the UK by Roughneck Recording Company and by City Slang in Germany. Roughneck was a subsidiary of Fire Records out of Glasgow and the single marked the beginning of a long and fruitful collaboration with the label. "Different Drum" was named Single of the Week, this time in *NME*, and was well received throughout the UK.

Atlantic wanted to release the record in the US as a CD EP with a few more songs. We gave them a pair of covers: "Step by Step," made popular by the New Kids on the Block, and an acoustic version of the Misfits' "Skulls." That may seem like an odd pairing, but to me the sequence tells a story. First, the cult member is recruited ("Ride with Me"), then they are indoctrinated ("Step by Step"), and finally sent out on a creepy-crawl murder mission ("Skulls"). As if that wasn't confusing enough, we called the EP *Favorite Spanish Dishes*. Why? Because that's the title of the book the model on the cover is reading. It's nice when things aren't as complicated as they seem.

I was going through a bit of a dry spell. I hoped that *Favorite Spanish Dishes* would get me going as a songwriter. The songs I was working on weren't flowing. I had ideas for how I wanted things to sound, but whenever I worked on the new material, I didn't like the way it came out.

We needed to deliver a record to our new label, and we were running out of time. We had a short European tour booked in the spring and a longer one in the summer. In between, we needed to record the new album. Jesse and David were a fantastic rhythm section and had great ideas, but they didn't contribute new material. I was on my own.

I'm not a natural songwriter. I have to work at it, which can lead to forcing the issue. I remember when I was old enough to help my dad around the house, he used to say, "Don't force it," when I was trying to solve a problem with strength rather than finesse. In songwriting, finesse is always better than force, even if you don't know what you're doing. It's a fake-it-till-you-make-it sort of thing. That doesn't mean you sit around and wait for inspiration. Ideas can come from all kinds of places, but you have to open the shop and make yourself available.

We went back to Fort Apache to make the album. It was a more drawn-out process than our previous records and the timing couldn't have been worse. While we were in the studio, Jesse and David had final exams and they were trying to finish out the school year, which was frustrating. We're making a record for a major label and you're worried about homework?

That made no sense to me. That's when I realized I needed to take control of the Lemonheads. There could only be one person calling all the shots. From that point on I was the Lemonheads and the Lemonheads was me. For better or for worse.

Unfortunately, my attempt at settling down wasn't working out as planned. I put all my focus and attention on the record and I spent a lot of time alone in the studio, obsessively going over all the tracks. I rerecorded some of Jesse's and David's bass and drum parts, which they weren't too happy about. Although asserting myself was new, playing drums was not. I'm the uncredited drummer for three or four songs on *Lovey*.

Lovey, our Atlantic debut, opens with "Ballarat," which takes its name from a ghost town in Death Valley not far from the Barker Ranch, where Charlie and many of his followers were eventually captured and brought into custody. The chanting of cheerleaders . . . let's get it together . . . from a soundtrack record, and then there's a squall of loud guitars. It's the perfect opening for *Lovey*: a little moody, a little menacing—sweet *and* sour.

"Half the Time" and "Year of the Cat" are followed by an electric version of "Ride with Me." I think the acoustic version on *Favorite*

Spanish Dishes is better than the version that made it onto *Lovey*, but that and five cents will get you a cup of coffee during the Depression. Side A finishes with "Li'l Seed," a pro-marijuana song.

The flip side opens with one of my earliest songs. I wrote "Stove" shortly after I moved into Ben's apartment in Porter Square. It's about the time this guy came to replace the stove. He took the old stove out and left it on the curb. It looked so forlorn out there that it stirred up all kinds of emotions in me. It reminded me of this book I had when I was a kid. It was about a crane that got thrown away but wanted to show the world that it was still useful. It made me sad when the crane got sent to the dump, and the stove felt like an embodiment of that story. Just seeing our little stove out there, waiting to get taken away, had an effect on me. There was something symbolic in that. It was a love song, about a stove that I had grown used to that was unexpectedly taken away from me.

"Left for Dead" is a remake of "Clang Bang Clang" from *Creator*, which imagines Charlie's life behind bars, ranting and raving in his prison cell.

Lovey has its share of spontaneous moments. I was playing the Gram Parsons song "Brass Buttons" in the studio. It's a sad, mournful song that reflected how I was feeling that particular day, and Corey said, "Let's do it!" so we did. "(The) Door" is a classic rock jam that's loaded with every hard rock cliché we could think of.

The untitled last track is a voice message from Polly Noonan, who had a bit part in *Ferris Bueller's Day Off*. It's kind of a throwaway to pad the record, but it wouldn't be Polly's last appearance on a Lemonheads record.

* * *

There are no rules in rock and roll except for one, and I broke it: never, ever bring your girlfriend on tour.

I didn't give it a whole lot of thought. As soon as we finished recording *Lovey* in early June 1990, we jumped on a plane to England and started our longest tour to date. We wanted to start away from the bright lights of London and kicked things off at the Zap Club in Brighton. As soon as our tour bus rolled into town the media descended on us. When reporters started asking questions about Kendra, I knew I'd made a terrible mistake.

While Gold Mountain handled things on the home front, we hired Tina van der Straaten to be our tour manager on the road in Europe. Tina was Dutch and knew the ins and outs of the European club circuit, which was cool, but chaotic. Our last visit to Europe had been stressful. The crowds were amazing, but everything else was a challenge. Small hurdles like overcoming language barriers and managing different currencies became difficult problems. Plus, we kept losing our drummer. Tina was a pro at navigating the bookers and borders and managed to keep tabs on all of us.

Unfortunately, Tina and Kendra clashed almost immediately. Kendra wasn't particularly confrontational, but the same could not be said for Tina. Whenever Kendra said anything, Tina shot her down. It didn't matter if her comment had any value, Tina wasn't interested.

When you're in a touring band there's an us-against-them mentality. It's you against the world, almost like a family. On tour, no one gets what they want 100 percent of the time, and you have to be okay with that, even when you aren't.

Kendra didn't understand that. She thought she was inside the circle; Tina made a point of letting her know that she wasn't, and she didn't pull any punches. Kendra wasn't particularly opinionated—she didn't have strong feelings about how things should go—but when she did make her feelings known, Tina treated her like her opinion didn't matter. This put Jesse and David in a difficult position because now every decision we made was colored by whether it was something Kendra and Tina were fighting about. It was unfortunate. It was exhausting. And it was all my fault.

Berlin was a low point on the tour. Luisa came to the show and wanted to see me. She was disappointed to learn that not only did I have a girlfriend, but I'd brought her along.

I did a lot of drugs on that tour. Rather than deal with the bad vibes, I mentally checked out. It also put a lot of pressure on Jesse and David, who wanted no part of the drama, but had to deal with it anyway. We all partied, but I was on another level. I was kind of on autopilot that summer, drifting through the tour in a haze of drugs.

"I like you on drugs," Tina said one day, "but not when you aren't."

That threw me for a loop. Was I more interesting on drugs? More manageable? Or did she mean I wasn't as nice when I wasn't high? I spent a lot of time trying to figure out what she meant. Should I be on drugs more? I decided she was right. I would take drugs.

By the end of the tour, Jesse and David had finally had enough and very publicly quit the band. After our last show, in Leeds, Jesse burned all of his effects pedals in a suitcase in front of the gig. The media on hand took pictures and the story ran in the music press.

Kendra and I were finished, too. The relationship dragged on for a while afterward, but she blew up my scene. Now more than ever I was committed to the lifestyle of a touring musician, and that was something I had to do alone.

* * *

RUMORS OF MY DEMISE

I needed to find some new players to do the American tour of *Lovey*. I didn't want to put an ad in the paper or interview a bunch of random people. I wanted what the Lemonheads had in the beginning: weird punk kids who'd grown up a bit, but not too much. I wanted Hüsker Dü or, failing that, Naked Raygun. What I got was the remnants of Squirrel Bait, a hardcore band out of Louisville, Kentucky.

Ben Daughtrey was a talented drummer who'd played on both Squirrel Bait records for Homestead. After the band broke up, he was in some bands with bassist Byron Hoagland. They came as a package deal.

We rehearsed a few times, and the newly reconstituted Lemonheads—seventh drummer, second bassist, and me—hit the road. The circumstances weren't ideal. We sounded okay, but the old Lemonheads had perfected the art of almost-but-not-quite falling apart. It was exciting to watch us teeter on the edge. There were plenty of nights I thought, *This could go either way*. The new version of the Lemonheads was fine, but there was none of the danger that made us compelling.

The shows didn't sell out. We did well in the big cities, but we had more than one gig in the sticks where the turnout wasn't too good. It was all very hit or miss. Touring was such hard work, and it wasn't paying off. The turnout wasn't all that different from our previous tours in the US, which we'd done on shoestring budgets with very little promotion. In fact, in some places it was worse.

I told Jesse and David I was sorry about the way the European tour had gone down and that I never should have brought Kendra along. Most important, I confessed that the Lemonheads wasn't the same without them and asked them to come back. They rejoined the band and the Lemonheads were back in business.

We did a run up the East Coast with a pair of bands on the indie powerhouse SST Records: Screaming Trees and Das Damen. There weren't that many dates and it came to be known as The Tour That No One Came To. My friend Dan Peters was drumming for Trees. The last time I'd seen him he was playing with Mudhoney. Drummers are the glue that holds a touring operation together. They're usually easygoing and down-to-earth. Dan was both of those things. I was happy to see him. He'd been all over the world and I needed his counsel.

There was a promoter who wanted to bring us to Australia and I had mixed feelings about it, considering how unsettled things were. There were so many Australian bands that I loved: Radio Birdman, the Screaming Tribesmen, the Saints. Everybody loved the Saints, but I *really* loved the Saints. We had a drinking game in high school and the only rule was every time Chris Bailey goes, "Come on!" or "All right!" or "Let's shoot the professor!" we had to drink. We got drunk as fuck listening to the Saints first record.

In spite of my passion for Australian bands, I had this notion that it would be like England, only hotter. So I told Dan the situation and asked him for his advice.

"What's this tropical-England bullshit all about?" I asked him. "Is Australia any good?"

"Fucking go," Dan said. "Don't even think about it."

"Really?"

"Australia is the best. Just go."

I told the promoter we'd do it.

*   *   *

Some strange things happened on that East Coast tour. During sound check at Tipitina's, the club in New Orleans where the Neville

Brothers often played, Dennis Hopper was there—just drinking at the bar at our sound check. Afterward, he talked to us for a while. He was into what we were doing.

To be honest, I needed the pep talk. After two long tours and all that time in the studio, *Lovey* had barely made a blip. In fact, we sold three times as many copies of *Lick* as we did *Lovey*. So much for major label marketing and distribution.

Lovey was a complete mystery to Atlantic. The label didn't have a clue what to do with us and sales reflected that confusion. It didn't help matters that the woman who'd signed us to Atlantic jumped ship and left us high and dry to start her own label. When a person brings you to a label, they're invested in your career because your success is their success. But if they leave the label, you get handed off to someone who potentially doesn't have the same kind of commitment or enthusiasm, and that can spell trouble. You don't need to know anything about the music business to understand that you want the people who represent you to be as passionate about your music as you are.

I lit into that executive during an interview in a fanzine, called her a parasite. The interview got back to the executive and she wasn't too happy, but that was the extent of it. Today it would be a huge deal and dominate news feeds for a few hours until the next crisis of the day. The more things change, you know.

I was very arrogant back then, which worked against me at times, but I didn't see the point in being humble. The Lemonheads weren't major sellers. We didn't have any kind of power. The record label called all the shots, and I didn't feel like the company was going out of its way to give us the boost we needed to break into the mainstream. But why would I think that, it's all up to the band.

The entire industry was in transition. Very few of the bands that had come up through the indie ranks had made it. The Replacements flamed out. Hüsker Dü broke up. But American guitar bands were huge overseas, and indie bands like Bad Religion and Fugazi were selling tons of records that they put out on their own labels.

But at the top of the charts it was the same old shit. It's easy to ignore the hits that are selling millions of copies when you're outside the system, but when you sign with a major label the reality is you're sharing resources with those bands. You're not exactly in competition with them, but it underscores how not all artists are treated equally. What chance did the Lemonheads have when artists like Phil Collins were sucking up the attention?

I have nothing against Phil, he's a drummer after all. One time I was kicked off a flight for being a bit too spirited. So I went and bought a first-class ticket to try to get from LA to Glastonbury on time. I was seated next to Phil Collins, and we compared notes about our experiences at Atlantic. I went on and on about his drumming, which he tolerated like a gentleman. He plays on one of my favorite records of all time, the Brian Eno record *Another Green World*. I was glad he wasn't *too* nice because I would feel obliged to go back and listen to things like "Sussudio."

Compared to *Lick*, *Lovey* was a commercial disappointment. *Lick* had two things going for it that *Lovey* did not, and Curtis at Taang! deserves credit for both: First, he was right about "Luka." That fucking song was a hit. Radio stations couldn't stop playing it—even when DJs admitted to disliking it. In fact, one radio station banned our version of the song from its rotation, which only made it more popular with listeners.

Second, Curtis licensed *Lick* to World Service for release in the UK. A shrewd move; it opened a whole new audience of Lemonheads fans. They loved us in the UK. Who knows what might have happened if Atlantic had released a proper single in the UK?

RUMORS OF MY DEMISE

Ultimately, *Lovey*'s commercial failure didn't change anything for me. It was the best Lemonheads record yet—that's what mattered. It's still my favorite. While it was discouraging that our improvement didn't translate to sales, that was out of our control. Our job was to make a good record, and as far as I was concerned, we'd succeeded. Although at times I felt like we were close to being dropped, Atlantic stuck with us. There wasn't anything we could do but write some more songs.

I SAID, "HIT IT!"

On April 23, 1991, I happened to be at a Richard Hell reading in New York with Syd Straw and Marc Ribot when we heard Johnny Thunders had died. Yes, Johnny Thunders of the New York Dolls. I got to talking to all of the roadies about how much I loved the Dolls and they invited me to the funeral, so I went. I wore a beige corduroy jacket and black trousers.

I got on the subway and made my way to Queens. There must have been 150 people packed into St. Anastasia Church. Everyone from the New York punk scene was there, but holy shit there was a lot of drinking happening on the way to the cemetery. Me and Johnny's former bandmates in the Dolls, Syl Sylvain and Jerry Nolan (who was also in the Heartbreakers), found a toilet down the hill from the cemetery, and by the time we got back Johnny was being lowered into the ground. Syl took this opportunity to perform the traditional Jewish ritual, and as he threw the first shovel of dirt onto the coffin he yelled, "You motherfucker!" Hanging out with Nolan and Syl, I was breathing rarefied rock and roll air. They were great people, and we had lots of fun. A pity about the venue. I was able to get a ride back to the city with them, and as I got out of the car,

Syl said with a wicked New York accent, "If you ever need a cheap producer..."

I was in between albums, so in May I went on a European tour with Juliana and Howe Gelb and John Convertino of Giant Sand, the psychedelic band from Tucson, Arizona. We went as a lark and organized everything ourselves. We found some cheap plane tickets—$200 round trip—and off we went. We had to fly to Chicago from Boston on the way to London, so it was a little more than a round trip, but we were young and psyched to be going.

We were a band in the loosest sense possible. We only practiced once, at a gig at CBGB. Howe has an incredible ability to carry on as if everything is organized chaos. I have learned more from Howe about life and music than pretty much anyone else. He is a mensch, and through him I came to love all of his buddies and Tucson. Our repertoire was L-hedz, Blakes, and Giant Sand songs. We should have called the band Giant Lemon Babies, but that would have made too much sense. Instead, I got down with my awkward self and came up with the truly enervating Fruit Child, Large. Who puts a comma in their band name? I remember the comma was very important to me.

I did. That tour was so much fun. It was the last doing-it-solely-for-fun, adventure, free booze, glory-of-expression, working-a-group-dynamic, the spills, the chills, bruises-and-hickeys tour before shit got professional. The band name implied the desultory, experimental, lost-as-fuck, four-U-turns-a-day reality of the tour. We got in the van and played all over Europe, mainly twelve gigs in Deutschland. Stephen Bonnar mixed the shows and he drove. We got lost every single day of the tour. The band members all had more experience in Europe than the stalwart New Zealand soldier at the wheel, but we didn't know the exact route, either. Whoops—there goes Dortmund. It wasn't so easy to find the clubs before GPS, even though I've missed more shows owing to GPS than using maps. Beware of cities with the same name when you're over in fortress Europe. Always use a postal code.

Giant Sand had a good following in Europe, which prevented the tour from being a total disaster. We did it for the fun of playing together. No pressure, no expectations. We even made a little money.

*   *   *

I told Jesse and David the Lemonheads had been offered a tour in Australia and New Zealand, along with some dates in Europe, and it was a turning point for the band, but especially for me.

Dan was right: Australia was as good as he said it would be. It wasn't just the people who I connected with, the whole vibe resonated with me. People tend to compare Australia to England or America, but neither comparison works. For me, Australia will aways be the myth of California that the Beach Boys sang about, but real.

Everything is a little off, a little different, and that difference was stimulating for me.

New Zealand, on the other hand, was a different story. People will tell you it's the other way around, that New Zealand is magical and Australia is kind of ordinary, but they're wrong.

Make no mistake, I like New Zealand. We played what was essentially a college tour and performed at all the universities. New Zealand is the first place where things were going so well I thought about trashing a hotel room.

Our record sold extremely well down there. We were so far from home I didn't expect the record to have any kind of impact, but I was wrong. I remember thinking, *How is this even happening?* Australians took hospitality to levels we'd never experienced before. It was almost heartbreaking how well they treated us, and not just the fans, but the promoters, the other bands and their friends, everyone. I was very sad to leave.

*   *   *

Corey Loog joined Jesse, David, and me for another Lemonheads tour in Europe to close out the summer of 1991. Edwin Heath was our tour manager and front of house. Tanco was the roadie who carried stuff. Both of them were from Groningen, home of to the legendary Vera Club. Dan Estabrook did merch and took photos. He would wear headphones in the van and was visibly in pain when we played our latest, greatest Neil Young/Buffalo Springfield mixtape. It was great to have Corey back with us and we played some very loud shows.

Late in the tour, I shared a room with Tanco in Belgium. In the middle of the night he climbed out a window and fell three stories to the ground. I didn't see it happen, but I heard him screaming as he fell. He survived the fall, but he was badly hurt. All I remember about that night is putting my T-shirt on a chair by the window before I went to sleep. Neither of us had any idea what happened.

That was a wicked scary experience. Hurting myself—or someone else—in my sleep was a big fear of mine. Did I do something to frighten Tanco? Or was he a sleepwalker, too? Maybe both of us were sleepwalking at the same time, like two somnambulists walking out of a bar . . .

I had a bunch of good smack and a weird wooden wind instrument. I picked up both in Needle Park in Zurich. It was a crazy place back then, like Vancouver with fewer people, who were better dressed, and real heroin. I was worried the smacked-out jazz I was playing on my wooden horn might have sent Tanco jumping out the window.

That wasn't the strangest sleepwalking episode of the tour. In Basel, Switzerland, I got up in the middle of the night and walked out of the hotel. I must have made a lot of noise on my way out because someone heard me leave and followed me out the door. They found me in a petting zoo a few blocks from the hotel. I'd climbed into the rabbit pen and was sitting down on the grass, surrounded by a circle of rabbits. Apparently, I was talking to them in my sleep.

Toward the end of the tour, I was on ecstasy at a club in Manchester when they played Nirvana's "Sliver" over the sound system.

Mom and Dad went to a show . . .

I heard that song and I knew my band was going to be fine because somehow my kind of music was suddenly getting popular. It felt like a turning point.

Here's why: the majors were signing so many indie bands it was only a matter of time before one of us broke through. Everyone knew it was going to happen. It was something that Juliana and I talked about all the time. Hearing "Sliver" that night was a buckle-your-seat-belt moment for me.

The Lemonheads were doing well in Germany, Australia, and England, and a lot of our friends had gotten big in Europe before they caught on in the States. Even Hendrix had to go to England first. So did the Pixies. I had faith the Lemonheads' time would come. In fact, it was right around the corner.

* * *

I loved Australia so much that I wanted to finagle a way back there as soon as I could.

I asked the promoter Steve Pavlovic to bring me back to Oz by October. I kept faxing him and he came up with the gear.

"How about opening for Fugazi?" he asked.

"Great! How long can I stay?"

"About seven weeks with breaks to write."

"Cool bananas, Pav. I'm in like Errol."

I had to borrow money from my mom to fly down there, but I paid her back after the tour. I grew up idolizing Minor Threat, so playing with Fugazi was a huge thrill for me. Of course, I'd get trashed and play the Minor Threat song "Guilty of Being White" every night at the end of my set. The crowd loved it, but what did Ian MacKaye think? After the show one night, he gave me a talking to, which was exactly what I wanted.

"I'm really flattered, Evan," Ian said, "but you shouldn't get so drunk before you play!"

"Okay, Ian!" I said, and then I did it again the next night.

I couldn't help myself. I felt like the luckiest guy on the planet, and I was truly happy just to be there. Fugazi's shows were amazing, and they were exceptionally nice and warmhearted people. What I thought was interesting was the band's straight-edge politics didn't apply to its crew (or to me, for that matter). I quickly figured out Fugazi's soundman liked to get high. Who cares if he did drugs? He was the best man for the job.

So, while Fugazi was eating their vegan food and being super straight edge, I was bashing out Minor Threat songs and partying it up with their soundman. As strict as they were with themselves, they never judged us.

As a band, Fugazi was untouchable. Not only was it exciting to watch them play, it was also inspiring. I'd never played on my own before, just me and my guitar. If I was going to be opening, I knew

RUMORS OF MY DEMISE

I had to bring it, and I did. This was a completely new experience for me as a musician. I felt like I was doing something quite brave. Playing by yourself is hard, but it's just you, so it's easy to finesse mistakes. It was an important step for me as a performer to realize I could do it, that I could hold an audience without a full band behind me. Not many people want to. I took my SG and borrowed a Gretsch from one of my favorite Australian rockers, Ian Rilen, from the band X. No acoustic guitars on that tour.

One of the first solo gigs without Fugazi was at the Annandale Hotel on Parramatta Road in Sydney. I couldn't believe all the people who came to play the show with me: Don Walker from Cold Chisel, Tex Perkins and Spencer P. Jones from the Cruel Sea, Kim Salmon from the Scientists. I loved meeting all these visionary musicians. I even ran into Rob Younger of Radio Birdman on a bus. Meeting what was left of one of my favorite bands of all time was a holy-fucking-shit moment. The Eastern Dark's Geoff Milne and Bill Gibson also came down to see me before one of my shows. That really got to me, because I loved them.

I stayed in Australia for several weeks longer than I'd planned, and I still didn't want to leave. After the tour, I hung out in Melbourne and then stuck around Sydney for a while, looking for the right kind of trouble. Sydney had a lot of good bands—and still does. I partied with my friends Nic Dalton and Tom Morgan. We'd stay up all night on speed and write songs just for the hell of it. It was an incredibly creative scene. Toward the end, I clocked thirteen nights without any sleep.

I couldn't stay in Oz forever. It had been a prolific period for me, and I wanted to keep this feeling of creativity flowing for as long as possible. I'd completely bought into the magic of Australia. It was summer in the Southern Hemisphere and I wasn't looking forward to winter in Boston. I was also feeling anxious about getting to work on the new album.

Sam Brumbaugh, one of my sister's best friends and with whom I share a birthday, came to visit. It was Sam who had made the really astute suggestion that the Lemonheads cover "Different Drum" by Mike Nesmith. When my flight was getting ready to leave, Sam was the voice of reason I needed. "Hey, Ev, you should go back and get to work. Go on home and finish your album." I couldn't argue with that.

* * *

When I got back to Boston I fell into a deep depression. The Big D. I didn't see the point in anything. The days were getting shorter, the nights were longer. It was bitterly cold and everything felt bleak. After being away for so long, Boston seemed foreign and strange. My mom was still in town, my dad was out on Martha's Vineyard and Holly was in New York. I was twenty-four, but I felt so old. I never felt older. Even though I knew coming home was the right thing to do, I felt cut off from everything I did in Australia. I'd felt like a new person in a new place on drugs, and I felt the loss of that person when I came home.

I moved in with Juliana on Brainerd Road in Allston. She urged me to go see a psychiatrist, so I called the doctor I'd gone to when I was in high school, Al Kahn, and made an appointment to see him at his office on Brattle Street in Cambridge. Everybody at Commonwealth went to see the psychiatrist at one point or another.

"Ev," he said, "just take it straight for a while. Don't drink, don't smoke pot, don't do anything. All these under-the-counter medicines are not doing you any good and you need a break from them."

RUMORS OF MY DEMISE

He wasn't judgmental at all. He was totally cool with me. Just listening to him was reassuring.

I followed his advice. I didn't get clean and sober; I took a break, just like the doctor ordered. When I was down in Australia, I wasn't getting any sleep because of all the speed I was doing. I needed to pull myself together. I used to call it brain stiching. Sleeping for weeks and getting your brain together again.

While I was hanging out with Juliana, I started writing about my friends in Australia and some of the experiences I'd had down there. I realized that by working on these songs, I could go back to that time and place. I didn't need drugs to recapture those feelings. All I needed was my guitar. I found that by slowing down and concentrating I was able to get back to work. This clean period became the genesis of *It's a Shame About Ray*.

* * *

After the Lemonheads' Australian tour, Jesse quit the band again to go to film school, and this time he meant it. He'd played his last show with the Lemonheads. With Jesse gone I was the last original member of the band, but David stayed with me.

I talked Juliana into playing bass on the new record. She agreed on one condition: she didn't want to go on tour with us. Actually, that's not true. She wanted to tour with her own new solo project as support, but not as a member of my band. Fair enough.

Most of the songs on *It's a Shame About Ray* were either written in Australia or inspired by my experiences there. A lot of stories about the origin of the title track have circulated over the years. I'm not saying that they're wrong, because I had a hand in spreading them, but this is how I remember it.

One morning Tom and I discovered a little gem in *The Sydney Morning Herald*. The headline was "It's a Shame About Ray." It was a priest's final comment about one of his students, a kid named Ray, who couldn't toe the line and kept getting kicked out of school. It became one hell of a catchphrase for us. We said it so often, it ended up as the chorus and title of a new song.

I had all the chords and riffs already. I'd written them back in Boston. Tom and I wrote the lyrics and melody together one morning. We kept singing it and brought a tape of the song to play for Nic at his store Half A Cow outside Sydney. Somehow, we played it live on the radio that same day at Triple R FM. It was a heady morning.

When the song started to cohere, it gave us chills. We knew we'd stumbled onto something much darker and deeper than a throwaway line from a newspaper. Tears were shed, from sleep deprivation, when we realized that this song we thought was about someone who was vanishing in plain sight was about *us* or something. We'd been up for four or five days doing speed—we also finished "Confetti" and "Bit Part" that morning—so the drugs may have had something to do with the intensity of our emotions, but we creeped ourselves out when the realization hit.

"Rockin Stroll" is a song about Milo, Robyn St. Clare's son. She's the bass player in the Hummingbirds, and Nic filled in for her while she was having her baby. For me, coming up with ideas for songs isn't the hard part, it's knowing what to leave out. That isn't always easy to know.

"Rudderless" is another song whose title I took from an Australian newspaper. This time it was a paper in Melbourne while I was on my solo tour. I'd never heard that word before and I liked it as a metaphor for being adrift in the world. Sometimes you spend a lot of energy to get somewhere, only to feel completely cut off once you arrive.

"My Drug Buddy" is one of those rare songs where the lyrics came first. I was trying to describe, in a very straightforward way, a night in Sydney when I went out to score some speed. No pretenses, no rhymes, nothing. I took a piece of paper towel and used a magic marker to write the lyrics.

A lot of my songs are about longing, and "My Drug Buddy" is about wishing I could go back to that night in Sydney. It's like a diary entry. There's a little bit of repetition to disguise the fact that there isn't a chorus. The song just kind of stumbles along. You'd think a song about going to score some speed would be faster, but it's mellow and slow. It came together in almost no time at all. I think it took about twenty minutes, start to finish. I was totally sober when I wrote it.

The best songs don't take long to write. I've had songs that took weeks, months, and even years, and they never ended up better than the twenty minute ones. If I have to work on it too much most likely it won't end up being one of my favorite ones.

"The Turnpike Down" is the Mass Turnpike and its "butterscotch streetlamps" marking my path. "Alison's Starting to Happen" is about Nic's girlfriend, Alison Galloway. "Hannah & Gabi" is about my last two girlfriends before I heaved ho for several years and, to paraphrase Diamond Dave, was jogging with the horned one.

"Kitchen" was one of Nic's songs and I put it on there to make it easier for him to get a visa so he could come to the States and play in the Lemonheads. I knew that having one of his songs on the album would help smooth things over with immigration. If anyone gave him any shit about his visa he could say he was a unique and necessary component of the Lemonheads' mechanism.

"Ceiling Fan in My Spoon" was also written in Australia. It's not a drug song, though I can see why people might think it is. I had more ups than downs in Australia, but I would still get depressed from time to time. The day I wrote it I was coming down from being up for too many days and feeling edgy and out of sorts. I was staying at Nic's house, and I needed some space to clear my head. I went to a café to be alone with my thoughts for a while. While I was waiting for the coffee to be served, I looked down and saw the reflection of the ceiling fan spinning in my spoon. The song evolved from that simple image.

"Frank Mills" is from the musical *Hair*. There's a strong element of self parody in covering this song. It doesn't rhyme, no choruses. It's right up my alley, and I felt called to do it.

Once we had all the songs, we made a demo for the label. Atlantic loved it, and they wanted me to come out to LA to make the record. Maybe they wanted to keep an eye on me in the studio. I remember thinking it would be cool to hang out in the Hollywood Hills with some movie stars. It's embarrassing to admit I actually wished for something like that, but I did, and then those wishes came true.

HERE'S TO YOU, MRS. ROBINSON

We celebrated the arrival of 1992 by rehearsing for an hour every day to ensure we had the songs down cold. While we were gearing up to make the record I was staying with Curtis at the Taang! House. We did a few gigs where we played the new songs, and then it was time to go to LA to make *It's a Shame About Ray*.

Even though this would be the Lemonheads' fifth studio album and our second for Atlantic, it felt like an adventure. After a harsh winter in the Northeast, I was looking forward to spending some time in LA. I also thought it would be fun to drop acid while flying across the country.

I took the LSD on the way to the airport and it started to kick in as we were taking off. At one point during the flight, I thought to myself, *I wonder what will happen if I open this little door?*—the little door being the emergency exit. I thought I was being low-key about it; I wasn't bugging out demanding to be let off the plane. I eased up against the door and put all my weight into it, but it wouldn't budge. The flight attendant was amused by the sight of me trying to open the cabin door while wearing yellow pajamas from Brooks Brothers.

"Those doors don't open when the cabin's under pressure," she said.

"Good to know," I said and pretended to go back to sleep in my seat.

I'm pretty sure she was on to me.

We went to see Hole at the Whisky a Go Go on February 11, 1992. Both Hole's *Pretty on the Inside* and Nirvana's *Nevermind* had come out the previous September, but *Nevermind* didn't knock Michael Jackson from the number one spot on the charts until late January. By then "Smells Like Teen Spirit" was on constant rotation on the radio and on MTV.

"You made a great record, man," I said to Kurt.

"Thanks!"

He had just gotten back from Australia, so I bought him a beer and we compared notes about our experiences Down Under. I told him that *Nevermind* was going to help so many bands, including mine.

It seemed to trouble Kurt. "Thanks for the beer," he said.

Kurt rejected the idea that he'd been anointed as the one who would break things open for indie rock. That didn't interest him in the least and I felt a little embarrassed. It was a memorable first night in LA.

Atlantic Records put the Lemonheads up at the Oakwood Apartments, which is semi-infamous because it's where music, film, and television studios like to dump their up-and-coming talent. It's also where Nirvana stayed when they recorded *Nevermind*. I'm equally uncomfortable in all places, so the accommodations at Oakwood were fine with me, but I didn't like the layout. I got lost in the parking lot every time I went home. It's complicated, and it's a mega-complex and all the apartment buildings look the same. I was constantly getting turned around and driving my rental car in circles as I searched for my building.

*   *   *

The Lemonheads rocked up to Cherokee Studios on Fairfax just up from Melrose. The studio was run by Dee, Joe, and Bruce Robb, aka the Robb Brothers. Cherokee had been an MGM recording studio of note. Billie Holiday, Frank Sinatra, Ella Fitzgerald, Elvis Presley, and Count Basie, to name a few, recorded there before the Robbs bought it in 1972. Since it had become Cherokee, David Bowie, Rod Stewart, the Jackson 5, the Replacements, X, Tom Petty, Van Halen, Suicidal Tendencies, Charly Garcia, and many others had recorded there. We were getting the full LA treatment this time and we were stoked.

The Robb Brothers talked about the old days of Cherokee Studios when it was located at the edge of the San Fernando Valley. They had the best stories about LA in the sixties. Before moving to Hollywood, the Robbs ran a home studio out of their ranch in Chatsworth, where Steely Dan recorded *Pretzel Logic*. I'm a closet Dan fan.

Their ranch sat at the end of the Santa Susana Pass not far from the Spahn Movie Ranch, which means the brothers had all kinds of interactions with Charlie and his followers. They told us stories about how the girls from the family would wander onto their property and take fruit from their orange trees. The brothers would run them off, but they always came back.

"Charlie says these are our oranges."

The Robbs were gun nuts, and, being unaware of these pretty little teenagers' reputations, would point automatic weapons at them. "Would you please leave and tell Charlie to fuck himself?" They stayed away. Even the Mansons understood that preserving harmony with your neighbors was prudent.

The brothers also told us about Shorty Shea, a stuntman they knew who lived at the Spahn Ranch. Shea was a friend of George Spahn and was concerned that the old man was being taken advantage of by Charlie and his followers. He was something of a protector and looked out for people. After warning Charlie to stay away from the ranch, Charlie had him killed. It's not a question of *if* they murdered him, but how many people participated in the grisly deed. Shea's body wasn't found for several years, so he isn't as well known as some of the other victims.

Inspired by these stories I decided to add a shout-out to Shorty Shea on the song we were working on that day, which happened to be "It's a Shame About Ray." I asked Juliana to sing the part, and at first she was reluctant.

"Why are you doing this? It's such a nice song and there's nothing evil on the record."

"Exactly," I said.

So, during the second chorus, after I sing, "Something needs to go away," Juliana comes in with "Shorty Shea!" That's it. It's a throwaway line that most people don't even realize is there. But it serves as a tribute to someone who did the right thing and paid the ultimate price.

Incredibly, there's a rumor that Shea had a son named Ray. Of course, I had no idea at the time. Whether you're writing a song or filming a fairy tale, the truth is bound to be stranger than whatever you're doing.

* * *

We didn't do a lot of drugs while we were making that record. We'd drink some beer and one of the brothers had these mild pain pills called Rugbies for emergencies. The drug of choice for *Ray* was Greenblatt's deli. Every day I'd have a turkey and Swiss sandwich with sauerkraut on marbled rye and a cup of matzo ball soup. Every single day. *It's a Shame About Ray* could not have been made without Greenblatt's. The restaurant isn't there anymore. I got so angry and sad when I heard that it was closing. How? Why? And where else am I going to find a $5,000 bottle of cognac?

Greenblatt's wasn't the only diner we went to. Dave and I were at a breakfast place on Melrose when I was recognized by a fan.

"Are you Evan Dando?"

"Yeah," I said, but as soon as I opened my mouth I realized this was no ordinary fan: it was a really handsome guy who looked like an actor. He explained that he had a mixtape with "Mallo Cup," "Half the Time," and "Ride with Me" on it, and introduced me to Isabelle Adjani, which kind of blew my mind. I didn't recognize him at first, but I knew he was somebody, and he had a warm presence.

"I'm Evan."

"I really like your music," he said.

Then it came to me: this was Johnny Depp. It turned out that when he was dating Winona Ryder, she'd made him a tape of Lemonheads songs and he liked it. We got to talking and he asked what we were doing in town, and I told him we were recording a new album. Johnny was excited to hear we were working on new material, and I invited him down to the studio. I was just being polite. I didn't think he would actually show up at Cherokee that evening, but he did. He came in at the tail end of the session, and afterward I could tell he wanted to hang out.

"Where are you staying?" he asked.

"The Oakwood," I said.

"Man, that's rough. You can come up and stay with me."

"Really?"

"I've got plenty of room."

"Okay," I said, and I moved into Johnny Depp's house in the Hollywood Hills for a couple months. Staying with Johnny was the perfect way to experience LA. He was in between girlfriends, had plenty of free time, and could get into any club or restaurant in town. And he was Johnny Depp. We didn't go out all that much because I was making a record and trying to keep things low-key. We'd hang out in his house, play music, and pop Xanax. I don't recall what we talked about so much as what we *didn't* talk about: Hollywood, rock and roll, fame. We talked about the kind of stuff you share with your best friend: the first time we had a crush on a girl or the way certain seasons trigger specific memories.

We also talked about books. Johnny had an incredible library and a real fascination for the writers of the beat generation. He even had a couple of suitcases that once belonged to Jack Kerouac. We'd read all the same books and could talk for hours. We'd climb into bed, pass the guitar back and forth, and talk like a couple of five-year-old kids at a sleepover. We called it sidewinding because we'd lie on his bed sideways. It was somehow different enough to not be weird.

You would think we would go to bars and meet girls, but we spent so much time together just hanging out at his house that some of our friends thought we were an item. When you're older, it's rare to make new friends. When you're a kid, those early friendships are stimulating, and so easy.

* * *

Johnny and I had taken some acid, and we decided to go on an adventure. We started by visiting my record label, and the building was under construction. An extensive renovation was underway on the top two floors and the building was covered in scaffolding. That sparked an idea. What if we climbed out onto the scaffolding and said hello to everyone through the windows from the outside looking in? That could be funny. Wouldn't that be hilarious?

I'm a pretty cautious person, especially on hallucinogens, so this was one of my more harrowing adventures. That's not to say I don't do crazy stuff but it's on a stunt-to-stunt basis. I work out what's safe and what's crazy and go for it. This didn't seem so bad.

By this time the acid was coming on. We needed to move. We went all the way around the building, passing the offices for the accountants, A&R reps, executives, and their assistants. Once we got the hang of it, navigating the scaffolding was pretty easy, and we did a couple of laps around the building, laughing, picking up speed as we went.

The timing was perfect. Everyone in the office was losing their shit because we were up on the twentieth floor, racing around the building, laughing our asses off. They were probably all imagining the headlines if something terrible happened to us. "Johnny Depp Plunges to His Death During LSD Freakout." What were they going to do? Call the police on us?

I think we may have had cocktails with us, but not cigarettes. We were dying for a smoke, so we climbed back inside and went to see my A&R rep. We sat in his office smoking cigarettes, all three of us pretending everything was completely normal, but the rep was pretty freaked out.

Back at Johnny's place, we had a good laugh about it. It didn't seem possible that we'd actually done what we did. It was the kind of thing that Johnny did in movies, not in real life, and certainly not with a head full of LSD. I loved that about Johnny. He was just an extra-fun friend. No star trips whatsoever. Although he had a lot to lose, he never acted like it.

*   *   *

After a vocal tracking session at Cherokee the night before the Rodney King verdict, I went to go see Diamanda Galás at the Palace with a friend who was visiting from Denmark. It was a wonderful show, and afterward we went backstage and I met the actor Bud Cort, who played Harold in *Harold and Maude*.

The next day, we were hanging out at Johnny's house, taking in the view. Johnny lived just above the house where Julian Lennon used to live. The tile roof still read PISS OFF from when he got married and the paparazzi were flying over his house in helicopters, trying to take pictures of him. My friend from Denmark pointed out these lines in the sky.

"What's that?" she asked.

"It's smoke," I said. I wasn't sure if that's what it was, but it sure looked like columns of smoke rising out of the city. Then it clicked: the Rodney King verdict had been announced that day. Four white cops were acquitted of the violent beating of a Black man. The uprising started in South Central LA and spread to other parts of the city. We turned on the news and watched it all unfold. It came from the roots of the city and just grew and grew and got worse and worse. There was no telling when it would stop or how it would end.

This was one of the scariest things I'd ever been through because it wasn't an external event, like a plane crash or a bomb blast. Watching the news, you got the sense that people were fed up with the system, it was from within, and it felt like the only way to fix it was to burn everything to the ground.

At Cherokee Studios, the Robb Brothers rigged spotlights, tipped over heavy picnic tables, and built barricades inside the studio in case looters decided to break in. That would have been a deadly mistake. The Robb Brothers had a massive cache of weapons that included Uzis and AK-47s. They also had a secret weapon at their disposal. One of their clients, Rick James, was also recording an album at the time, and he spent the LA uprising holed up at Cherokee. They gave him an Uzi, and whenever a black van of armed intruders rolled up, James fired up a megaphone and shouted, "Get the fuck out of here!" in his unmistakable voice. The interlopers would drive off, freaked out and confused.

I stayed with Johnny, and we were joined by a few others who came up to his place to ride out the riots. There were five or six people, plus their pets in cages. We'd sit in the hot tub and watch the news. We had telescopes, so we could watch things unfold in real time.

"Oh, shit, this building is going up!"

"This one is about to collapse!"

We tried to make the best of the situation. We blasted Public Enemy's "Burn Hollywood Burn." It was kind of a party. A party for a city that was going up in flames.

*   *   *

We finished the record and hit the road. If I had to sum up the *It's a Shame About Ray* tour in one word, it would be "chaos." Not the kind of major label debauchery that rock and roll is famous for, but the kind of mayhem where you feel like you're on the verge of losing control.

Even though Juliana plays bass on the record, she had made it clear that she would play with her own band in the opening slot on our tour. So she got Bob Weston from Volcano Suns to play with her. Nic arrived from Australia to play bass with the Lemonheads. The tour kicked off in Vancouver and went all over North America, but we couldn't outrun the chaos. It followed us everywhere.

The US border with Canada is brutal for touring bands. The guards search everywhere, inventory everything, and if you don't have your paperwork in order you're in for a long night. They know every trick in the book, so there's no getting over on them. This time they tried to plant a joint on us. None of us had any drugs because we all knew better and it was the beginning of the tour, but they put a joint on the tour bus and insisted that it was ours. We pled our case to the Canadian authorities for hours before they finally let us through.

We had an unusual amount of trouble on that tour. We were opening up for Soul Asylum, a ridiculously good live band that had played as a guest performer at the Rock 'n' Roll Rumble the year we were in it. The show was in Chicago, which wasn't too far from their hometown of Minneapolis, so we knew we had to be on top of our game. We had just finished our set. I was wearing pajamas for some reason. As I came off the stage, I saw all this ruckus going on backstage. My friend Springa, the singer for Boston hardcore legends SSD, was wrestling around with some guy. I ran over and pulled him off Springa.

"Hey, what are you doing?" I yelled. "That's my friend!"

What I didn't know was that Springa had been down in the basement doing blow in the bathroom. This other guy was actually an undercover cop who was in the process of arresting him. The funny thing was he didn't look like a cop. He pulled out his badge, but he had it on a lanyard around his neck, and in the heat of the moment I thought it was an all-access pass.

"Nice backstage pass!" I said and slapped the badge out of the cop's hand.

Because the badge was attached to a lanyard, it went whipping around his neck, choking him. The cop let go of Springa and grabbed hold of me. His eyes were bugging out of his head like a cartoon. I don't know if it was because he was mad at me or because he was choking, but it was not a good situation for either of us.

By this time the stage manager had finally caught on that something wasn't right and got between me and the cop. In the tangle of limbs, the cop lost his balance, and we all went tumbling down a set of steel stairs that led to the exit, with me, Springa, and the stage manager all riding along on top of the cop like a surfboard. That cop's head must have hit every step on the way down.

When we reached the bottom, Springa took off running and I wasn't too far behind him. The cop was too woozy to give chase. We hid in the tour bus, and I helped Springa dispose of the evidence while the tour manager tried to smooth out the situation with the police. The crew packed up our gear as quickly as possible. After we were all loaded up and ready to go, Springa didn't want to get off the bus.

"I'm not going out there!" Springa yelled. "That guy fucking knows what I look like!"

Springa was certain he was going to jail if he stepped off the bus, but he couldn't stay on it forever.

"Come on, Springa," I said. "Ride with us!"

"I can't! I gotta work tomorrow!" Springa complained.

"Come with us!" I insisted.

As the bus pulled away from the club, Springa tried to cook up a plan with the driver to drop him off on the other side of town. The bus, however, was heading in the opposite direction. When we sailed past his exit, Springa knew he had no choice but to come with us.

"Oh, fuck," he said. "I'll go."

Like it or not, he was stuck with us.

Even on nights when there was nothing going on, trouble had a way of finding me. One night in Cleveland there were two strippers staying in the hotel room next door. I had been searching the hotel for signs of life—girls, drugs, etc.—when I heard Nirvana's "Come as You Are" drifting through the hotel room's wall. The women had no idea who I was, so it wasn't a groupie situation, but I ended up partying with them all night. I was wearing a blue-and-white polka-dot shirt that belonged to Howe Gelb of Giant Sand, which the girls teasingly called "poke me dot," and I was happy to oblige both of them. They had a cute silver .22 pistol, a lovable little dog called Miss Thang, and a ton of cocaine.

* * *

Now, you may have noticed that there's been no mention of our dicky cover of the Simon & Garfunkel hit "Mrs. Robinson." That's because the song wasn't included on the original release of *It's a Shame About Ray*. In fact, when we embarked on our tour it hadn't even been recorded yet.

Here's how that happened. We were asked to provide a cover of the song for the twenty-fifth-anniversary release of *The Graduate* on VHS. When we had some downtime during the tour, we went into a studio to record the song. We messed around with it a little bit to see if we all knew the parts and then we let it rip. We played the song all the way through from beginning to end exactly once. We nailed it on the first try. By the time we left the studio we had forgotten all about it.

The first single Atlantic released from the album was "It's a Shame About Ray" and it didn't go over well at all. But our cover of "Mrs. Robinson" was released as a single in the UK and quickly blew up. We were offered a string of European dates and special performances as a result. We played in a lot of the spots we'd played before, two-thousand-seater venues, like the Town and Country in London, and they were sold out and packed to the rafters. Everyone wanted to hear "Mrs. Robinson," and we gave it to them maybe five times. We didn't take the song seriously at all. When we played "Mrs. Robinson" on *Top of the Pops*, I sang the last bit in a Morrissey impression.

It was "Luka" all over again. But a hit single wasn't enough for our corporate masters. Danny Goldberg, who ran Gold Mountain, had been named president at Atlantic and he had big plans for the song. He wanted to put "Mrs. Robinson" on *It's a Shame About Ray*. We didn't know you could do that. Wasn't the record out already? How could you retroactively add a song to a record that was currently in stores? Wasn't that like adding a chapter to a book after it has already been published?

"I'm putting the song on the record," Goldberg said.

"Please don't," I said.

"I'm doing it."

"I really wish you wouldn't."

"It's done."

Atlantic reissued the record and added "Mrs. Robinson" against our wishes, which made it hard to feel good about the song. "Mrs. Robinson" was never meant to be on that record. Creatively, conceptually, whatever criteria you want to use, that song didn't belong on *It's a Shame About Ray*.

But there it was.

That's the way things happen in show business. These people get together in a boardroom and decide in advance who is going to be popular and what's going to be a hit, and then they spend boatloads of money trying to make it happen. They try to be strategic about something that is completely subjective. I quickly learned there's no place for idealism in the music industry.

On the other hand, what did I know about making a hit record? I thought all the songs on *It's a Shame About Ray* were better than "Mrs. Robinson."

In a way, we manifested our cover of "Mrs. Robinson" into existence. While recording "Alison's Starting to Happen," I included a sample of Katharine Ross, who plays Elaine Robinson, Mrs. Robinson's daughter, in *The Graduate*. It's the moment where she yells, "Ben!" The Lemonheads filmed a video for the song. I didn't want to do the video, but I didn't put up much of a fight, either. I said, "I'll do it if you bring me a 'Hello, My Name Is' sticker." I wrote *Luka* on the sticker and wore it in the video. That was my little protest.

For many people "Mrs. Robinson" was their gateway drug to the Lemonheads. Call it karma or whatever you want, but Goldberg's plan worked. Thanks to "Mrs. Robinson," *It's a Shame About Ray* went gold in the US. A lot of people who bought the record because of "Mrs. Robinson" didn't know anything about the Lemonheads, and they discovered they liked the moody groove we'd laid down. Or maybe their girlfriends liked it.

With our rise in popularity came a rush of critical attention. Critics tended to view *It's a Shame About Ray* as a great leap forward for the Lemonheads, and maybe it was. When you make a bunch of albums but haven't produced a hit, you're regarded as a cult favorite. When you finally get that hit, then you've matured. Music journalists were spouting all this nonsense about how the Lemonheads were finally delivering, like we'd been deliberately holding back all these years. Considering that all this adulation came *after* "Mrs. Robinson" was added to the record, it was a little hard to take.

I tend to think *It's a Shame About Ray*'s popularity was a case of being in the right place at the right time. The environment was finally right for bands like the Lemonheads to thrive. From the label's point of view, we'd reversed course after *Lovey*'s disappointing sales, and our numbers far exceeded *Lick*.

We were on the right track, whatever that meant. The label was happy, so we were happy, but the label wanted more.

YOU GIVE DRUGS A BAD NAME

You give something of yourself away when you put your picture on the cover of a magazine. That's not in the contract, and it's not something that anyone ever tells you, but it's definitely part of the deal. You lose it and you never get it back.

The PR people at Gold Mountain were determined to turn me into a cover boy. The magazine covers helped with publicity, but the emphasis on my looks over my music set the tone for how people would come to view the Lemonheads.

The first cover shoot I did was for *Spex* in Germany. The German music market is massive—bigger than the UK, bigger than Japan. In the early nineties, as long as the music had loud guitars—punk, post-punk, alternative, indie—it was big in Germany. But *Spex* wasn't a punk zine. *Spex* was a big, slick glossy magazine that put celebrities on its cover—actors, models, pop stars. The Lemonheads didn't exactly qualify, but I was still naive enough to believe that any exposure was good exposure.

Interview was my big breakout as a cover boy. I did the shoot with fashion photographer Bruce Weber on the beach in Miami. Bruce was responsible for those famous Calvin Klein underwear ads in the eighties. Once he took my photograph, all the other photographers wanted to get in on the action. The *Interview* cover shoot signaled that the Lemonheads were worthy of serious attention, which is ironic because music journalists didn't take us seriously at all.

For the *Interview* cover shoot, Bruce had me take off my shirt and sprawl in the sand. They covered me with lemons so that all you could see was my head and part of my torso. Lemon. Head. Get it? When the issue came out the word "squeeze" was curled around my nipple. I didn't know if I should laugh or be offended.

The people at Gold Mountain were thrilled that we were going to be on the cover of a big glossy magazine with a serious art pedigree. *Interview* was important, they told me, so I went along with it. But when I saw the results, I was embarrassed by how lame it was. I felt conned.

As a musician, you have to go along with what the critics say about you. That's part of the deal of being an artist. You put your work out there for people to judge, take your lumps, and keep your mouth shut. Not everyone is going to like what you do, and you have to learn to accept that and be gracious about it. That's the beauty of art. When you find something that moves you, it's profound, even life-changing. The reality is most art isn't going to have that kind of impact. You can fire back at a critic who doesn't like your work, but it makes you look like an ass. I mean, is there anything more insufferable than a rock band arguing with an interviewer over what they sound like or why they matter?

"No, that's not what's interesting about us. You've got it all wrong!"

It's like fighting the ocean. You have to let the waves wash over you.

This was different. This wasn't criticism. This was marketing. But it wasn't the right kind of marketing because it had nothing to do with how the band sounded but how I looked. These magazines were used to dealing with people who either aspired to be part of the image factory or were already pros at it.

That wasn't us. We were a bunch of boisterous, drug-addled musicians who were only a few months removed from gigging for rent money and sleeping on floors.

Gold Mountain wasn't sympathetic. They didn't understand why we'd be unhappy with the kind of attention we were getting. As far as they were concerned, we were out of line. They'd worked to get the publicity our band was receiving—with results, they were quick to point out, that other bands would kill for. It was a catch-22. They didn't know what to do with us, and we didn't know what to do with all the attention that was suddenly coming our way.

The focus on my looks quickly went from annoying to absurd. In *Interview*, they described me as a "hippie dippy dude." *Melody Maker* called me a "punk pin-up." One critic dubbed me the "slacker sex kitten," and another came up with "Elvis Costello with cheekbones." Cheekbones! What do my cheekbones have to do with anything?

In the indie rock underground, a writer would get ridiculed for writing dreck like this. The fanzines and weekly papers may have suffered from poor funding, lousy distribution, and inexperienced staffers, but they genuinely cared about the music they wrote about. These zines and indie newsweeklies strove to be as cool as the bands they covered.

There was nothing cool about the way the slick music and fashion magazines treated us. When they ran out of words they made up new ones to describe me: "alternahunk," "bubblegrunge."

After *Interview*, *NME* and *Melody Maker* came calling. Because we'd played in the UK so many times and had enjoyed some success there, we knew how hard it was to land a cover for these weekly music magazines because you never knew if Morrissey or Bono was going to break a nail and scrap your cover shoot.

It was absurd. One time they put me on the cover because I got a haircut. There was probably some poor indie band thinking they were going to get their big break and then fucking Evan Dando gets a haircut. It was stupid then and it's stupid now. I don't think much has changed since the early nineties. I saw it as part of the job. And I fucked it up completely.

NME named me "Man of the Year," which was cool, and then they put me on the cover shirtless in bed with the headline "Juicy!" My cover photo for *Sky* magazine was more demure, but the headline read "Reluctant Babe Magnet." Well, no. I don't recall any reluctance on my part. The reluctance came from having to steer interviews away from my looks, my hair, and what I was wearing, to the music we had worked so hard to create. It seldom worked.

I pushed back in my own weird way. I wouldn't wash my hair, or I'd hide my face behind it while we played. I'd wear long winter coats and parkas to photo shoots or even onstage. I committed the cardinal sin of wearing the same red jacket on a pair of television appearances. I thought I was protesting the publicity machine, but all this did was contribute to the Dippy Dando narrative. If one magazine wrote about me in a certain way, then the rest of the magazines got in line to serve up the same treatment. Once that story was established, I couldn't change it.

This fixation on my looks had been there from the beginning. We were in *Sassy* magazine in February 1991 under the banner "Cute Band Alert." We got to know all the people at *Sassy* and it became an inside joke. Bullet Lavolta was the first Cute Band Alert, Run Westy Run was second, and we were third. In one issue *Sassy* put a thumbnail photo of me at the end of every article. They were poking fun at the publicity machine even as they perpetuated it.

All that silliness about my looks peaked when I was named one of *People* magazine's 50 Most Beautiful People. I was in a good class of people: Kate Moss, Uma Thurman, Stephanie Seymour. I think I was number forty-nine, and I remember feeling bad for whoever was behind me at fifty.

None of this took us by surprise, but it was still kind of dispiriting. There was so much energy and enthusiasm around the indie explosion of the early nineties. There were so many great bands making compelling music. Surely there had to be something more interesting to write about than my hair. The label figured if people thought I was cute, then maybe they'd buy our records. But it was a weird way for people to find out about the Lemonheads. I wasn't an actor or a model. I was a musician. How I looked shouldn't matter.

As the interview requests and photo shoots piled up, I made it a point to remind myself why I was doing this. I had no desire to become famous. That wasn't my ulterior motive. All I wanted to do was to keep doing what I was doing. I started writing songs as a way to figure out my problems. I think that's why early in my career I couldn't always access the part of my brain where the songwriting came from. Writing songs was a way to comfort myself, and it turns out that if you try hard enough you reach a universal chord that comforts other people, too, and that's pretty cool. The realization that these songs I found so soothing could bring happiness to others made the whole endeavor worthwhile.

I thought of myself as a songwriter who happened to be good-looking, not a good-looking person who happened to write songs. I thought that was a distinction worth fighting for, but I didn't want to ruin the one thing that truly made me happy by alienating the press and being pretentious and aloof. I just wanted to be myself, my slightly weird and somewhat self-indulgent self. (Okay, maybe not somewhat.)

It's hard not to be hurt by the things people say about you. Even *Sassy* magazine occasionally took things too far and referred to me as "His Beautiful Blond Sadness." Maybe the key to being an intelligent person is to not read the things people write about you.

Drugs were the one thing that music journalists found more interesting than my looks. Talking about drugs was how I derailed my deal with the devil. My friends in the industry tried to warn me about being so cavalier with the press. They said it would come back to haunt me some day: "You're going to get a lot of things, but you're going to lose more."

I didn't listen. After five studio albums, I thought I knew something about the record business, but I still had a lot to learn. I was very naive—about the media, about celebrity, about the difference between being famous and notorious.

I made a big mistake during my interview with *Interview*. When the subject turned to drugs, I was completely honest with the reporter. I told him that while I didn't condone drug use for anyone else, I had no regrets about the experiences I'd had on drugs. I didn't think I said anything that was particularly shocking, but the story came on the heels of the release of our second single from *It's a Shame About Ray*, "My Drug Buddy," which didn't go over well with record stores or radio stations. Instead, DJs played "Confetti," the song on the flip side. I guess all those D.A.R.E. T-shirts and This Is Your Brain on Drugs videos succeeded in cowing the corporations into believing that Just Say No was the only way to go. They weren't ready for a song that said yes to drugs.

RUMORS OF MY DEMISE

*   *   *

When punk broke in the autumn of 1991, Atlantic Records established a committee devoted to kissing my ass. Imagine my surprise when that all came to an end too soon on April 8, 1994. Nirvana's *Nevermind* had changed the course of rock and roll, stuff like Debbie Gibson, synth-pop, and hair metal had been bested for a spell. Everyone in the international college slumber party, all my rock and roll friends and I were to benefit.

The biggest change took place not on stages or in record stores but in the boardrooms at major labels. After Nirvana, record executives broadened their definition of popular music, which was long overdue. They started taking a closer look at their rosters with dollar signs in their eyes. Gold records weren't good enough anymore. They wanted blockbusters. Instead of nurturing the careers of bands they truly believed in, the labels went on a feeding frenzy, throwing money at every band with an edgy-sounding demo in the hope they would become the next Nirvana.

Atlantic was banking on bigger things from the Lemonheads. This wasn't about recouping the losses from *Lovey*; this was about striking while the iron was hot and cashing in. When you make a record that underperforms, you feel pressure to make a record that sells, but it's a low-key kind of pressure because the label has more or less written you off. You can take your time because no one cares about what you're doing.

But now we were in a completely different situation. Thanks to "Mrs. Robinson," we toured nonstop for over a year on *It's a Shame About Ray*. When we weren't onstage, we were doing interviews and photo shoots. The Lemonheads were getting a ton of attention, and the label intended to capitalize on it. Goldberg wanted another record and he wanted it right away. We had very little downtime to write new material. So not only were the expectations higher, we were on a tighter schedule and under a lot more scrutiny. We only had a few weeks off during the summer to record new music, but we had to do some festivals in the middle of August and then come back and finish the album.

We wrote *Come on Feel the Lemonheads* on the road. I went back to Oz to see my friends and write some more songs with Tomas Martin Morgan. He was like the fourth member of the Lemonheads.

We returned to LA in 1993 to make our sixth studio album, our third for Atlantic. We stayed at the infamous Chateau Marmont on Sunset Boulevard in West Hollywood. I was excited to be at the Chateau because of its rock and roll reputation—both good and bad. John Belushi died in bungalow 2, cause of death: speedball mishap. He's buried on Martha's Vineyard in Abel's Hill Cemetery.

They gave me the big room—room 64. It had two bathrooms and a huge balcony. I got that room so everyone could hang out after we'd wrapped up the day's work in the studio.

Although it seemed like hardly any time had passed since our last visit, LA felt like a different place. Before, it had been rainy and lush. Now it was hot and dry. You could feel the tension that had risen to the surface during the uprising was still simmering, and it seemed as though all the friends I'd made had left town.

If we weren't hanging out at the Chateau we'd go to Johnny's, where Gibby Haynes was a frequent guest. I'd met Gibby at Johnny's the year before and we hit it off immediately. I was a huge fan of his band, the Butthole Surfers. It was kind of a big deal becoming friends with him. We both love "Outdoor Miner" by Wire. I would play it on guitar and we'd both sing "The egg timer!"

RUMORS OF MY DEMISE

We realized pretty quickly we could go off on tangents together without fear of the other person thinking he was dealing with a total weirdo. He's hilarious and eccentric and full of surprises. One day we were in Hollywood when he announced, "I want a seersucker suit."

Even though I'd just met Gibby, I had a lot of money, more than I'd ever had in my life, so I said, "I'll buy you a seersucker suit!" I think he needed it for a wedding.

We went out and bought the suit. Gibby put it on and said, "Sears made it. Sucker bought it."

It became an early bonding experience for us. That's Gibby in a nutshell. He sees the world differently than the rest of us do. He has a unique way of stringing ideas together that's very relatable to me. I don't want to say we could read each other's minds, but our brains worked well together. There's almost no one I'd rather talk to than Gibby Haynes.

When Johnny was in Texas shooting *What's Eating Gilbert Grape*, Gibby and I flew out to visit him on set in Austin. We became tight during that trip, and we discovered that we had similar appetites. Johnny would drink every now and then, but Gibby and I were the poster boys for saying yes to drugs.

In Austin, Johnny rented a huge house on a hill from a rich guy. We called it the Big Gay House because it was filled with homoerotic art, which was a little much to deal with all the time, so we rounded it all up and stashed it in a closet.

The origins of the song "Big Gay Heart" can be traced back to that house. I'm straight, but I tried to write a song for gay people, gay truckers specifically. In the early nineties, heterosexual America was still grappling with homosexuality as a civil rights issue, and many closed-minded people were freaking out about AIDS. Holly was on the front lines of the AIDS crisis as a social worker, and I was really proud of her and the work she was doing to help people with HIV/AIDS in New York City. She helped me understand the struggles so many people were going through and the many ways the government made the situation worse. The potential for the song to backfire was much greater than the possibility of a hit, but Lemonheads fans got it. I like to think they're a little bit ahead of the curve.

When Johnny came back to LA from filming *What's Eating Gilbert Grape*, he gave me a copy of the novel by Peter Hedges that the film was based on.

"I used you for my character," he explained. "I used your mannerisms."

"Oh, cool."

"Gilbert is fifty percent you, fifty percent someone else."

I went to the premiere and I have to say I did see a little of myself in Gilbert Grape, but I never did find out who that other person who influenced the character was. Maybe it was Gibby.

*   *   *

I didn't go to LA to hang out with Johnny and Gibby, but to make another record with the Robb Brothers at Cherokee Studios. They'd been around long enough to see trends come and go. With *It's a Shame About Ray*, they were in favor of showcasing the songs instead of burying them under a lot of noise, which was what many bands were doing then. They were also opposed to digital technology. They just didn't trust it yet. The result was a warmer, softer sound that gives *It's a Shame About Ray* a kind of timeless feel—even if it sounds a little more like AM radio than FM radio. A lot of music of the early nineties feels dated to me, but the Robb Brothers wanted to make a record that would stand the test of time, which it has.

Not all of the songs were finished when we went back to Cherokee for *Come on Feel the Lemonheads*, which added to the pressure. Nic helped shape many of the songs on the new record. We returned to our love of the Velvet Underground, and he got me into a bunch of stuff I didn't know about but probably should have, like Gene Clark's *Roadmaster* and *Triptych* by the Bevis Frond—a psychedelic one-man band I learned to love.

We front-loaded the album with the songs we thought would make the best singles: "The Great Big NO," "Into Your Arms," and "It's About Time." The first single was "Into Your Arms" and was written by Robyn St. Clare. She wrote the song for the Love Positions, a band that Nic had played in back in Sydney. "Into Your Arms" is actually about him. I don't think of it as a stereotypical cover song because it was never a radio hit and not a lot of people knew it—especially in the US. I thought it was a perfect little pop song that would be a great single. MTV agreed with me and the song was picked for its Buzz Bin.

"It's About Time" is a tribute to Juliana. Juliana is a natural songwriter. Her songs are simple, but elegant. Tom and I tried to write a song in her style, but along the way it kind of became about her. Juliana is a super-talented musician and one of my oldest friends, who happens to be one of the best songwriters I know. We came up together. We toured together. We never would have lasted as a couple.

Juliana follows her own path, and she won't budge for anybody. I like that about her, that conviction. Lots of times when she'd rather be alone, she'll go along to get along and just kind of keep to herself. Sometimes she'll be off in a corner, doodling in her journal, just doing her thing.

I think the reason we were able to stay so close throughout the eighties, the nineties, and beyond is because we never slept together. She's a real steady person, a calming influence in the studio or on the road. It's good to have people like that in your corner in those situations. I'm glad we had that line that we never crossed. Marianne Faithfull used to say that about Bob Dylan: "We never had sex and I'm so glad because he's so dramatic." I imagine that's how Juliana feels about me.

If *It's a Shame About Ray* draws from my experiences in Australia, *Come on Feel the Lemonheads* was inspired by LA. A lot of the songs are peppered with insights from my new reality as a "rock star." For instance, the line "Have your people call mine" sounds trite, but it speaks to the lack of autonomy so many people in LA seem to have. It always surprised me how many people were willing to hand the reins over to agents, lawyers, and handlers and let them steer their career. For better or worse, I didn't do that. I just did whatever I felt like doing, day by day and hour by hour. I have driven a few industry people crazy along the way with my free-spirited attitude, but I don't know any other way to be.

"Paid to Smile" makes my feelings known about my role as the music industry's cover boy. Because of the references to getting stoned, people think "Style" is a drug song, but it's actually about being anxious and indecisive. I've read some interesting theories about the song over the years, but me and Tom dashed it off in five minutes, and then, contrary to the song's message, immediately got stoned.

I wrote "I'll Do It Anyway" for Belinda Carlisle, but we didn't get it to her in time for her to use it on her record, so we used it on ours. She sings backup vocals on the song, though it's meant to be more of a duet. I don't think we've ever played it live. Gram Parsons's sideman Sneaky Pete Kleinow plays steel guitar on "Big Gay Heart," which was our third single from the album, as well

RUMORS OF MY DEMISE

as on "Being Around." I just love the sound of his guitar on those songs. Acoustic versions of "Being Around" and "Into Your Arms" originally appeared on the B-side of the "Mrs. Robinson" single. If a cover of "Mrs. Robinson" was the Lemonheads at its phoniest, those acoustic versions provide a glimpse of where my head was at in those days, intimate and offbeat songs about opening your heart.

The end of the record devolves into a rowdy mess with a series of secret tracks hidden inside "The Jello Fund." Critics hated it, but there was a method to our madness. The fifteen-minute-long track was a way to sabotage any attempts to add additional songs to our record. If Atlantic wanted to tack on another single, like they did with "Mrs. Robinson" on *It's a Shame About Ray*, it would follow fifteen minutes of dead air and experimental jams.

Come on Feel the Lemonheads has a bit of an escapist feel. It's not the most grounded record, but after all that time on the road, how could it be? Everything was happening so fast—too fast—and we were in a rush to finish it.

*   *   *

Even though I had my room at the Chateau, I spent my share of nights at Johnny's house, where Gibby was staying while Johnny was out of town. We were respectful of Johnny's house, but we kept losing things. We lost the remote that controlled the front gate. Whenever we came back to his house, we had to leave our vehicles in the street, climb up the embankment, and hop over the fence.

My rental car—a white Chevy—was somewhere in Santa Monica. I'd left the car with Martyn LeNoble of Porno for Pyros and it was MIA for about a month, so we drove Johnny's Porsche around Hollywood. We were extra careful with it, but because we'd lost the remote control to the gate we had to leave the car in the street, which wasn't ideal. What if someone stole Johnny's Porsche?

If we could, Gibby and I would get someone to take us where we needed to go or—more accurately—get us the drugs we were looking for. We hung out with a musician friend of mine, Tom, quite a bit. He had a Nissan Pathfinder with a cracked windshield that we called the Nissan Crackfinder. I usually stayed home while Tom and Gibby went out to get the crack. I never wanted to go score the drugs. I would pay extra just to stay home. That scene wasn't for me.

I went with Gibby and Tom to score exactly one time and it was a heavy situation. We went down to a place in Compton and as soon as we pulled up to the spot all these guys bum-rushed the car. They were all in competition with each other and wouldn't take no for an answer. That's why Tom's windshield was broken, from crack dealers jumping on his car, and not just one or two, but four or five, all of them yelling at us.

"My stuff's the best!"

"Buy from me!"

It was too chaotic for me. When it comes to illicit behavior, I like rules. I like knowing that if I follow the proper procedure I won't get into trouble, and if I don't follow the rules I like to not get caught.

People like Gibby don't give a shit about any of that. He used to thrive on that stuff. He'd throw himself into any situation without thinking twice. I called him Gibby Danger, from the Stooges song "Gimme Danger." I've met people who like scoring drugs more than actually doing them. Not me. I'd get too nervous, and that kind of negative energy can be bad news during a drug deal. When someone's anxious and doesn't want to be there, people pick up on it and start jumping to conclusions.

We didn't do hard drugs at Johnny's house. For that we went back to the Chateau. We'd hang out and watch *Jurassic Park* over and over again, and one of the girls who was with us dropped one of Johnny's *Edward Scissorhands* props. Thankfully, it didn't break, but Gibby and I were not cut out to be caretakers.

When we got word that Johnny would be home in a few days we scrambled to get the house back in tip-top shape. We hired some house cleaners to restore some semblance of order. I went out to the beach to see if I could get my rental car back from Martyn.

The Lemonheads and Porno for Pyros played a lot of the same festivals and we spent a lot of time together in Europe and LA. I was struck by how nice Perry Farrell was. I was expecting him to be a total LA weirdo and he was actually a very normal-seeming guy. I liked him a lot as both a person and a performer. One of my favorite LA bands is Love, and I think Perry channels Arthur Lee better than anyone else.

Speaking of which, one night Arthur came over to the Chateau with members of Ride and Primal Scream. We hung out at the pool, playing music long into the night, and we kept all the guests awake. People were yelling at us, "Turn that fucking shit off!" but we kept playing. I played the song "Big Gay Heart" for Arthur, but it was a little too much for him. He was kind of an old-fashioned guy and I don't think he was ready for it.

Johnny's Porsche wouldn't start, so we had it towed to a mechanic's shop and got it fixed up in time for his return. I wasn't there when the day of reckoning came. All I know is we never did find the remote control to his gate.

MARKED FOR LIFE

We had some epic times at the Chateau. I partied with Lou Barlow of Dinosaur Jr. and Sebadoh fame and he lived to tell the tale.

"I'll try this hard drugs thing for a night," he said to me.

So we did. We smoked crack and heroin and then played music together all night long. It was more like a drug-fueled jam session than a party. We didn't sit around and stare at the clock until it was time to take another hit. Music was always the priority. We played lots of Dinosaur Jr. songs together, like "The Leper," and Lou had all these new songs he'd written for Sebadoh. I made a tape of that night for posterity. I eventually lost it, but I used to listen to it all the time.

The next time I saw Lou, at the Reading Festival, he had a surprise for me.

"Evan, I wrote a song about that night!"

We were in a little trailer with fifteen people and he took out his guitar and played it for me. It's called "Skull" and it's a perfect little song about the many ways in which the Chateau Marmont is haunted.

After five weeks in LA, my bandmates packed up their gear and left. Nic split for Sydney and David went back to Boston. Even Juliana, who'd recorded some backing vocals and is a steadying influence on any project she's involved in, went home. I was left to finish the record by myself. We were on a tight deadline and all we had left were the vocals and the overdubs. I needed my voice to be in shape.

Naturally, I went on a crack bender, which is the worst possible thing a singer can do to their voice because it deadens the vocal chords. "Bender" isn't the right word for it. I didn't vanish into the underworld of dangerous drugs as has been reported. I was hanging out in my swanky suite at the Chateau. I'd smoked crack prior to this trip to LA, but that was my first extended dalliance with the drug. I got into the whole ritual of it: prepping the pipe, loading it up, taking a hit. The crackling of the rock, blowing clouds. For five minutes you're flying high and then you need to smoke some more, so I did. Over and over again.

When the smoke cleared, my voice was shot. I freaked out because I was afraid that I'd done permanent damage to my vocal chords and I still had to finish recording the album. I went to the doctor and explained the situation.

"I think I messed up my voice," I said.

"How did you do that?" he asked.

"I may have smoked some crack."

"I see."

"And a little heroin."

The doctor checked me out and reassured me that the damage was only temporary. He said all I needed to do was rest my voice for a week, and by rest he meant no singing, no talking, and, of course, no smoking crack.

RUMORS OF MY DEMISE

I was so relieved. While I wasn't looking forward to telling the Robb Brothers or my handlers at Gold Mountain that I would be out of commission for a week, I could manage it. I'd hole up in the Chateau, spend a week with my guitar, and be ready to go. Unfortunately, that was the same week the British music press sent something like twenty reporters out to LA to talk to me about *Come on Feel the Lemonheads*.

I should have canceled the interviews. I should have let the label handle it. I should have had the PR team release a statement about how exhausted I was and stash me somewhere while I "recuperated."

I foolishly went ahead with the interviews. I wanted to do the right thing. I didn't know I could just say no to the press. Because I couldn't talk, I scribbled my answers on little scraps of paper. I didn't hold anything back. I told them everything. *Sorry I can't talk, but I was smoking crack and damaged my voice. What do you want to know about the new record?*

Of course, after I told them that, they didn't care about the new record anymore. They wanted to know all about my adventures with crack cocaine, and like an idiot I told them. I got into the weeds and told them everything there is to know about the drug. How to prepare it, how to smoke it, what it feels like, and how it can fuck you up. I wrote it all out for them on these little pieces of paper. I basically gave them a tutorial. Crack 101 with Evan Dando.

It was all pretty bizarre. Now I can see the humor in the situation, but it was apparent almost immediately that I'd made a huge mistake. Most reporters look the other way if you drink or smoke pot. Hell, many are more than happy to partake with you. That's rock and roll. But if you do heroin you're a cliché, and if you smoke crack you're a monster.

This story has gotten repeated a lot and the details have blurred over time, so let me set the record straight. When those reporters wrote their articles, they made it seem like I'd just stumbled out of a crack house, was in the throes of a horrible addiction, and was physically incapacitated.

None of that was true. It's not like I was in some hyper-narcotized state where I was physically unable to speak. I was simply following my doctor's orders so I could get back in the studio as quickly as possible. Nor was I high for the interviews. I was anxious and uncomfortable because I knew the writers had come a long way to interview me and I had to write everything out for them, but I wasn't impaired. They had a job to do, and I genuinely felt terrible about not speaking with them.

What I failed to realize at the time was that I'd given those reporters a gift. Instead of having to manufacture a boring puff piece about a record they hadn't heard, I handed them a sensational story and served it up on a silver platter. I even wrote the quotes for them.

I wasn't completely naive about the media. I'd had some fun with reporters at their expense. I'd sit down and make stuff up and they'd print it. Sometimes they'd get mad when they found out I was pulling their chain, but if they were cool, we'd laugh about it later. There were some writers who tried to understand where I was coming from. I became good friends with a few writers, like Mark Blackwell of *Spin* magazine. He grasped the absurdity of the post-Nirvana indie explosion. Sometimes I'd get the reporters to do acid or speed with me and we'd turn the interview into an adventure. Why ask me a bunch of meaningless questions when we can go out and have a real experience together?

If they were uptight and serious, I'd give them bullshit. If they were real with me, I'd be real with them. I'd let my guard down, which I probably did a bit too often, and tell them what was going on in my life and in my imagination.

You have to be wary, especially with reporters who are overly nice to you, because they're the ones who write the most scathing articles. Or we'd have a good time together and their editors would turn the story into something completely different. That happened a lot.

You can't say, "I love doing blow and having threesomes." Maybe down the road you can say it, after you've had your moment in the sun, but not when you're in it. You have to play the role of the genius artist, the dedicated troubadour, and the grateful performer who can't believe his good fortune. In other words, you have to lie.

I used to love to read interviews by the Dublin band My Bloody Valentine. They were always honest and forthright. They didn't fake it. They spoke the truth of their reality. I remember thinking, *I'm going to do that. I'm going to tell it like it is. I'll tell the truth!* I found out the hard way the truth can get you in a lot of trouble. Those interviews established a narrative: Evan Dando is a druggie. Rumors about my drug use were already circulating, but now it was on the record, and reporters asked me about it over and over again.

"Are drugs good for you?"

"Should everyone do them?"

"What about your fans?"

"What about the children?"

I couldn't win. They didn't want me to talk about the music, they wanted me to tell them about getting high. I was marked for life. I was someone who gave drugs a bad name.

The British press is good at building you up so they can take you down. In the beginning you can do no wrong. Then they put you under a microscope until they get tired of dissecting you. For instance, after the crack episode, *NME* put me on the cover with Björk with the headline "Venus and Dopehead," which was just mean.

I went from indie darling to drug addict overnight. The thing about labels is that over time they lose their stick and flutter away. At the end of the day all an artist has are the things they make, not what others say about them. But the British invented tabloid journalism and have elevated cruelty to an art form. When they put you in their crosshairs, watch out—it's going to be a long, ugly ride.

* * *

River Phoenix overdosed at the Viper Room not long after *Come on Feel the Lemonheads* came out. Johnny Depp was part of a group that had bought the place earlier that year, and he invited me to play at the grand opening of his Hollywood playhouse. In fact, I bought the very first drink ever served at the Viper Room—a greyhound—and they put my twenty-dollar bill in the frame with the liquor license behind the bar.

I brought my dad as a guest, and Gibby was there, too, in the seersucker suit I'd bought him, which lent an air of danger to the proceedings because you never knew what might happen when Gibby was cutting loose. Strangely enough, Gibby and my dad hit it off and they had a great time hanging out together at this Hollywood shindig.

What a lot of people don't know is that Gibby was a basketball star in high school and was just a few credits shy of earning his MBA before he fully committed to the Butthole Surfers. He can easily blend in with lawyer-types like my dad. He was mad, bad, and dangerous to know, but he was genuine. There isn't an inauthentic bone in his body. I admire that about him.

My dad had a quirky side to him, too. For instance, he loved to get me drunk. Five fingers of gin with a few drops of Angostura bitters was the standard initiation if we hadn't seen each other for a while.

Gibby, Johnny, and Bob Forrest of Thelonious Monster were in a band called P with Flea and John Frusciante of the Red Hot Chili Peppers. P had invited River to perform on the night that he overdosed. Someone gave him a cocktail spiked with drugs. He was only twenty-three years old.

River's death set a chain of events in motion that would have an impact on just about everyone I knew in the film, music, and entertainment business. Most of it was bad, but some of it was good, which was hard to reconcile.

*   *   *

The first time I didn't sleep with Courtney Love I was touring with Hole. *Come on Feel the Lemonheads* had just come out. Nirvana was in Europe, so Gold Mountain put Hole and the Lemonheads on a West Coast tour, which was a terrible idea. I think they were trying to stir up trouble, and I think Courtney put them up to it. Don't get me wrong, Courtney was a lot of fun to hang out with, but she was a chaos agent of the first order.

"Hey, Evan," she said apropos of nothing. "I made Kurt cry last night."

"What happened?" I asked.

"I told him we were having an affair."

"Fuck, Courtney! Why did you do that?"

Courtney and I were not having an affair. We'd never slept together or fooled around or anything of the sort. We'd done drugs together, which had its own kind of intimacy because

Courtney always needed help shooting up, but nothing more. I thought it was a terrible thing to say to Kurt.

Courtney laughed it off like it was no big deal. Then she did it again, or at least she said she did, but I believed her. I'd been touring pretty much nonstop for years. It got to the point where the road *was* my life. I always had plenty of female companionship while I was touring, but I missed my mom in Boston and my sister in New York. No matter how ridiculous my life got, they knew the real me and were always a grounding influence. I knew how hard it was to be apart from the people who love you, and I was appalled that Courtney would do that to Kurt while he was on the road.

Also, I didn't want Kurt to be mad at me. I didn't know him all that well and I was afraid it would drive a wedge between us. I knew that what Courtney said to him wasn't true, but did Kurt?

I never saw Nirvana play because we were always on tour at the same time. Kurt and I only met twice. The second time was after a solo gig at the Seattle Art Museum with Sarah McLachlan. After the show Dave Grohl and Krist Novoselic came back to the dressing room and kidnapped me.

"Where are we going?"

"The Stouffer Hotel to pick up Kurt. We have practice and you're invited."

So we went and got him and they rehearsed *In Utero*. Then I jumped on the drums for a new song that Dave had. Kurt said I was a good drummer.

After the session we went to a nearby 7-Eleven, but the store had already closed. Kurt knocked on the door and after a while the people working inside recognized who it was and opened up for us. Kurt bought Munchos, Winston Lights, and an orange Gatorade. I think I got a Charleston Chew.

RUMORS OF MY DEMISE

Even though I didn't know Kurt particularly well, I felt like I did because Courtney talked about him all the time. That's what you do on the road. You talk about the people you left behind and the people you want to see when you get home. I liked hearing about Kurt. I respected him and wanted him to respect me, but I didn't want to get dragged into any drama between them. How could we ever be friends if in the back of his mind he was always wondering if I'd slept with his wife?

One thing Courtney said to me on that tour has stuck with me.

"Evan, we're rich! We can take out hits on people!"

"Hooray," I answered confusedly.

I wasn't at all attracted to her physically. She was fun to talk to and just hilariously funny and smart. One night at the Commodore Ballroom in Vancouver she felt like the audience was flat, so she smashed her guitar and screamed at them.

"You don't know that it's cool to like us! So we'll come back when you do and you will be lining up!"

She was always throwing bottles. If I wanted to hang out with other women, she'd get jealous, even though there was nothing going on between us. I got pretty good at dodging whiskey bottles aimed at my head.

I don't want to make it seem like it was all bad, because I genuinely like Courtney. I always made time to hang out with her to keep the peace, but I was glad when the tour was over. Too much drama.

Maybe Courtney's paranoia was rubbing off on me, but I was starting to get the sense that the people I trusted to handle my career didn't always have my best interests at heart.

* * *

Come on Feel the Lemonheads hit the UK charts at number five and got as high as number fifty-six on the *Billboard* 200. "Into Your Arms" also did very well on the singles charts. I like the album, but hate the cover. It's more like a magazine layout than the cover of a record album, and it reminds me of all the photo shoots I had to do.

When it was time to make the video for the second single, "It's About Time," the producers put out a casting call and assembled a tape of seventy women who responded. After watching all the audition tapes, I picked Amy Smart and Angelina Jolie. Amy and Angelina had been in critically acclaimed movies, but hadn't had a big break yet.

They were used to being on camera, and we had a fun time shooting the video. It starts out with me and Angelina making out in a convertible, which is a terrible idea if you're trying to keep your romantic indiscretion a secret from your girlfriend. I get caught and try to win Amy back, and she slams a door in my face. In the end, we climb into a bathtub with all our clothes on in front of a roaring fireplace. Like all music videos, it doesn't make a lot of sense.

Most of the video is "live" shots of me, Nic, and David playing in a room that is completely covered in green fur. It has a little bit of an *Alice in Wonderland* feel to it as we bash away on our instruments in a way that looks totally fake, especially for a song that's so mellow.

In 1994 the label released two more singles, "Big Gay Heart" and "The Great Big NO." Billy Bragg used to cover "Big Gay Heart." He was a fan, but that song almost got me into trouble in Chicago. "Big Gay Heart" isn't a gay anthem so much as an attempt to remove the stigma from the word "gay." When I was growing up, "gay" was a slur. With Sneaky Pete's piercing steel guitar, it feels like a gay country and western love ballad. It's got a provocative line, "I don't need you to suck my dick," which is an important part of the story.

RUMORS OF MY DEMISE

We'd just played a free festival in Grant Park in Chicago and I was hanging out with Springa backstage when I was approached by this weirdly aggressive dude.

"What was that you were saying about sucking cock?" this guy wanted to know. "You want to suck my dick?"

At first, we thought he was coming on to me in his own weird way, but after he started rambling about families and children, it quickly became clear that he wanted me to repeat the lyrics back to him. He was an undercover cop, and he was looking to bust me, but he'd misheard the lyric.

"What were you saying up there?" he kept asking.

He thought I was soliciting the crowd, and now the creep was trying to trick me into saying "Suck my dick."

We slowly backed away from him, and when someone stepped in to diffuse the situation, we hid out in the tour bus. It seemed like I was always hiding from lunatic cops on the bus with Springa.

On another occasion, the Lemonheads were playing Summerfest, the annual music festival in downtown Milwaukee. Summerfest draws thousands of people, and the crowd is always diverse: college kids, soccer moms, and even some Hells Angels were in the mix. We were psyched to play.

Festivals can be a mixed bag. The big crowds are fun to play in front of, but there are no guarantees they will know who you are or appreciate your music. There's no bigger drag than playing to thousands of people who wish you would pack up your gear and go home.

Thankfully, that wasn't the case. We took the stage, and the crowd was into it. They sang and danced along to the songs. Unfortunately, the bouncers didn't get the message. They were all meatheads who looked like college football players. They didn't understand that even though the crowd was going nuts, that didn't mean they were out of control.

But there was more to it than that. Earlier that summer the Lemonheads had played with an art band that sang these satirical songs that were meant to antagonize the audience and it worked a little too well. Some of the bouncers from that show were working Summerfest and they were definitely not happy to see us again. To retaliate, they were randomly beating up on kids in the crowd. In the middle of our set, a couple of the bouncers pulled down this guy who was crowd-surfing and started wailing on him. I could see what was going on from the stage and immediately stopped the show.

"What are you doing?" I shouted through the mic. "Fucking leave that kid alone!"

The goons stopped pounding on the guy and put him in a headlock instead, like that was an improvement.

"I'm not playing until you let that kid go!" I shouted.

The crowd started razzing the security. I kept talking shit, which made the crowd more brazen. Security was there to protect the band, not attack the crowd. But now the crowd was turning on them.

Instead of letting the kid go and chilling the fuck out, they turned to the stage. One of our guitar techs spat at one of the security guys and hit him right in the face. When the first guard came up onstage, I took off my guitar to protect myself. I had no intention of hitting anyone—I'm not stupid—but I was hoping to create enough of a delay for the people backstage to figure out that shit was going down.

That's when Springa sprang into action. He came running out with this huge bucket of ice and beer and launched it across the stage.

"Run, Evan!" he shouted.

RUMORS OF MY DEMISE

While I made my exit, security was slipping and sliding all over the place as they tried to cross the stage filled with melting ice and cans of beer—not to mention the live wires everywhere.

Once again, we ran to the tour bus and hid inside. That might have been a mistake this time. There were several guys we were trying to get away from and they'd all just seen me onstage, so they knew where I'd be. Our tour manager rounded up the rest of the band and got them on board while the crew loaded up the gear. But the goons weren't ready to give up. They had no intention of letting us go and were actually rocking the bus back and forth, demanding that I come out.

In all of the confusion, Springa slipped off the bus and went looking for the Hells Angels he'd seen in the crowd. Somehow, he was able to convince a bunch of the bikers to help us out.

I was starting to freak out when the bus stopped rocking and all these bikers rolled up on their motorcycles and began revving their engines. It was like a scene in a Roger Corman film. The security guys thought they were dealing with a skinny rocker, and instead they had the local chapter of the Hells Angels to contend with.

Springa jumped on board, and the Hells Angels escorted us out of Wisconsin. When we were in the clear, I asked Springa what he'd said to the bikers to get them to help us.

"I said you were Charlie Manson's biggest fan!"

* * *

Come on Feel the Lemonheads took us all over the world, including Japan, which was a first for me, David, and Nic. Japan was wild because there were groupies waiting for us everywhere we went. These women would literally line up for a chance to come back to our hotel with us. That kind of blew our minds and we'd joke about it: "Excuse me, but are you sure you have the right band?" It felt like there'd been some kind of wonderful mistake.

In Japan, we weren't part of a festival or touring with a group of bands; we were completely on our own. All of our interactions were with Japanese people. Granted, as touring musicians we were pretty pampered, but in Japan, as soon as we hit the street or got on a train, that safety net disappeared. After so many weird interactions with the press in the US and the UK, it was a relief to just be a person for a while, one of the billions of bodies bouncing around the planet.

Come on Feel the Lemonheads did better than *It's a Shame About Ray*—both records went gold—but fell short of Atlantic's expectations, which were unrealistic. When the album didn't make a quantum leap and ship 5 million copies right out of the gate, the label more or less gave up on us.

Was it the ideal follow-up to *It's a Shame About Ray*? I don't know. It's hard to follow a strong record because people will want to compare the two and decide which one is better. It's human nature, which is why I think it's good to let a little time go by between albums. The artist needs to reset and recalibrate, and so do the fans.

After *Come on Feel the Lemonheads* was in the can, I learned some things that made it obvious that Atlantic cared about the record more than about me. After the crack incident, it got back to me that the label was pressuring the producers to hurry the record along in case I overdosed, but the Robb Brothers had my back.

"Evan needs more time," they said.

The response from Atlantic was all too predictable. "Don't worry about Evan."

"Evan's not right."

"It doesn't matter. Just finish the record!"

RUMORS OF MY DEMISE

That wasn't the worst of it. There were people at the management company who would say things like "Evan's a cash cow. We're going to blitz him for three years and chuck him out on his ass." They used to say shit like that to other artists they were managing and it would get back to me. They'd let them use my account, so I'd get charged for long-distance calls and van rentals and things like that. They had no respect for the Lemonheads.

I'm not bitter about this, because I keep the music and the money separate. All the highs and lows I've experienced as a performer have nothing to do with the music I've created. Playing music is its own reward. That's the main thing that's kept me going all these years.

They just wanted me to get the record done before I overdosed. That's the cold, hard reality of the music business. My reps at Atlantic had read the stories about me just like everyone else. They watched me take laps around the building with a head full of LSD. They could have reached out to me, asked me if I was okay. Instead, they called the producer and cracked the whip. That told me everything I needed to know about their priorities and changed my relationship with the record business. But forces greater than me and my problems were about to turn the industry on its head.

NEGATIVE CREEPS

On April 8, 1994, Kurt Cobain was found dead in his home in Seattle, a victim of an apparent self-inflicted gunshot wound. It was one of those moments when everyone in our scene knew where they were when they heard the news.

The Lemonheads were in Massachusetts to play a gig at a college. I think it was in Worcester, but that doesn't narrow it down. Tom's band Smudge was on tour with us and we'd just gotten back from eating at the Old Spaghetti Factory with the Australians before the show. It was me, Nic, his girlfriend Alison of "Alison's Starting to Happen" fame, Tom, and Smudge's bass player. We were approaching the end of the tour and were kind of taking stock of things, discussing plans for what would come next.

What made that afternoon so eerie was that we'd been talking about Nirvana. We were bitching about how cool everything was before Nirvana blew up the scene. We put the blame for the whole indie thing going to shit at Kurt's feet. We didn't have anything against Nirvana, our feelings for the band hadn't changed, but the general theme of the conversation was *The scene was cool before Nirvana.*

Afterward, we drove back to our hotel, and Dave, who'd stayed behind and had been watching MTV, gave us the bad news.

"Kurt's dead," he said.

I immediately turned to Nic and said, "It's the end of an era."

For those of us in the know, Kurt's death was shocking, but it wasn't a surprise. He'd been struggling with his heroin addiction, which was complicated by his chronic stomach troubles. My first reaction wasn't one of sorrow or incomprehension, but anger. I was always more of a fan than a friend, and like a lot of fans I was angry that I was never going to hear a new song from Kurt. It took a while to sink in.

After *Nevermind*, there was a period when everyone in the industry was trying to figure out who would be the next Nirvana. All around the world, kids were cranking up the volume on their guitar amps. Glam metal, makeup, and spandex were out. Long hair, scruffy beards, and flannel shirts were in. It couldn't last and everyone knew it, but for a brief window of time it felt like something magical had happened. Cool music was on the radio again. Suddenly there were opportunities for loud, noisy rock bands. People from our scene, including me, were able to make a living. It felt like we'd won, and we owed it all to Nirvana.

Kurt's death upended the entire music industry. He never wanted to be the figurehead for the indie rock explosion of the early nineties, but when he died it all fell apart. We all knew the record industry would find a way to ruin everything, and it did, but we figured it would take a while. We were wrong. The fallout from Kurt's death was immediate. The course correction happened fast, and there wasn't anything subtle about it.

My friend Ben Kweller, who came up through the indie ranks,

got dropped immediately after Kurt's death. The label bought out his contract and kicked him to the curb.

A move like that sends a message. It wasn't "We don't believe in you anymore." It was "You're no longer useful to us." It was a cutthroat move that spoke volumes about the character of the people I was dealing with. They didn't give a fuck about anything but the bottom line. The music business is basically run by bankers. The people in charge will tell you they love making music, but that's only true when it sells. The money comes first. That's just the way it is, and shame on you if you lose sight of that for a second.

It may sound callous to talk about the impact of Kurt's suicide on the music industry, but I was way too close to the fallout. Gold Mountain gave me a front-row seat to the aftermath. Shit was changing, and it was clear that I wasn't going to be included in whatever would happen next.

I was contracted to deliver another record to Atlantic, but I felt like I could be dropped at any moment. The prudent move would have been to buckle down and put some money aside, but I did the opposite. I did loads of drugs and spent my money frivolously. It was like tossing confetti into a hurricane.

I tend to view money as the enemy, and I try to get rid of it as quickly as possible. I don't like to be idle, so spending all my money forces me to earn more when it runs out. My dad used to lay this heavy trip on me about managing my money better. He was one of those people who believe that success is a ladder that you have to climb one rung at a time. To him it didn't matter how high you got as long as you were making progress. He was very careful with his money and was afraid of losing what he had.

"You have to run scared," he told me.

Fuck that, I thought.

I wanted to enjoy my money, not be afraid of it. Money puts you in a prison and I wanted to be free. My dad's advice had the opposite effect of what he intended.

Things got warped beyond belief after Kurt's death. A lot of people thought that something was going on between me and Courtney, including many of our mutual friends, which fanned the flames of the rumor. If even my friends thought we were having an affair, then the rumors had to be true, right?

Wrong. A lot of people thought we slept together while we were on tour. Courtney tried to make that happen, but I didn't go for it. Nothing happened between us, but she told people that it had, and they believed her.

I reached out to Pat Smear, who'd been brought in to play with Nirvana, to ask him something that had been bothering me.

"Did Kurt think Courtney was cheating on him with me?" I asked.

"Yeah, man," Pat said. "He thought you and Courtney were having an affair."

"He didn't really think I'd do that to him, did he?"

"Afraid so."

Oh god, I thought. *Kurt Cobain went to his death thinking I'd slept with Courtney.*

Pat was a friend of mine. He told me he'd tried to reassure Kurt there was nothing going on, but apparently Kurt wasn't convinced. Even though things got weird toward the end, deep down I think Kurt was a good man. Just knowing Kurt was carrying that with him when he died was deeply upsetting to me.

* * *

Courtney was fixated on me, but she wasn't the only one. It was always strange. It happened again when Kathleen Hanna of Bikini Kill put out a zine called *My Life with Evan Dando, Popstar*. The zine reflected her frustration with the media, to which I could certainly relate, but it was also weirdly personal.

I wasn't offended by it, but her fans thought it was an attack on me and felt obligated to take action and mobilize a protest against me. Riot Grrrls would come to my shows and not enjoy themselves as a statement. They'd stand around in groups and yell, "Evan Dando sucks!"

The funny thing was they didn't do this outside. They bought tickets and did it during the show. As long as you pay your way in, you can protest all you want.

Kathleen and I actually knew each other. We'd met by chance at the Portobello Road market in London. We literally bumped into each other and hung out for a while. It was totally cool and completely innocent, but you'd never know that reading the zine. She took a weird obsessive angle. It was kind of funny, kind of mean, but it was art, so it was cool. It just had very little to do with our encounter that day.

By the way, *My Life with Evan Dando* wasn't the only anti–Evan Dando zine on the market. *Die Evan Dando, Die* beat Kathleen Hanna to the punch. When people don't like me, they go out of their way to make their feelings known. I can relate. Sometimes I don't like me either.

* * *

The second time I didn't sleep with Courtney, I was hanging out with her the summer after Kurt died. She was supposed to go on the aptly titled Live Through This Tour, but the death of her bass player, Kristen Pfaff, made that impossible.

People in the scene kept slipping away, mostly from drug overdoses. In terms of my own drug use, I was very much in denial. I did a lot of drugs with Courtney the summer after Kurt died.

I'd say something like "We'll party after the show."

"What we're onto is way beyond partying," Courtney said.

She was right, but I wasn't ready to admit that I had a habit, that I looked forward to that first shot of the day a little too much, that the only time I felt right with the world was when I was high. Those realizations were coming, but in the summer of '94, they were still a long way off.

Courtney kept trying to make something happen between us. I would tell her no and she would sulk about it for a while and I'd avoid her. Then she'd ask me for a small favor, the kind that any friend would do, especially after what she'd been through, and I'd do it. I felt bad about rejecting her all the time considering the terrible situation she was in.

She was grieving. Maybe she felt the bullshit she had to deal with from the media and the fans couldn't possibly be worse. People were literally stalking her and showing up at her house at night. It was a horrible situation, and I cared about her as a friend. I wanted to be there for Courtney during this very dark time. That's how I fell into her trap.

"Here, take this," she said one night, handing me a bag.

"What is it?" I asked.

"Some of Kurt's clothes. I want you to have them."

"Why are you giving this to me?"

"Everything is so fucked right now. Just take it."

So I did. I didn't think it was strange at first. I thought Courtney was giving Kurt's stuff away to keep his possessions in her circle of friends rather than have them disappear and show up for sale somewhere. Everyone wanted a piece of Kurt. I took the clothes, and I wore them occasionally because we were more or less the same size. There was a ratty-looking trench coat that I wore onstage a few times and a blue cardigan sweater. One thing that bands from the Northeast shared with bands from the Northwest was an appreciation for a good sweater.

At the time, I didn't understand how famous Kurt's sweaters were. There was a whole field of sweater detectives who kept track of all the different sweaters he wore. Eventually, I wised up to the fact that Courtney wanted me to be seen wearing Kurt's clothes. I'm pretty sure the sweater Courtney gave me is the one he's wearing in the photo on the back of the greatest hits album. In the pantheon of Kurt's sweaters, it's definitely up there. Courtney knew what she was doing when she gave it to me.

Then there was the bear.

Courtney had a stuffed teddy bear in which she kept Kurt's ashes. It was part teddy bear, part backpack, so she could carry it around with her wherever she went. At first, I liked the bear. I liked knowing that Kurt was close, but eventually it started to give me the creeps.

A bunch of us were in Courtney's hotel room in Manhattan. It was me, Courtney, and some members of Juliana's band. It wasn't a party, but people were partying.

"Let's take a picture together," Courtney said.

"Okay," I said.

"Let's pretend like we're making out."

I didn't want to do it. We were on her bed and even though there were lots of people around and nothing intimate was happening, I knew people would get the wrong idea if they saw the photo. It was just an awkward situation, and I wanted no part of it.

"I don't want to," I said.

"Come on, Evan!" Courtney said. "It will be funny in fifteen years." She kept saying that: "It will be funny in fifteen years."

I shook my head, but she wouldn't let the matter drop.

"Come on, do it!"

Finally, it got to the point where I felt like it would be less strange if I just did it than her asking me over and over again. It was my camera, and I figured no harm would come of it if no one ever saw the photo.

"All right," I relented.

We kissed and took the picture. Our lips barely touched, like the way you'd kiss a close friend or relative.

Anyway, like so many other things, I forgot all about my kiss with Courtney. I didn't even think about it when my camera went missing a few days later. A bunch of us were staying in the hotel to support Courtney and our stuff was spread out in different rooms. I figured it would turn up eventually.

About a week later the photo of me and Courtney kissing in bed was splashed all over the *New York Post*. Even though you can tell the photo is posed, there was a huge uproar over it. People were not cool with that photo. Fans felt like it was disrespectful to Kurt's memory, and it made me look like a sleaze who was taking advantage of Courtney during a vulnerable period of her life.

That was the best-case scenario. For some, that photo was proof that the rumors Courtney had been spreading about us were true and that I was a first-class scumbag. I figured it was someone working at the hotel, or someone posing as a hotel worker. Paparazzi spy tactics. Real cloak-and-dagger shit.

Later, someone told me that Courtney sent the photo to the tabloids herself, which made me sad. I wanted to believe that she wouldn't pull a stunt like that.

Mom, Holly, me.

On the fundamentalist gondola with Dad. Skiing and surfing were our religion.

19 Western Avenue, Essex, Massachusetts. Lovely Colonial with the dirt floor basement. I spent nine great years here.

"I have rabies (stay away from me)!"
—Chris Doherty, Gang Green

Ladies used to approach my mom and me and say, "I want that!," meaning my hair color scheme. This was how it looked in autumn. I had a natural reaction to the seasons. My hair changed color on the quick side! (Why are you reading this book?) Oh, that's my stuffed animal Ozzy the ocelot.

The Dandos' 1977 Christmas card, snapped at Côte des Basques beach, Biarritz, summer '76.

Madrid, 1976.

Albert Jeffrey Dando on the bass. He had a passion for bass lines.

Me and Holly with my mother's painting behind us.

Divorce and Christmas collide in the Back Bay.

Me and Mama.

North Neck, Chappy, circa June 1980.

In front of the West Tisbury house on the Whiting farm with my fly-fishing catch, circa 1981.

Schooly D(ando) with a little bass; I threw him back. Menemsha, Massachusetts.

The Lemonheads supporting the Ramones, 1986.

Me, Ivan, John Bing, Jesse, and our favorite diner. Commonwealth days.

Going for that sweaty post-gig feel of our favorite MC5 photos.

Ben, Jesse, John Strohm, and me, on our summer '87 tour.

Ever politically aware, John and I got our tits out so the girls didn't have to.
Blake Babies press photo, 1988.

Being in the Blake Babies was serious fun. At the Condo Pad, 1988.

So sad when you "find" clothes you loved in photographs. Early shirt of Ernie and Bert.

Me, David, and Nic. Handmade Public Enemy shirt on me, and Nic's got on his star pants that he made. Boston, 1992.

Me and Juliana.

Me, Holly, and our beloved Robert Plant on a national radio show in 1993.

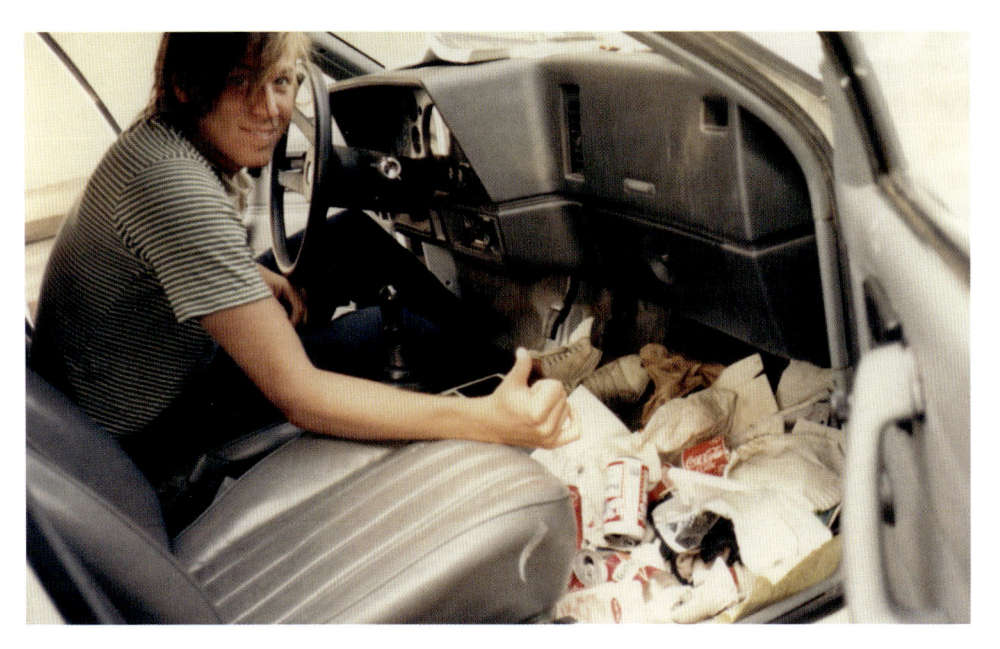

Tidy as ever in my white Chevy station wagon, aka the "Ride with Me" car. (The song was written about a drive to the Florida Keys. My only stop was a show by Boston favorites Christmas in Chapel Hill, North Carolina. True soldier of love.)

Come on!
Feel the Lemonheads!

Only low self-esteem and drugs could cause a man to gesture thusly.

GET IN THE BACK OF THE VAN!

My Gram Parsons T-shirt, given to me in Perth, that B(something) made, and the SG I bought for three hundred bucks. Our guitar tech Steve Morgan looks on.

"Where you been is good and gone,
All you keep's the getting there."
—"To Live Is to Fly," Townes Van Zandt

Lemonmania in Ulster.

Beware of the spindle-legged troubadour in the park.

In the middle of the *It's a Shame About Ray* recordings, I was struggling with overdubs. Nic said, "Get a reggae hat." This is all I could find on Melrose. It worked, but looked bad.

Japan, where groupies never died. Alex, our tour manager, wrote, "Not my nuts" on the back of my kimono, joking if I had to meet any groupies' fathers the next day.

Me, wearing a T-shirt onstage, playing an SG.

Sweater rock in its declining years.

Performing in the noughties with Valerie from Glasgow, a handmade guitar strap, and an Iron Maiden T-shirt given to me by Jeordie (Twiggy) of Marilyn Manson.

Iggy to the rescue. Such a mensch; I love that man. Nic Dalton, a really famous footballer, and Courtney Love making the scene backstage after a Roseland show.

Loved Suede live at the KROQ Weenie Roast. Great band!

A platinum voice, but only gold records. Janet Billig, Michael Krumper being presented for *Ray* and *Come on Feel*. I left them at CBGB and Hilly was like, "Okay . . . you could have had them engraved to the club!"

Smoking in the greenhouse.

Me and Gibby.

The Aquinnah House, Martha's Vineyard. Across from Philbin Beach.

Twilight gloaming of the alternahunk. "I've been looking to the future, thinking about the past and present getting closer." —Eugene Kelly

RUMORS OF MY DEMISE

I think on some level we all care what people think about us. When you're the subject of intense media scrutiny, you have to figure out a way not to care or you'll go crazy. But this was different. Courtney was trying to plant an idea that simply wasn't true. It wasn't fair and it wasn't cool and there was no getting away from it.

Unfortunately, I'll always be a part of the sad, strange story of Kurt and Courtney. That photo implicated me in all kinds of conspiracy theories about Kurt's death, which persist to this day. Even Courtney's father insinuated as much in Nick Broomfield's so-called documentary.

My real friends know what happened, but Kurt's fans, Courtney's fans, and some of my own fans were mad at me. Even though I've told the story many times, people still think I had something to do with the circumstances that led to Kurt's death. I felt like the only thing I could do was run away.

* * *

After River Phoenix died, I got his part in the James Mangold film *Heavy*. It wasn't something I auditioned for or even went after. They approached me and asked if I wanted to do it. I found out I got the part that River was going to play after the fact. I play Liv Tyler's rocker boyfriend, which wasn't a stretch for me. It's a small role, a bit part.

It was something to do, a way to stay busy and hang out with some interesting new people. My first day on the set, Liv and I prepared for our scene together on a bridge in Port Jervis, New York.

Mangold said, "Okay, you two. We're gonna chain you to the bridge and you're going to make out."

Wow, I thought. *This is a fun job.*

Liv was stunning. Even though she'd been in the Aerosmith video for "Crazy" with Alicia Silverstone, I had no idea who she was when I was cast in the movie. It's impossible to be that close to someone for that long without getting to know something about them. We had a lot in common. She hadn't done much acting, but had been modeling since she was fourteen years old. Her mother was a model, too, and had been living with Todd Rundgren when she had an affair with Steven Tyler of Aerosmith and got pregnant. Liv grew up thinking Rundgren was her biological father, but she eventually figured out the truth.

Liv and I were chained together not so that she couldn't run away from me but so that we wouldn't fall off the bridge and plunge into the Delaware River below. It's the last scene in the movie and lasts for only a few seconds, but it took us five hours to shoot. Five hours is a long time to make out with someone. If all acting was that enjoyable, I'd still be doing it.

I got to meet Deborah Harry, who plays Liv's antagonist in the movie. I also did three songs for the soundtrack: "Hot Coals," "Frying Pan," and "How Much I've Lied"—my first recordings as a solo artist. Thurston Moore and the Plimsouls also contributed songs to the album. The film did well at Sundance and Cannes and launched Mangold's career.

Heavy isn't my only acting credit. I also have a cameo in *Reality Bites*. I play an actor named Roy. They were going to use one of our songs in the movie, but for some reason Atlantic Records wouldn't allow it, which was pretty stupid because the soundtrack did well and eventually went double platinum. For a lot of people, that record is not just the soundtrack to the movie but to the nineties as well. Dinosaur Jr. and the Juliana Hatfield Three got in there, but not the Lemonheads. For me, it underscored the fact that no one in the entertainment business knows what they're doing. They pass the buck when shit goes south, take credit for things they had nothing to do with, and when a golden opportunity comes along, they bungle it.

After we wrapped shooting *Heavy*, Liv insisted I meet her friends Marlon Richards and Lucie de la Falaise. Lucie was a model whose father was a furniture designer. Marlon also had a famous father: Keith Richards of the Rolling Stones.

"You're going to love them, and I know they'll love you!"

I was living in Manhattan at the time. In between *It's a Shame About Ray* and *Come on Feel the Lemonheads*, I'd gotten a place in the city but wasn't there all that often. It was somewhere to go between tours. After Liv introduced me to Marlon and Lucie, I started to spend a lot more time in the city. We met for dinner at Bar Pitti and I realized right away that Marlon wasn't some entitled scion sliding through life on Keith's coattails. On the contrary, he was a talented photographer and graphic designer and was just as creative as his father. When he was a kid, he weathered some storms with his family that forced him to grow up in a hurry. That's his story to tell, but it resonated with some of my own experiences.

We hung out a lot and got to be good friends. We'd run around the city and go to clubs together. He knew a lot of models, so he could get us into all the happening spots. We went to so many parties with rock stars and fashion models. Musicians and models understand each other because it's such a crazy way to be in the world. Ridiculous schedules, high-pressure gigs, the crush of celebrity. Everybody knows you, or at least they think they do, but few ever take the time to really get to know you. They never bother to look deeper than the surface.

Marlon made the effort. I think he understood that I was going through some things. I'd been on the road for two and a half years and I was worn out from all the traveling. Even though technically I was "home," it didn't feel like it. Holly was living in the city and would come to gigs, but she was concerned about my lifestyle. Her job as a social worker had given her a close-up look at all the ways that drugs can ruin a life and she worried about me.

I was a bit ragged and forlorn. Being on the road that much messes you up. While you're away you feel cut off from your life. The only thing that matters is the next stop, the next venue, the next show. I'd traveled so much that all my time home was wrapped up in getting ready for the next tour. That's when people crack up and bands implode. I needed a break. I'd been through the indie wars, but I didn't know where to go or what to do with myself.

When Marlon and Lucie invited me on their honeymoon in the Caribbean, I jumped at the opportunity. We weren't traveling to some fancy resort, but to Marlon's father's house in Jamaica—Ocho Rios—a place steeped in Rolling Stones history.

After going on the road in support of *Exile on Main St.* in 1973, the Rolling Stones went to Kingston, Jamaica, to record *Goats Head Soup*. It was the same year the soundtrack to *The Harder They Come* and the Wailers' *Catch a Fire* came out. It was an electric time to be in Jamaica, and Keith bought his house there after the Rolling Stones were done cutting the album. It became his home away from home.

Keith's house in Jamaica was not just a getaway, but an archive of incredible material. When Keith moved into the house the Rolling Stones were scattered all over the globe, and for the first time they tried working on new material remotely. Keith kept all the correspondence from this period, including letters from Mick Jagger in which he shares ideas and makes recommendations for the new album. Keith reflected on these letters and wrote his replies in a journal for safekeeping when they were back in the studio together.

RUMORS OF MY DEMISE

The house was also full of notebooks the band kept during their recording sessions. Keith had made all these notations about the songs as they were writing them. There were at least three notebooks for *Some Girls* that were incredibly detailed. I'd pore over these journals like sacred texts.

And then there were the tapes: racks of unmarked cassettes that had different mixes of all the songs from that phase of the Rolling Stones' career: *Some Girls*, *Exile on Main St.*, and *Tattoo You*. I spent hours listening to the recording sessions for *Some Girls*. I'd pop in a tape and listen. They recorded different mixes of every song on those records. So inspiring!

Between the notebooks and the tapes, it was like a master class in songwriting, and it gave me a deeper appreciation of the effort that went into crafting them. Those songs aren't classics by accident. When the Rolling Stones met in Paris to make a new record, those sessions produced material for three albums: *Some Girls*, *Emotional Rescue*, and *Tattoo You*. Boom, boom, boom. They got three albums out of those sessions.

I have always loved *Some Girls*. It's got an amazing sound with cool guitar effects and great performances by Keith. At the time of the recording, the band was starting to fall off a bit. It had been six years since they'd capped that incredible run of *Let It Bleed*, *Sticky Fingers*, and *Exile on Main St.* Three strong records. *Some Girls* was a return to form. Almost like a comeback record. Plus, they had all the other material. The only song they had to rerecord was "Start Me Up" for *Tattoo You* because it was originally conceived as a reggae song called "Never Stop." Calling it a reggae song is a bit of a stretch, but you can hear the Jamaican influence on Keith's playing in the original version.

I wasn't the only misfit on this excursion to Ocho Rios. Tarka Cordell was another troubled soul who Marlon brought along on the trip. Tarka was a musician and producer like his father, Denny Cordell, who'd worked with a zillion bands and discovered Tom Petty and the Cranberries. After a while, me and Tarka were sent to a hotel way up in the mountains called Murphy Hill so that the newlyweds could have some time to themselves. Apparently, this hotel was built on the site of a pig farm and they still had a few running wild on the grounds. Marlon had a sense of humor about it.

"It's time for you guys to go sleep with the pigs," he said, and off we went.

Kingston can be a dangerous place, and if you go looking for trouble you might find more than you bargained for. We stayed in our hotel in the mountains for about three weeks, until we ran out of Xanax. I knew better than to try to score on my own. All night long we heard gunshots along the highway.

As inspiring as it was, I was sad that my Jamaican sojourn was over. It was time to be a Lemonhead again.

SILVER HILL

The highlight of the rock and roll calendar was festival season, which unofficially began with Glastonbury in June and ended with Reading in August. The big rock festivals of the nineties brought together musicians from all facets of the music industry, which led to some wild times behind the scenes. At a festival in Denmark, I was invited to the little tent where Lemmy Kilmister of Motörhead and Shane MacGowan of the Pogues were cutting up enormous lines of speed. Those lines were fucking huge—over a foot long—and on that particular day I was up for the challenge.

The first time the Lemonheads played Glastonbury, in 1993, we almost missed the gig due to travel delays, but there were all kinds of rumors about why we were late flying around: the airline wouldn't let me board the plane because I was too fucked up, cops arrested me for creating a disturbance on the plane, the band was sick of my shenanigans and broke up . . . None of this was true. The British press didn't need a reason to print a salacious story about me. The fact of the matter was we made it to Glastonbury on time, but when I took the stage wearing a dress with my hair in pigtails, the media went wild.

By the time of the Lemonheads' third appearance at Glastonbury, in 1995, the press had had enough of me, so it's not surprising they reported that I was a no-show. That's not entirely true. I was there. In fact, my performance has been judged as one of the festival's all-time worst, which is hard to do if you're not there.

Let me back up a bit. The Lemonheads arrived at Glastonbury a day early. I was all checked in and watching Jeff Buckley's set from backstage when I was ambushed by a pair of beautiful women. Things quickly unraveled from there.

I had an on-and-off relationship with a famous couple who were both women. One was a model; the other was an athlete who'd turned to music. We'd bumped into each other a few times, but they were more into each other than they were me. I didn't know they were coming to Glastonbury and they surprised me backstage. They had a car and wanted to whisk me away to their hotel.

"Just for a little while," they promised.

I was apprehensive at first, but they were very persuasive, and I crumbled like a house of cards. I got in the car and off we went.

I wasn't driving, and I was a bit distracted, but we drove for what felt like hours. We just kept going and going, and when we finally stopped, we were very far from Glastonbury. We went into their hotel room and the hours kind of melted away. I lost track of time, which can happen when you're under the influence of heroin and being held prisoner by a pair of beautiful women.

Night turned into morning and morning turning into . . . Holy shit! What time is it? We tumbled out of bed and into the car and drove back to Glastonbury, which seemed to take even longer under the somber gray skies.

We didn't quite make it in time, and I missed my slot at the festival, which is the lamest thing you can do as a musician. I let the fans down. I let the promoter down. I let the label down. Most important, I let the Lemonheads down. Every time the festival organizers came around with a panicked "Where's Dando?" all David and Nic could do was shrug their shoulders. My bandmates had been through this many times before. Usually, I showed up at the last minute, but not this time.

The way the festival was set up, we couldn't jump onto someone else's slot because Nic and Dave had gone back to the hotel after all our gear was cleared off the stage. I was about to throw in the towel when someone hit on the brilliant idea to have me do an acoustic set. I was up for it because I felt terrible about missing the gig, so I decided to give it a shot.

That proved to be a big mistake.

Fans had been crammed into this hot, sweaty tent for hours, waiting for Portishead to play. When I came out onstage the mood soured. People were there to see an acoustic set from Portishead, not an American plunking away on a guitar like some wanker at the pub. People actually started throwing bottles at me, which I didn't appreciate. I picked one up and threw it back, and that put a stop to that. I'd actually scared them somehow, but it was a chaotic situation. As the bottles were replaced by boos, I was quickly hustled off the stage for my own safety. Amazingly, there isn't any footage of my very brief performance.

Meanwhile, backstage, Russell Warby, my longtime promoter in the UK, was going absolutely mental. He was furious about the acoustic set and actually kicked the guy whose idea it was to shoehorn me into Portishead's slot. He understood from the jump that it was a terrible idea to put me in front of a hostile crowd like that. He got wicked violent and they booted him out of the festival. I left before they threw me out, too.

Glastonbury is a lot of fun, but there's a certain sameness to the festival, especially if you're the guy the paper sends to write about it every year. Well, I'd given the writers a gold mine, and my antics at the festival were the lead story the next day. You'd have thought I'd taken a sledgehammer to the stage and brought the house down.

But you know what? I'd probably do it again. I like to think I'm smart enough to make sure I'd stay on-site, or at least take the party back to my own hotel.

* * *

I felt like I was losing my spark. I was still deeply troubled by Kurt's death and all the messiness of the aftermath. Playing a show involves a lot of hard work, and if you lose sight of that you'll be in for a rude awakening. My focus was drifting, and I was letting the negative attention for things I had no control over distract me from making music.

I was doing tons of drugs, and I wasn't trying to hide it from anyone. I was in denial about having a habit. When I'm on a run like that, the last thing I'm thinking about is overdosing, but I knew that thought was in people's heads. First River. Then Kurt. Who's next? Will it be Dando?

There were some weird vibes swirling around. In many ways my life was pretty great. Marlon and Lucie had welcomed me into the wider circle of their family and friends. Marlon introduced me to his dad, "Uncle Mick," and the rest of the gang. Once I was in with Keith, I was in with the whole crowd. It was like having a second family.

I was also acting in movies and hanging out with Milla Jovovich. We'd met after one of my shows at Roseland in New York. She wasn't super famous yet. She'd only been in *Return to the Blue Lagoon*. She was uncannily beautiful and I kind of fell for her. We fooled around a little bit, but she had a boyfriend that I didn't know about who was the bass player in Jamiroquai, so it was complicated. She invited me to come visit her in Spain and I missed the plane, which was a blessing in disguise because she was there with her boyfriend.

In addition to being an actress and a model, Milla was a talented musician who'd released an album called *The Divine Comedy* with lyrics she'd written and music she'd composed. It's folk rock, but her label tried to make her out to be a pop star, which was so off the mark it was almost comical. We played some festivals together, including a gig in New Orleans in the summer of '94. For reasons I'll never be able to explain, we were using Jimmy Swaggart's PA system. All the gear had these little metal plaques that said "Property of Jimmy Swaggart." I stole one and put it on my guitar. I thought it was the funniest thing, but that little plaque was like a talisman that would trigger all kinds of weirdness.

I had some time on my hands. I had plenty of money and nothing to do, which isn't a good combination for me. Working keeps me focused and sane. Left to my own devices, I was doing a lot of heroin and little of anything else. I felt the best thing for me would be to get out of New York for a while.

I decided to go to Sydney to recapture some of the magic I'd experienced on my previous visits. Australia was a place that had been good to me and good for me. I thought if I unplugged from the toxicity of the music business for a bit, which went hand in glove with the media machine, I'd recharge my batteries before hunkering down to tackle the next record. By leaving the continent I'd be leaving my troubles behind. But that's not the way it works.

It's hard to describe what happened on that trip. I've told multiple versions of the story over the years. The details have gotten jumbled up, but here's what I remember. I flew to Sydney and checked into a hotel. Instead of resting up for a few days, I went out and scored some speed. I told myself it would help me manage my jet lag, but as I would soon find out, I was fighting more than exhaustion.

I was way too wired to sleep, so I left the hotel and went looking for something stronger. All I could find was ecstasy. I took some, but it wasn't working for me, so I topped it off with some LSD. All the drugs did was make me restless, so I walked around the city by myself. I wasn't sleepwalking, but I wasn't *not* sleepwalking, either. I had no idea what I was doing because I wasn't fully present. I was on some strange kind of autopilot, but this was not a blissed-out trip. I felt terrible. I was literally puking in the streets and sweating through my clothes. I couldn't figure out what was wrong with me. I was so out of it I forgot I had a habit.

I was withdrawing from heroin.

By the time I got back to my hotel the sun had come up and I was tripping hard. I managed to get ahold of some Valium, boxes and boxes of the stuff, but it was too late. I lost the plot. The objects in the room took on a strange significance, none weirder than the "Property of Jimmy Swaggart" plaque on my guitar. I believed I'd made a deal with the devil and now my soul belonged to Jimmy Swaggart. I pried off the plaque and tossed it aside like it was possessed. Next, I fixated on the money in my wallet. Why does it say "In God We Trust" on the American dollar bill? Why is God on the money?

Everything was a sign. Everything was connected. The "Property of Jimmy Swaggart" plaque and the "In God We Trust" message on the money felt like they were related, they had to be, but how?

I felt like I was *this close* to understanding. Conspiracy 101.

I was in bad shape and started to bug out. It became imperative that I get home before I completely disconnected from reality. I left the hotel with my guitar and suitcase. I was feeding coins into sewer grates thinking that would do the trick and I'd be teleported back to the United States. Poof! I'm home. I was in the grip of some weird magical thinking, a full-on psychotic breakdown.

I jumped in a cab and asked the driver to take me to the airport. I had my passport and my ticket, but I hadn't showered in days, and I wasn't wearing any shoes. Also, I didn't have money to pay the driver. That caused a scene. I wanted to compensate the driver for all the trouble I was causing, but I had no idea how to do that without Jimmy Swaggart's money.

"Get out of my cab," the driver said. "Just go."

I thought the driver was giving me a break because, somehow, we were already at the airport, but when I got out of the cab there were police officers waiting in the terminal. Why were the cops at the airport? Did they know I was coming? Did Jimmy Swaggart send them?

As I approached the terminal, they all turned and looked at me. I tried to force my way inside, but they weren't having it. It took five cops to wrestle me into submission and slap a pair of handcuffs on me. I didn't understand what was happening. I got cut in the skirmish and I was getting blood all over the place, but I didn't realize it was coming from me. In my aggrieved state I thought the cops were stopping me from going home, which was now a matter of life or death. Why wouldn't they let me go home?

I was at the center of my own conspiracy.

Thankfully, the police didn't arrest me. In fact, the cops were extremely nice to me, which wasn't something I expected or deserved. They took me to a little room and asked me a bunch of questions, which brought me back to reality. After they were done interrogating me, they dropped me off at my hotel and wished me well. I can only imagine what would have happened if I'd pulled a stunt like that at JFK.

The episode scared the hell out of me. A million different things could have gone wrong. I didn't know what to do so I called Holly, who'd already been contacted by some of my friends.

"I need help," I said.

"What is it?" Holly asked.

"I want to come home."

"We'll get you home, Ev. Don't worry."

I explained what had happened to me, but I wasn't making much sense. Holly told me later that most of what I said was gibberish. I was convinced I had to fly home on the exact same route I'd taken a few days before—only backward. I'd lost my mind and the only way to find it was by retracing my steps, so to speak.

Holly tried to talk some sense into me, but I wouldn't back down. She got in touch with a friend of mine in Sydney named Mandy, who flew home with me and made sure I got to Boston in one piece. I don't know what I would have done without her. I popped a bunch of Valium and slept the whole way.

When I arrived in Boston, my dad, mom, and sister were all waiting for me at the airport. They'd hired a limousine and we all drove to the hospital together. They were worried to death about me. I could barely talk and there was nothing to say.

Holly got me set up in a superexpensive sanitarium in Connecticut called Silver Hill. My dad paid for the whole thing. Apparently, Edie Sedgwick did a stint at Silver Hill, which Holly knew I'd appreciate. She wanted to make it "fun" for me.

Well, it wasn't fun.

When I arrived at Silver Hill, the intake staff took all of my belongings away from me—my wallet, my shoes, my belt. Anything

I might use to run away or hurt myself. Holly had already taken away all the Valium.

My first night there I couldn't sleep—I was terrified of sleepwalking in the sanitarium—and the staff checked on me every fifteen minutes. Was I on suicide watch?

Maybe, but I didn't want to die. That wasn't my deal. I'd always interpreted my sleepwalking as a symptom of my desire to live, like my unconscious mind was trying to warn me that something terrible was about to happen and I needed to get away.

"Ssshhh, Evan," the duty nurse said to me. "Get some rest."

People were always telling me that I needed to rest. Nurses, family, friends. *Just relax for a while, Evan. Get some rest and catch up on your sleep.* They didn't know that while I was sleeping my demons were catching up on me.

Like a lot of people who find themselves in rehab for the first time, I didn't think I needed to be there. I blamed my crack-up Down Under on a lack of sleep. It was the cocktail of speed, ecstasy, and LSD combined with the heroin withdrawal that pushed me over the edge.

My problem was with heroin. I'd developed a habit and underestimated the effects of withdrawal. When you have a habit, you have to feed it or suffer the consequences—both physical and psychological. I thought by changing up the scenery and taking lots of other drugs I could avoid the comedown.

I went to Silver Hill to recover from my misadventures in Australia, but I didn't want to stop getting high. Not then. Not ever. Rehab was an opportunity to come back to myself, but it wasn't this big, life-changing experience for me. Rehab never is. For some people rehab clearly defines their lives in terms of before and after. It wasn't that big of a deal for me. I treated my visit like a mental health break, a chance to get my shit together, not an opportunity to take a good hard look at myself, which was probably what the situation called for, but I wasn't ready for that yet.

My sleepwalking hadn't been as bad in recent years, which I attributed to all the drugs I was taking. They kept the party going and the night terrors at bay—a win-win situation.

While I was at Silver Hill I had a terrifying thought: *What if the madness I'd experienced in Australia was the night terrors breaking through to my conscious mind and taking over the controls?*

I knew that I'd gone to a very dark place in Australia. You lose sleep, but you never get it back. It's gone, and if you're not careful your sanity can go with it. I never wanted to experience that again, but I also didn't want to open the door to a new chapter of sleepwalking.

I was twenty-seven years old—the same age as Brian Jones, Jimi Hendrix, Janis Joplin, Jim Morrison, and D. Boon when they died. Now Kurt had joined the dead in the 27 Club.

This realization prompted a strange revelation, but it was more than that. I'm reluctant to call it a spiritual moment because I don't believe in those things, but it was much stronger than an epiphany. I don't have the words to describe what it was, so I'll just tell you what happened.

While I was at Silver Hill, I felt very close to Kurt, closer than I'd ever felt to him when he was alive. I didn't think he was watching over me or anything like that, but it was a very peculiar feeling, very intense. I felt like now that Kurt had crossed over, he understood the truth about things in his life that he didn't have access to while he was alive. I felt this very strongly. Although my experience in Australia had made me wary of messages from beyond and that sort of thing, this felt different. Wherever Kurt was, I felt like he wanted me to know that he knew the truth.

RUMORS OF MY DEMISE

It feels weird to write about this, because I don't want to give the impression that Kurt came to me in a vision while I was in rehab at Silver Hill. That didn't happen, but the effect was the same as if he had. I felt like a burden had been lifted and I didn't have to carry around all that negativity anymore. I didn't have to worry about what anyone else thought about me and Courtney and Kurt because we all knew the truth and that was the only thing that mattered. I could just let it all go.

I was absolutely flooded with gratitude. Not only toward Kurt and his family but to my own family as well. They were there for me when I needed them most. They pulled me out of a very dark place and helped me get well again.

I felt I'd gotten all I was going to get out of rehab. I don't remember how many days I spent there, but it was less than two weeks. Most of the time I hung out with suicidal teens who didn't care who I was. That was my little clique: me and the kids who were pissed off at the world. I made a few friends, but we didn't hang out afterward. We tried, but it was weird. Getting together was a reminder of the lowest point in our lives, and that's not something we wanted to hang on to. Rehab was a chance to start over, to turn the page, and that's exactly what I did, but I was reading a different book than everyone else.

* * *

The first thing I did after I got out of rehab was go to Milla's apartment. She had a new place over near the Macy's on West 34th Street. She lit all these candles in her apartment, like fifty of them, completely transforming the space.

All I wanted to do was smoke a big fat joint. Even though I was dead set on quitting heroin, that didn't mean I wanted to stop getting high. I had no intention of climbing aboard the sobriety wagon. That ride wasn't for me. After the intensity of rehab all I wanted was to hang out with Milla and be around her energy.

I had an idea for a song that had been kicking around while I was at Silver Hill, and it needed to come out. I took my guitar, climbed into Milla's bathtub, and went to work. I wanted to write a Mazzy Star–sounding song, and the result was "Hospital." I didn't know what it was about when I was writing it, and when I was done, I realized all the different meanings it could have, like the line "green leaves falling from the trees" could be about AIDS, young people dying, or even Kurt. It was one of those intuitive songs that didn't require a whole lot of thought.

I moved into the Gramercy Park Hotel for a while. I was in a new phase of living and wanted to stay someplace that was as transitory as I felt. I didn't know what my next move would be, but whatever it was I didn't want to rush it. My experience at Silver Hill led me to reassess my place in the music business. I didn't want my life to keep going in the same direction. I had to change how I conducted myself with the media.

When the Lemonheads signed to Atlantic, I thought the whole rock star thing was a game, and I treated it like one. I embraced it wholeheartedly. I was comfortable with the cliché because I liked the attention. I was more than happy being a character, a cartoon, and I was accommodating to anyone who helped me achieve that end. I think people took advantage of my willingness to go along with that—of course they did—but I didn't care. I enjoyed everything about the rock and roll lifestyle: playing shows, traveling first-class, going to music festivals, hanging out with beautiful women, and being high on alcohol and drugs for most of it.

But people want their rock stars to be edgy and mysterious. When you're open and honest and reveal that you're just as vulnerable and insecure as everyone else, they turn on you. The press puts you on a pedestal, and if you don't live up to their image of what a rock star should be, they knock you off it. No one forced me to play that game, so I had only myself to blame when the music media turned on me. Fair enough.

After my breakdown in Australia, my priorities changed. I had three goals: stay out of the news, jail, and the insane asylum. While I was in Silver Hill, I realized I was taking myself a bit too seriously. My bitterness toward the music business was getting in the way of having fun. I still owed Atlantic another record. I could suffer through it and deliver a record everyone would hate, or I could start having fun again.

I started doing interviews on my own terms. I still said things I shouldn't have said, but I stopped acting as if it mattered. I'd be cagey or coy, distracted or dishonest. Giving a "good" interview was no longer a priority for me. That was up to the writers to figure out. Sometimes I'd even turn the tables on them while they were interviewing me:

"So, what are your literary influences?"

"What?"

"Is there anyone special in your life?"

"You can't ask me that!"

If I was doing a bunch of interviews in a row, I'd serve up the same non sequiturs in every conversation just to see how many made it into print.

"The ocean is the internet!" was one of them.

Boston legend Jonathan Richman of the Modern Lovers gave me some tips for dealing with the press: don't talk about world events, use short sentences to prevent being misrepresented, and when you start to get bored with the interview it's time to wrap it up. All great advice.

I began to establish boundaries for myself. No interviews after an all-nighter. No self-promotion on an empty stomach. That sort of thing. Today they would call it self-care, but my critics didn't care for it one bit. They thought I was being difficult and confrontational, and for a while I kind of was, but I was enjoying myself.

In return for making their lives difficult, many writers set out to make me look like an idiot. What can I say? I gave them plenty of material to work with. It's kind of funny that my big takeaway from rehab wasn't to stop doing drugs, but to stop talking to the media about doing drugs. I was too much with myself, but it was too late to be anyone else.

SINKING FEELINGS

I had one more record to write to fulfill my contract with Atlantic, and the Lemonheads were in a state of disarray. David and Nic left the band. After more than three years of almost nonstop touring, they wanted out. David moved to LA to be a writer, and Nic returned to Sydney to run his record label.

Rather than start the band up all over again, I thought I'd write the new record myself, use session musicians in the studio, and recruit some players when it was time to tour. It didn't work out that way, but when I wrote the songs for the new album, the Lemonheads were a one-man band.

Car Button Cloth, the Lemonheads' seventh studio album, is my most personal record. I wrote "It's All True" after my misadventures at Glastonbury. The song opens with four truths that are obvious lies. These tongue-in-cheek statements poke fun at the wild stories that various newspapers and magazines wrote about me after my so-called meltdown at Glastonbury:

> I haven't cried baby since I learned to talk
> Haven't fallen down since I learned to walk

>   And I don't get bored watching the tube
>   And I never had a rock in my shoe

"If I Could Talk I'd Tell You" was inspired by the interviews I did with the British press after my crack binge in LA. When I responded to one of the journalists' questions with the note "If I could talk, I'd tell you," I knew right away I'd use it in a song. I wrote the song during a jam session with Eugene Kelly from the legendary Scottish punk band the Vaselines and it just fell together.

"Break Me," "Hospital," and "Losing Your Mind" all draw on my breakdown in Australia and my time at Silver Hill. The first two sound almost happy-go-lucky, but "Losing Your Mind" goes to some mental caverns without glamorizing the experience. The song sounds the way depression feels.

>   What a comfort to find out you're losing your mind
>   When you re-realize that it's not the first time

When I can't go out on the road and play, it starts to feel like there's something missing in my life and that gets me into trouble. I get into plenty of trouble on the road, too, but it's only when I'm completely cut off from music that the absence becomes intolerable. "Something's Missing" is about those dark periods when I'm not right with myself or my music.

I nearly included a song I cowrote with Noel Gallagher when I went on tour with Oasis, but it was scrapped. I met the Gallaghers at a festival at the end of the *Come on Feel the Lemonheads* tour. They invited me to come with them to Amsterdam, and since I wasn't ready to stop touring, I went along for the ride. I'd hang out, get loaded, play the tambourine on the side of the stage. The English press hated me for that, which I'll never understand. The Australian press did the same thing to Kylie Minogue when she came to see the Lemonheads in Melbourne and we hung out for a few days afterward. They tried to make it into more than what it was. Can't people just have fun and enjoy each other's music?

The song I cowrote with Noel was called "Purple Parallelogram," but it was pulled at the last minute, sparing everyone involved a good deal of embarrassment.

Car Button Cloth has its lighter moments, like "The Outdoor Type," a song Tom wrote and recorded with his band Smudge, and "6ix," which is my tribute to Gwyneth Paltrow's character in the movie *Se7en*. These songs balance out the heaviness of the Louvin Brothers' murder ballad "Knoxville Girl," which Nick Cave and the Bad Seeds have also covered. I wanted to do the song after Nick told me my music wasn't evil enough.

While I was working on the songs for *Car Button Cloth*, I dreamt I was standing on a stage in front of a huge crowd, strumming my guitar and singing the words "one more time" over and over again for what felt like hours. When I woke up, I grabbed my guitar to see if I could capture the song before it slipped away. I dream about songs all the time, but I almost always forget them when I wake up. This time was different. I was able to remember the basic melody. I had a tape recorder handy, and I managed to capture it before it disappeared. That song became, wait for it, "One More Time."

The album title comes from an experience I had as a kid. For a school project I filled up the bathtub and dropped things into the water to see what would float and what would sink. I gathered up a bunch of my stuff and dumped it in the tub, one at a time. A toy car, a button, and a piece of cloth all sank to the bottom. So I called the album *Car Button Cloth* and the cover re-creates the experiment with the caption "All of these things sank."

At least that was the story Atlantic made me tell. In fact, I found the cover on Byres Road in Glasgow on one of my many trips to visit Eugene Kelly. A clue to the truth of the child's drawing is the two-pence coin. My parents had bags of foreign coins, but only from places where you can surf. Try surfing in Glasgow. I reverse engineered the story in the name of corporate cowardice. They were actually worried that the kid would sue us!

Writing out your feelings in a song can be a great way to process heavy emotions, but recording them is a different story. You're basically bottling up your emotions and uncorking them every time you play live.

When it was time to record, I scrapped my plan to use session musicians because I'd found some exceptionally talented people to play with me. I convinced another Australian to replace Nic on bass—big Bill Gibson of the Eastern Dark. But I had to have at least one punk rocker in the band. After Murph was kicked out of Dinosaur Jr., I invited him to join the Lemonheads. Murph was up for it and he became the band's eighth drummer. That was a powerful rhythm section.

We made the record at Dreamland Recording Studios, which is in an old church, not far from Woodstock, New York. Bryce Goggin, who'd made some great albums with Pavement and the Breeders, produced the record. Bryce is also a talented multi-instrumentalist with a lot of out-of-the-box ideas. One day I went into the studio and I just didn't have it. After weeks of recording, I was completely fried, and I curled up in a ball under the console.

"I don't think I can sing today, Bryce."

"No problem," Bryce said.

RUMORS OF MY DEMISE

He gave me a pillow and a blanket and taped a microphone under the console in case the urge to sing came to me. After I chilled out for a while, I started to experiment with the microphone and thought my voice sounded pretty cool down there. We did a couple songs that way.

Car Button Cloth is more somber than *It's a Shame About Ray* or *Come on Feel the Lemonheads*, but I wouldn't call it downbeat—far from it. The first four tracks deal with some of the most harrowing experiences I'd had in recent years, but the songs themselves are kind of jaunty and upbeat. I think *Car Button Cloth* is the Lemonheads' best-sounding record.

* * *

"Did you hear Evan Dando died last night?"

I was eating dinner by myself at an Italian restaurant that I used to go to all the time on the Lower East Side when I overheard a conversation between two people at the next table.

Rumors of my demise had been circulating for years. I was in the middle of a run of more bad nights than good. Two years after Kurt died people were still talking about me like my death by overdose was preordained. No one said it to my face, but they wrote about it in the paper and talked about it behind my back. The rumor took on a life of its own and I could feel it weighing on me like a curse.

It took me many years to realize you can't outrun a rumor. I wasn't completely blameless. At the time, I was house-sitting for my friend Frank, a club impresario par excellence, at his place on Canal Street while he was away in Costa Rica. Frank lived with a gorgeous model from Alabama, and their apartment was a haven for party people who liked to smoke crack, people like me. We called it Basecamp.

EVAN DANDO

All the regulars at Basecamp had some kind of dumb nickname. There was Count Crackula and Rock Hudson and so forth. We'd smoke golf ball–sized rocks that we called three-dimensional snow cones. The people who hung out at Basecamp were the type who could smoke crack three, five, even seven days in a row like it was some kind of perverse contest.

We were all a bit deranged at Basecamp.

It was a sick boys' club, but there were girls, too, models mostly, which was a big part of its charm. The crack by itself wasn't anything special. The girls who were part of the scene, the amazing-looking club kids, actresses, and supermodels who were always around, kept it going for me.

The apartment was on the third floor and was covered with expensive Persian carpets. We shared Basecamp with a brazen colony of rodents that liked to eat the carpet. Rats will eat anything, but these were different because they were black and white, like they'd escaped from a science experiment gone horribly wrong. We wrote a song about them set to the melody of the Beatles' "Girl." As much as we made light of it, those rats freaked me out. They say you're never more than six feet away from a rat in New York City, but the rats at Basecamp were fearless.

At the restaurant, I looked over to see if the people at the next table were making some kind of a joke about me. People knew me at the restaurant because I went there a lot, but the couple having a conversation about me had no idea I was sitting next to them. They weren't messing around with me. They really thought I'd died.

I kept listening because you never know. Maybe this is how the afterlife works. You go to a restaurant and instead of getting a menu and some breadsticks you find out you're dead.

RUMORS OF MY DEMISE

According to the people seated next to me, I'd overdosed after the Smashing Pumpkins concert at Madison Square Garden the previous evening. That made sense. My reputation as a moody, drug-addled musician persisted mainly because I didn't see the point in hiding it.

I had been at the Garden the night before. My friends Dennis and Jimmy Flemion of the Frogs were playing with the Smashing Pumpkins. Dennis was filling in for Jonathan Melvoin, the keyboard player who'd overdosed and died. During each night's encore, Jimmy performed "1979" with the band, and members of the audience would come up onstage to dance along to the song. I'd gone down to the Garden to hang out with my friends, and they invited me to dance during "1979," which I did. It's a great song.

Immediately afterward, I transformed into a human cannonball. I was in a strangely aggressive mood that night, which is rare for me. I'm usually pretty mellow when I'm high, but I took too much Adderall, which isn't good for me. I drank a lot backstage, and after the show I started doing bad things, like throwing food around. My cool completely vanished and security got involved. They removed me from the backstage area and tossed me out of the Garden. They literally threw me out of the building. They picked me up and chucked my ass into the street.

I was also tripping on acid, which I'd forgotten about until the moment I went airborne. Time seemed to slow down as my body went hurtling through space.

Oh, no, I thought. *This is going to hurt.*

I bounced on the pavement and rolled away. It must have looked worse than it was and that's how the story of my death got exaggerated; I don't know, because it didn't hurt at all. Instead of trying to fight my way back into the building, I took off running. To the best of my knowledge, I didn't cause any more trouble that night. I went back to Basecamp and slept it off.

The scene at Basecamp went on for way too long. I wasn't doing much creatively, even though I always had my guitar with me. I was constantly coming up with things, bits and pieces, but I wasn't serious about making new music. Like any scene, people would fall in and out. Regulars stopped coming around, new people took their place, and then they became the new regulars. For me, a binge typically ends when I run out of money, or my dealer gets busted, or the supply dries up. The worst is when I get to the point where I just don't want to do drugs anymore. It will occur to me that I can't remember what it smells like to breathe fresh air or be out in the country. That moment is always unbearably sad. That's when I know I need to get out of the city.

I don't like cities. I'd almost always rather be outdoors. Drugs make cities tolerable. I'll hole up in a hotel room, an apartment, a crack den—and make it my nest. I like my nest to be a bit disheveled. There's comfort in losing sight of the big picture and forgetting about the rest of the world for a while.

And then the cloud lifted. I came to my senses and realized I was living in a rat-infested apartment, smoking crack all day.

I wanted out.

*   *   *

On the eve of the *Car Button Cloth* tour I destroyed a house. I rented a cottage on Martha's Vineyard for the summer. It was the same cottage in Aquinnah I'd stayed at the previous summer, which was a very Martha's Vineyard thing to do. There are families that have been summering on the island in the same place for generations.

RUMORS OF MY DEMISE

Being on the island brought back some of the happiest memories of my teenage years, a throwback to a time when I wished the summer would last forever. I wasn't planning on renting the same place again, but the owner reached out to me and lured me back.

Even though I'd toured all over the world and had been playing shows for over a decade, I still got very anxious before hitting the road. That feeling you get when you're planning a party and the whole time you're secretly wondering if anyone will show up—that's what going on tour is like for me. The night before, I'm a wreck. I'll sleepwalk or get wasted or do something foolish. Like destroy stuff.

I was trashing places long before I became a musician. When I was ten years old, me and my best friend in Boston, Frederick, got drunk and shattered a plate-glass window while we were on a ski trip with my parents. His parents had given him a couple bottles of wine that were meant to be a gift for my mom and dad.

"We're not going to give these to your parents," he said.

"We're not?"

"We're going to drink them ourselves!"

"Okay!"

We opened the wine with a church key bottle opener. I'd never gotten drunk before, but I'd been around alcohol all my life. I liked the way it tasted, maybe too much, because we got hammered, and Frederick threw a cribbage board through the window. Instead of freaking out about the broken glass or the snow flurries drifting into the chalet, I was mesmerized by how beautiful it was. Somehow, we convinced my parents that it had been an accident, while keeping our drunkenness a secret.

Frederick brought out the worst in me and we got into a lot of trouble together. On one of our adventures, we found this old decrepit greenhouse at the bottom of a hill. We stood at the top and threw rocks at it until we'd shattered all the windows. Every single one. Who does that?

On more than one occasion we randomly picked one of the neighborhoods in Boston, filled our pockets with rocks, and ran down a street breaking a window in every single house. Not just a couple of the houses, but every house on the block. SMASH! SMASH! SMASH!

The amazing thing was we got away with it. Maybe if we'd gotten caught, it would have put a stop to my destructive urges. We were horrible little savages, but we kept getting away with it. *Run, run as fast as you can. You can't catch me. I'm a gingerbread man!*

That summer on Martha's Vineyard before the *Car Button Cloth* tour, I had some friends from Indiana visiting me and we were drinking vodka like it was water. That's what we called it:

"You want some water?"

"More water, please."

We drank way too much "water" that night. We were also smoking crack, which probably had something to do with the way things careened into chaos.

While I loved being back on the island, I wasn't crazy about the cottage because it was falling apart. The knob on a drawer would come loose or the hinge on a cabinet would give way. It was always something. This went on all summer. I don't know if it was nerves or drunkenness, but I'd had enough of the place. We smashed windows, punched holes in the drywall, and tore doors off their hinges. We were totally out of control. We absolutely wrecked the place.

Surveying the wreckage the next day, I knew it massively exceeded my limited handyman skills. So I left. What was I supposed to do, leave a note? *Sorry I destroyed your house.*

After that, I was persona non grata in Aquinnah for a while. Finally, after months and months of legal entanglements with the landlord, we settled out of court. The house is gone now. They completely leveled it. They finished the job for me.

Destruction has been a recurring theme in my life. I've wrecked rental houses, practice spaces, hotel rooms. I once did four thousand dollars' worth of damage to a rental car with just my feet. I kicked the shit out of that car and hurt my knee in the process. It didn't stop when I turned eighteen, or twenty-one, or even thirty. Those destructive urges followed me around for a long time. It would be easy to blame it on my parents' divorce, but I was a terror before they split up.

Most people do something like that once, pay the price, and get it out of their system. But I had a problem destroying things. There's something joyful about breaking stuff. It's fun, but then someone's gotta clean up the mess, and if you get too carried away you end up hurting yourself. Mysterious bruises on your body; blood mixed in with the debris. It's cathartic in a way, but it comes with a price.

I'm happy to say my destructive urges have finally left me. I think after you've been bloodied and battered enough times it does something to your desire to break things. Even though I've changed my ways, my legacy lives on in Martha's Vineyard, where everybody knows your business.

*   *   *

For the *Car Button Cloth* tour, ex-Lemonhead John Strohm joined us on guitar, and for the first time since he left the band, we were a foursome again. Bill Gibson played bass and Murph punished the drums. It was nice going out on the road with a bunch of pros who knew what they were doing. Plus, John already knew all the old stuff. We brought Matchbox Twenty and Australian rocker Ben Lee with us.

Back in the early nineties, Ben was in the Bondi Beach band Noise Addict when he wrote a song about me called "I Wish I Was Him." It's a sarcastic piss-take full of affectionate ribbing. It was a breakout song for him, and we became good friends as a result, but I didn't get to know Ben until the tour.

In the UK, we were invited to play on Chris Evans's *TFI Friday* show. We were stoked to be on TV and performed the new song "Hospital," but didn't get to finish it. They cut us off right as we started clicking. That rubbed me the wrong way and summed up a lot of my frustration with the entertainment business. You tell secrets about yourself in a song and stand naked on the stage while you sing your guts out, but if the show runs over, they pull the plug on you and cut to a commercial so the network can make money. At the end of the song, I jumped into the crowd and collided with someone in the audience, which I felt terrible about afterward.

Car Button Cloth didn't take the world by storm. We released three singles in the UK that did okay, and the album briefly charted in the US. The record didn't produce any hits, but considering the way critics had been lining up to take cheapish shots at me, they actually said some nice things about the record.

It wasn't a surprise when Atlantic quietly declined to re-up the Lemonheads. I'd felt for some time that the cosmos had already spelled out my fate. If anything, I was grateful to have had the opportunity to make another record when they could have dropped me. If I hadn't owed Atlantic a record, I might not have had the wherewithal to turn my struggles into songs. If *Car Button Cloth* was going to be my last record, I was proud of what I'd made.

DISASTER MAGNET

I stood in the front row at St. Peter's Church while the pastor prattled on and on and on. We'd gathered for the christening of Marlon and Lucie's daughter Ella Rose. My head throbbed from last night's fun, and I felt like I could pass out at any second. All I wanted to do was go back to my hotel and crawl into bed, but I didn't want to let down my friends. I had to keep it together.

The ancient church was warm and stuffy. It was 1998, but without air-conditioning it felt like medieval times. I couldn't get over how old the place was. If you picked it up and set it down in the States it would instantly become the oldest building in all of America, which is kind of a trip when you think about it. Here it wasn't a big deal, there were old churches all over the place, and where was I again?

England. I was in England.

"On behalf of the whole church," the pastor droned, "I ask you: Do you renounce the spiritual forces of wickedness, reject the evil powers of this world, and repent of your sin?"

This was my cue. "I do," I said.

I would, I thought.

I'd try.

My friends had just had a beautiful baby girl. She was their first daughter, and out of all the people in the world, they'd chosen me to be her godfather. One of them, anyway. Ella Rose was so special she had two sets of godparents: Liv Tyler and Mark Wrong, and Kate Moss and me. Guess which one didn't belong? If you guessed Wrong, you wouldn't be right.

I met Kate in New York the night of Eartha Kitt's birthday party. I wasn't friends with Eartha and it was a PR stunt. I was meant to be Eartha's arm candy, which I didn't mind at all because we were seated at the same table as Kate and Naomi Campbell. Kate and I actually had crushes on each other before we even met, but it was a little weird because she'd dated Johnny Depp. We had a couple of wild nights together during Fashion Week in Paris. A two-week fling with lots of ecstasy and champagne. We figured out pretty quickly we were meant to be friends, which we are to this day. I can honestly say that Kate is one of the funniest, most intelligent people I've ever met.

Once Johnny found out about me and Kate, he wasn't so keen on me anymore. He must have still had feelings for her, but I couldn't ask because we didn't hang out like we used to, which is a shame. In my mind once you experience a brush with death with someone, that supersedes everything else. Were we that close to death the night we took acid high above Sunset Boulevard? I don't know, but I think Van Halen was right. When you go out to the edge, you lose a lot of friends there, baby.

The pastor again: "According to the grace given to you, will you remain faithful members of Christ's holy church and serve as Christ's representatives in the world?"

"I will," I said.

I could hear someone laughing in the back of the old stone church. I didn't have to turn around to know who it was, but I wanted to see it with my own eyes, to burn it into my memory, because I knew I'd be telling this story for the rest of my life.

I turned and there he was, Keith Richards, chuckling darkly as we made our promises before God and heaven to renounce all evil and be a good Christian example for his granddaughter Ella Rose.

It was Keith's fault I was in such a pitiful state. The night before he and Anita had thrown a party at Redlands, Keith's country estate in West Wittering. When I was growing up, Redlands was like a mystical place to me, the place where the police busted Keith Richards and Mick Jagger while they were coming down from an acid trip, Marianne Faithfull opening the door naked and draped in a bear rug.

So many times, I'd wished I could go to Redlands and see it with my own eyes. It was a fabled place in my imagination, like Mount Olympus only cooler, and now I was a regular guest.

Keith was fond of Fanta Orange and Absolut. It was the house drink at Redlands. We drank tons of it the night before Ella Rose's christening, but that's not the only thing we got up to. I was drinking my Fanta Orange and Absolut, minding my own business, when Keith approached me.

"Meet me at the bottom of the stairs in two minutes and eleven seconds," he said in a conspiratorial tone, like we were a couple of Cold War spies.

After two minutes and eleven seconds passed, I went to the landing and there were Kate and Liv at the bottom of the stairs. We'd all gotten the same message from Keith. When the man arrived, he looked at me with a gleam in his eye. I knew he was up to some kind of mischief.

"If I can have Kate and Liv," he said, "why do I need you?"

Good question.

Keith tried to run away from me, with Kate and Liv in tow, but the rock god tripped and fell *up* the stairs. I chased after them and stumbled over Keith, stepping on him. *Oh shit*, I thought, *I'm stepping on Keith fucking Richards!*

I apologized and helped him to his feet, but he brushed me off and we continued up the stairs to do some of his amazing blow.

Keith used to mess around with me because I was one of his son's friends. It didn't matter who I was (not that it should). As far as he was concerned, I was just one of Marlon's mates and it was his duty to fuck with me. We were all in our twenties and wanted to make a good impression on Keith. We desperately wanted him to like us, which he knew and used to his advantage.

One time, he was showing me and a group of Marlon's friends his sword. Of course he has a sword. He's Keith Richards. He was also smoking a joint. Keith pointed the sword at me.

"I want to show you something," he said.

"Me?" I gulped.

"A trick to smoking a joint that will get you really high."

That got my attention.

"First you inhale," he explained, "and then you crouch as low as you can go." Keith demonstrated by squatting down until his ass was practically on the floor. "Got it?"

I nodded.

"Give it a go," he said.

I took a hit, squatted, and exhaled.

"No, no, no," Keith protested. "You're doing it all wrong. You've got to hold it in until you're standing up again."

I tried it a second time, but that didn't meet with Keith's satisfaction. On my third attempt, as soon as I squatted down, Keith knocked me over, grabbed his sword, and pressed the blade to my throat.

"You're not on television now, mate. I'll slit your fucking throat and throw you in the moat!"

Several thoughts rushed through my head. *Keith Richards is threatening to kill me! How cool!*, which was replaced by *Keith Richards is threatening to kill me! Oh no!*

There really is a moat at Redlands by the way. Who knows how many bodies are in there.

Keith laughed and put the sword away.

"Don't worry, mate," he said as he helped me to my feet. "The last person in that moat was Brian Jones."

Eventually, Keith warmed up to me. Back at Ella Rose's christening, he took me aside for a chat.

"Ah, yeah, I'm sorry I was a dick, but you were one of Marlon's friends," he said with a shrug, like the matter was out of his hands. Those days were over. I was more than an annoying American songwriter; I was part of Keith's family now.

After that day, Keith was always very warm to me. "I've been watching you from afar," he told me.

His good will almost went up in smoke after I nearly burned Redlands to the ground.

Whenever I was in the area, I'd go to Redlands to visit. One time I was getting ready to start a tour and I went there to relax and hang out with Anita, even though Keith was out of town. I loved Anita and she treated me like one of her own. She was like an aunt to me.

It was during Fashion Week and there were all kinds of people I didn't know staying there. I sat by the fire with a cup of tea, reading the paper. The British tabloids can be intense, and something in the paper upset me. Without thinking about what I was doing, I balled up the newspaper and tossed it in the fire.

Well, you can't do that. Those old English country houses aren't equipped for it. The place started to fill up with smoke. Anita phoned the fire department, and if she hadn't rung them up when she did, the firemen told us afterward, we would have lost the house and everything in it.

Keith treasures that place. There's no question that if I'd burned down his beloved playhouse, I would have been better off going up the chimney than face Keith's fury, because then I would have ended up in the moat.

*   *   *

"This is our last show!" I yelled at the crowd at the Reading Festival.

It was 1997 and the Lemonheads were finished. We hadn't been a real band in a long, long time, but with the contract with Atlantic complete, there was no longer a reason to keep up the charade. The festival was the perfect way to go out. I didn't want to be at the beck and call of a label anymore. I wanted to start doing things on my own terms.

After our big blowout at Reading, I made the most of not being tied to a label by working on a bunch of projects. I collaborated with my favorite Bens, Ben Lee and Ben Kweller, and jammed with the Blake Babies for a bit. I also worked on my own songs—when I got around to it. I put out a live album from a solo performance in Cambridge called *Live at the Brattle Theatre* for a label in Australia. I even toyed with the idea of releasing a solo album of country covers, but did an EP instead called *Griffith Sunset* with songs I recorded in Sydney by Fred Neil, Lawton Williams, John Prine, Townes Van Zandt, and the Louvin Brothers.

Because I was a wanted man on Martha's Vineyard, I stuck to Manhattan, where I was introduced to Elizabeth Moses in '98. From the moment we met we were inseparable.

Elizabeth was from Tyneside, the coal-mining region in the northeast of England. She was literally a coal miner's daughter and grew up dirt-poor. She was tall, pretty, and extremely smart. A natural model. A lot of people thought we looked alike, but with her piercing blue eyes and blond hair, I thought she looked a little bit like Kurt, especially when she was wearing his blue cardigan. Elizabeth had tickets to see him right before he died, so I gave her the sweater. I was ready to part company with it, and I knew she'd take good care of it.

Elizabeth and I were a good team. She was a grounded, no-bullshit kind of person. Whenever I'd get anxious about something, she'd bring me back to earth and tell me exactly what I needed to hear.

We got married at the end of the millennium at the Boathouse in Central Park in front of about four hundred of our closest friends. We walked down the aisle to an instrumental version of Lou Reed's "Street Hassle." (If you know the words, you know why it had to be an instrumental version.) After we exchanged vows, we fired up the dry-ice machines and blasted "Electric Funeral" by Black Sabbath. If I was going to settle down, it had to be with someone who liked Black Sabbath as much as I did. Then the party started with music from J Mascis, Ben Kweller, and Speedball Baby.

We moved into an apartment building at 72 Broadway. We were in spitting distance of Alexander Hamilton's gravesite in the Trinity Church Cemetery and directly underneath the Twin Towers. It was a happy time for us.

I was doing a lot of one-off shows, just me and my guitar, and learned something important about myself: I wasn't very reliable on my own.

Things tended to go wrong when I toured by myself. I might oversleep, get lost on the way to the gig, or take too many Klonopins. In my opinion, it's better to do a bad show than no show at all. I've had a few bad ones—not too many—but when I fuck up, I go all the way.

One time in Germany I completely lost my singing voice. I sounded like a robot, so I improvised. I said, "This is Darth Vader from CNN," and then I fell off an eight-foot stage. That was a little scary because I felt like a piece of my mind went along with my voice.

* * *

In 2001 I went up to Cornell University in Ithaca, New York, to play a solo show. I like Cornell. I have friends in Ithaca and my dad went to school there. I like to think of him hanging out on the lawn outside the library with his guitar. It was the beginning of the fall semester, the weather was starting to turn, and they'd just opened this fancy new building where I was going to perform with my friend Mary Lorson of Madder Rose.

It was a chaotic show. I drank a bottle of Fernet-Branca, which will do that. I'd been hanging out with the Madder Rose crew that day and things got a little crazy. Back when they lived in the Village, they were friends with the artist Jean-Michel Basquiat. He used to come by their place and give them paintings. Madder Rose liked to party, but they held on to the art he gave them. Eventually, they sold the paintings and used the money to buy a house in Ithaca.

Mary started the show with an acoustic set. Afterward, I dragged this hay bale onstage to sit on while I played. A nice, idyllic scene, right?

I pretty much forgot about the hay bale until the end of the show, when I ripped it open and started tossing the hay all over the place, which upset the local authorities. After the gig, the campus cops came and started clearing people out of the hall—except for me. One cop in particular wasn't happy with me.

"Clean that up," he said.

Some of the students offered to help, which seemed to irritate him.

"Hurry up!"

"Fuck off," I said. I didn't see the harm in aggravating him further, since the show was over. He slapped some handcuffs on me and took me to the station on campus. Apparently, there was a rule on the books about bringing bales of hay into buildings, which I loudly protested. In the end I was charged with being drunk and disorderly.

No argument there. I woke up the next morning with a nasty hangover and a court date for September 11, 2001.

* * *

Everyone remembers September 11 as a beautiful day, and it was. The sky was bright blue, and it was unseasonably warm. Elizabeth and I were putzing around the kitchen in our apartment, making coffee and reading the paper, when an airplane crashed into the North Tower of the World Trade Center.

We went up onto the roof for a closer look. It was such a nice day, it seemed like half the building had the same idea. I thought it was an accident, a Cessna that had wandered off course. Word spread that it wasn't a small airplane but a commercial airliner. When disaster strikes, there's a certain vibe that's unmistakable. You can hear it in people's voices: excited, but also a little hysterical.

I'd been in LA for the uprising in '92, but I also happened to be in Paris when Princess Diana was killed in that horrible car accident in '97. The night it happened I took a train to Fontainebleau to stay with Marlon's wife, Lucie, and her grandmother Maxime and her father, Count Alexis, at their estate outside of Paris. Early the next morning, Count Alexis, a very distinguished gentleman who resembled Gregory Peck, came into my bedroom to tell me, which made the sad news even stranger.

I also happened to be on Martha's Vineyard in '99 when John F. Kennedy Jr.'s plane crashed. Me, Holly, and Elizabeth were at Philbin Beach. We didn't see the plane go down, but we watched some people farther along the beach pull a wheel out of the water. The rumor was they found part of John's sandal wedged into the wheel. As far as the locals were concerned, that pretty much closed the case as to whether John Jr. had really been on the plane.

I'd seemingly developed an uncanny knack for being in the worst place at the worst time—a disaster magnet—and the scene up on the rooftop felt eerily familiar. I remember thinking, *Here we go again* . . .

Elizabeth went down to our apartment to get her camera, and when I turned around, I saw the second plane go screaming across the sky and plow into the South Tower. There wasn't a blast or even an explosion. The plane just disappeared inside this hole that suddenly appeared in the tower above my head as if it were made of foam. It barely made a sound.

I briefly wondered if I was dreaming, and in that moment the realization of what was happening popped into my consciousness: *This is it*. Before I had the words to describe or even understand what was happening, I knew. The terrible thing I'd been running from all my life—the night terrors, the sleepwalking, the screaming in my sleep—had finally come.

It was the strangest thing. As I went down the stairs to find Elizabeth, I felt weirdly calm, like I knew what was going to happen next. Maybe that's how it works when something of that magnitude occurs. You have to trick your brain into thinking you're ready for it, but I had an unshakable feeling that I was meant to be there, almost like a premonition. It's hard to put into words, but it felt like I was fated to witness this tragedy. I just *knew*.

Somehow my wife and I passed each other on the stairs and she went up on the roof as I went down to our apartment. When she returned, she was visibly shaken. She told me she'd seen people jumping out of the towers. We were so close to the South Tower, she could look into their eyes as they jumped. It was a lot to process.

We looked out the window. The hole in the side of the building seemed to be getting bigger. We were drinking the coffee that we'd abandoned earlier, when the North Tower suddenly crumbled and fell into what seemed like a volcano of ash. Then our building started shaking. When it stopped, we ran like hell.

It was total chaos in the stairwell. People running, screaming, pure panic. Outside, it was even worse. We couldn't see the sky. We didn't know if we were going to live or die. We headed uptown to the Bowery, where Marlon, Lucie, and Ella Rose lived. By the time we got as far as Chinatown, the air had cleared a bit. Someone gave us paper masks to put on. That night at Marlon's, the immensity of it all took its toll and we drugged ourselves into oblivion.

We spent the first week after 9/11 at Holly's place, and Elizabeth had to borrow Holly's clothes. It was weeks before we could go back to our apartment. When they finally let us back in, it was worse than we could have imagined. Every morning, we woke up to this weird, smoking hole in the ground, a reminder of what had happened. All these people came to look at it. Tourists gawked at the fires that smoldered for weeks. We didn't understand any of it. Why would someone want to see that? We realized we didn't live on Broadway anymore. We lived at a place called Ground Zero.

Our impulse was to stay. "We're gonna tough this out!" I said.

"We're going to stay in the building!" Elizabeth agreed.

"We're not fucking leaving!" I insisted.

That may have been a mistake.

We had this beautiful balcony that overlooked the whole scene, and it was completely covered in ash. We swept up the ash and it was there again the next day. Then again the day after that and the day after that. Where was it all coming from?

It went on like that for weeks, sweeping up the ashes that never stopped falling. It was very fucked up and it started to get to us because we knew what was in those ashes. We spent a lot of time talking about it, too much actually, and then one day the phone rang.

"Mr. Dando?"

"Yeah?"

"This is the Ithaca City Court."

"Oh shit." I'd forgotten all about my court date. Now I was going to have a "failure to appear" on my record.

"Under the present circumstances we don't feel it's necessary for you to deal with this. We realize you have bigger problems right now. Case dismissed."

My first reaction was to celebrate, but it didn't feel right considering everything that was going on. We got into doing nitrous oxide, which was definitely not a good idea, especially when combined with the Vicodin we were already taking in great quantities. We started to have these weird visions. One time this phantom bird lady came into the apartment through the balcony. We knew she wasn't real, but we both saw her. A few days later, we found a single gold hoop earring on the balcony that we'd been sweeping for weeks. How'd it get there?

We lost touch with reality for a while.

It all got to be much too much.

WALKING MASTERPIECE OF REMEMBERED PAIN

I thought it would be a good idea to get back to work. After cranking out record after record for so many years, I worried about burning out. It wasn't so much that I needed a break from music, but I figured the public could use a break from me.

After the horror of 9/11, I wanted to occupy my mind with something. I was so grateful to have been spared the carnage of that awful event and something inside me changed.

I embraced the freedom of writing songs without the pressure of working on a new album. I took my time, casting about. I collaborated with old and new friends, and when I had enough songs I decided to release them as a solo album under my own name. People didn't believe me when I said the Lemonheads were finished. Maybe they would believe me now.

Baby I'm Bored was recorded in much the same way the songs were composed: all over the place. I recorded the album at three different studios: Sage & Sound in Los Angeles, Trout Recording in Brooklyn, and WaveLab in Tucson. As a result, I worked with a lot of musicians and producers. I collaborated with singer-songwriter

Jon Brion on four tracks. John Convertino and Howe Gelb of Giant Sand also helped out with a few tunes. Royston Langdon of Spacehog pitched in as well. It was like a series of reunions with old friends who I enlisted to play on the record.

Critics unfairly use the word "schizophrenic" to describe my kitchen sink approach to putting the album together. Even though *Baby I'm Bored* was recorded at different times at different studios, it's more consistent than some of the records I did for Atlantic. I think it's a good-sounding record. In terms of the audio quality, it's up there with my best.

There's nothing dashed off about *Baby I'm Bored*. One song on the record took years to write and required multiple collaborators. It's called "The Same Thing You Thought Hard About Is the Same Part I Can Live Without," which is maybe not the best title. I started that one with Tom and finished it with Ben Lee. The whole thing took five or six years. At no point did any of us think we were onto something special. It was more like a riddle that needed solving, but I like how it turned out: a fuzzed-out ode to regret. Ben wanted to change "part" to "thing" to balance out the title, but I said, "Fuck it"—it's already a long, unwieldly title, and we left it alone. Basically, it means "What matters to you doesn't matter to me." It's not like it's a big secret. Why should Fiona Apple get all the wicked-long titles?

Ben was living in New York, and we spent a lot of time at the apartment he shared with Claire Danes. It was a fun place to hang out and we wrote a lot of songs together. The difference between Ben and a lot of other musicians was that we didn't just talk about writing songs—we did it. He was a steadying influence at a time when I needed it.

Ben also contributed two of his own songs to *Baby I'm Bored*. "All My Life" is a beautiful little ballad, and I don't say that because it's the second song Ben wrote about me. *All my life I thought I needed all the things I didn't need at all.* That line is right on the money, but at the time I would not have been capable of that level of self-awareness. I think it's one of the most honest songs on the record, but there's no way I could have written it. It could only come from an outside perspective.

The other song that Ben wrote was "Hard Drive," a meditation on the split between the mechanical and the natural world. Not only did he write two of the standout tracks on the album, he kicked my ass when I needed to get into songwriting shape. I was blocked up and looking for something to break me out of it. Working with Ben was like a shock to the system. I don't know what I would have done without him.

Even though I got a ton of help with the record from songwriters, musicians, and producers, I only gave one shout-out in the liner notes: "Thanks, Springa." All these years later, that still cracks us up.

I'm happy with how *Baby I'm Bored* came out. I think of it as my *Some Girls*, my comeback album. It's just a consistently mellow record. If only I could say the same thing about the rest of my life.

Unlike other projects where we barely had enough material, we had a lot of songs that didn't make the cut. (That makes all the extra tracks on the reissue pretty compelling, in my opinion, but none more so than the instrumental, "Walk in the Woods with Lionel Richie.") Although I had trepidations about releasing a solo album because of the stigma involved, I'm glad I did it. The way the music industry is these days, the term "solo" is even more meaningless than "band." It's all so diluted, it doesn't matter what I call it.

The only thing I didn't like about the experience was going on tour and selling T-shirts. My name on a T-shirt?

That was weird.

EVAN DANDO

Those who were confused that I'd put out a solo record were really mixed up when I released a Lemonheads record that was just me and my acoustic guitar a few years later. It's called *Hotel Sessions* and was a recording I made in my hotel in Bondi Beach through a Walkman condenser mic in the early nineties. It was recorded late at night, when Sunday turns to Monday. You can hear all kinds of things inside my hotel room and outside the window: the hissing of the tape, the cars going by in the street, the waves on the beach, and even the occasional seagull. It's a cool little audio document.

Hotel Sessions wasn't received particularly well by the critics, but it holds a special place in my heart. It's got a couple of songs that never made it onto any of the other records, and I prefer this version of "Into Your Arms" to the one on *Come on Feel the Lemonheads*. *Hotel Sessions* chronicles how things were always falling in and out place.

* * *

When I found out that Detroit proto-punk legends the MC5 was reforming and was looking for a new singer, I told my manager I wanted the gig. Actually, it was a bit more complicated than that.

My manager at the time shared an office with Wayne Kramer, guitarist for the MC5, who was spearheading a world tour in support of a new DVD about the band. They got Mark Lanegan of the Screaming Trees to sing, but he and Wayne got into an argument about something, and Mark bailed at the last minute. Mark would have done an amazing job, but they needed another singer—fast.

My manager told me what was going on as it was happening. Since I knew all the songs, I called up Wayne and started singing to him on the phone. He had no choice but to say yes, and I was able to sneak in the back door. It ended up being one of the best experiences of my life.

Every indie rocker owes a debt to the Motor City Five for paving the way for hard-rocking alternative music in the United States. Whether it's punk, heavy metal, or uncensored rock and roll, the MC5 broke down all the barriers when Rob Tyner screamed, "Kick out the jams, motherfuckers!"

The MC5 broke up in 1972 after being dropped by their label. When Tyner passed away in 1991, that put the kibosh on all of the original members of the band ever reuniting. But then, in 2004, the band reformed as DKT/MC5 with three of the members who'd recorded *Kick Out the Jams* in 1968 and a bunch of special guests. Marshall Crenshaw took the late Fred "Sonic" Smith's spot on rhythm guitar, and me and my old friend Mark Arm of Mudhoney were the singers. Rob Tyner was so dynamic, it took two of us to fill his shoes.

We practiced in Toronto, and then we hit the road. The first couple of gigs me and Mark were a bit too overconfident. We didn't have the lyrics nailed and some people in the crowd gave us shit for it. One night, we kicked one of the hecklers in the front row. Wayne, who was a bit of a hard case, sat us down for a friendly chat.

"It's okay," he said, "but please don't do that ever again."

It wasn't a request.

Wayne Kramer was an amazing guitar player and it was incredible to share the stage with him every night. I especially liked hearing him play "Looking at You." It's a great song, maybe even better than "Kick Out the Jams." It's like a jumped-up Black Sabbath song with a whole lot of soul. It's just two chords, but Wayne made that guitar smoke.

The highlight of the tour was playing on *The Late Late Show with Craig Kilborn* as the musical guest. Mark and I tore it up while singing "Kick Out the Jams" together. That tour was some of the most fun I've ever had as a musician, even though I was kind of the ne'er-do-well of the group. The MC5 were notorious hell-raisers, and I took it upon myself to play that role in the twenty-first-century version of the band.

That didn't go over very well with Wayne and some of the older heads. None of the other guys on tour were partying except for Nick Oliveri, whose band, Mondo Generator, was the opener.

I got along with MC5's drummer, Dennis Thompson, and bass player, Michael Davis. They had some incredible stories about the MC5 and Iggy Pop from back when rock and roll was truly radical. Everywhere we went, a guest guitarist would jump onstage to jam with us. In Seattle it was Kim Thayil of Soundgarden, who ended up joining the band a few years down the road.

I'd forgotten what it feels like to just cut loose and have fun onstage. That's not a knock on the solo stuff I was doing, but it was nice to leave the guitar in the case for a few weeks and just let it all out.

The good times came to an end in Japan. We were on a plane, and I was complaining about one of the songs. I can't remember which one, but I was making a case for taking it off the set list, and Wayne fired me on the spot. I was like, "Now wait a minute," but Wayne didn't back down.

Actually, it was a blessing in disguise. We'd played forty-one gigs in the US, Australia, New Zealand, and Japan. The band was headed to England next, which I wasn't so crazy about, so my firing worked out perfectly.

Of course, I would have preferred leaving on my own terms, but forty-one nights was more than enough for me. You gotta leave some jams for the next guy.

* * *

RUMORS OF MY DEMISE

In 2005, I was touring in Brazil with All Systems Go! The singer, John Kastner, used to be in the Doughboys and was also my manager. He had Karl Alvarez of the Descendents playing bass with him. One of the gigs was a festival where a bunch of Brazilian punk bands played Lemonheads covers. I had so much fun that it got me thinking about putting out a new Lemonheads record. Everyone rallied around the idea. I approached Karl to see if he and Bill Stevenson, his bandmate from the Descendents, would be interested in making a record with me.

"I bet Bill would want to do that," Karl said.

That's how I got what is arguably the best pop-punk rhythm section of all time to be our sixth bass player and ninth drummer.

Back in 1994, Tim Rogers of the Australian band You Am I put out a single called "How Much Is Enough." The song is all about me and my relationship to fame. My friends in Sydney all thought I was superambitious, which I always found amusing. In my own way, I suppose I was, but compared to other American bands, the Lemonheads were total slackers. I'm not named in the lyrics of "How Much Is Enough," but when you know the intention behind the song, the references are clear. It's got a great line about joining a collective, and it changed the way I thought about the Lemonheads.

In the beginning when it was just the three of us—Ben, Jesse, and me—the Lemonheads were a real band. Not in terms of our abilities, but with respect to where we were coming from and what we were trying to achieve. The dynamic changed when we started bringing in different players. It wasn't better or worse—just different.

After the majors got involved and things got corporate, I took charge of all the hiring and firing. I knew where we were headed, and I knew what I wanted to do with the band. Things got hectic for a while with all the different members and ex-members and ex-ex-members. The list of people who have played in the Lemonheads is pretty long.

For all the people who have ever been in the Lemonheads—from Ben and Jesse to the musicians who played on my last record—the version of the band they knew didn't exist anymore. Each iteration of the Lemonheads was no less valid for having new players. For the time that we were together, we were the Lemonheads, but life is short, and time is fleeting, and we get called to do different things at different times.

To put it another way, after those first three records, the Lemonheads were more of an idea than an actual band, and though I wasn't always the driving force, especially in the beginning, I'm the only one who has been there for every iteration. I think the word "band" has too much baggage for the way the Lemonheads function. I think Tim Rogers was onto something. "Collective" gets to the heart of who and what we are. The Lemonheads are musicians who gather for a common purpose: to make music and play songs. The players change, but the ambition remains the same. Or maybe it's just a fancy way of saying me and whoever's around at the time.

Call it what you will. It's a thing with a name and that name is the Lemonheads. What that means is up to you. I'd been asking myself "How Much Is Enough" for most of my adult life and I still didn't have any answers.

How much money?
How much fame?
How much heroin?
How much pain?

* * *

RUMORS OF MY DEMISE

We assembled to make the Lemonheads' first studio album in a decade at the Blasting Room, Bill Stevenson's spot in Fort Collins, Colorado.

While everyone knows about Bill's prowess on the drums as a member of Black Flag, the Descendents, All, and many other bands, he's also an incredible songwriter. He wrote all those super-catchy early Descendents songs: "Myage," "I'm the One," "Catalina," and so many more. He's into Cole Porter, and like me he's a closet Steely Dan fan. I guess I'm outing him now.

I went out to Hermosa Beach for a couple weeks so we could write some songs together. I love hanging out in Hermosa. The vibe there is a little different than the rest of LA. Hermosa Beach is Black Flag's hometown and ground zero for American hardcore. The first thing I asked Bill to do was to take me on a fishing trip to Catalina Island, but he wouldn't do it, which is probably a good thing considering I was in no shape for a boat trip. We had some very productive songwriting sessions out there at the beach. Bill wrote "Become the Enemy" and "Steve's Boy" and we collaborated on "Let's Just Laugh."

J Mascis's guitar is immediately recognizable on Tom Morgan's song "No Backbone," but on "Steve's Boy" he's joined by another Hermosa Beach legend, SPOT, who produced so many great albums for SST Records and is a pretty amazing guitar player in his own right. I was so stoked to have Bill in the band that I didn't play any drums on a record for the first time since *Creator*. There was no need for me to sit behind the kit when I had the fastest right hand in punk rock in the Lemonheads.

In the song "Poughkeepsie" there's a line lifted from the writer Flannery O'Connor that I always loved: "Walking masterpiece of remembered pain." I put it in the song just to see if I could get away with it, and I did. No one has ever asked me about that line.

We had so much fun making that record. I was like a kid in a candy store having such great players to jam with every night. Bill and Karl are phenomenal musicians who brought fresh thinking and new ideas to the studio every day. I titled the record *The Lemonheads* because I felt that Bill and Karl rekindled the spark of the original Lemonheads. With each record, I was trying to redefine the band. By calling it *The Lemonheads* I was making a statement about the band coming full circle back to where we started.

Unfortunately, no one cares about that sort of thing.

I should have called the record something else so that people understood it was a new record and not a rehash of old stuff. Back in 1998, Atlantic released a compilation, *The Best of the Lemonheads: The Atlantic Years*. Our self-titled record made it seem like the new record was another comp. I can see how our fans might have gotten confused. I've thought about it a lot, but I still don't know what I would have called the album.

* * *

I stopped drinking in my late thirties. I still take a drink from time to time, but I don't drink like I used to. It was getting to be a problem. In an effort to curb my drug use, I was drinking up to thirty drinks a day. In New York it's part of the culture. I was going out every night. Bars, clubs, parties. There was usually some extra stimulation involved as well.

People think when you're a musician you get to drink for free every night. It's not that easy. If anything, you pay for more drinks because you're picking up the tab for your friends, and when you're a celebrity at the bar, everyone's your friend. I've always preferred to get my own drinks because you never know what someone might be giving you. Plus, you want to take care of the bartender. All too often the guy who likes to act like a big shot by buying drinks for everyone will stiff the bartender. That just makes everyone look like an asshole.

I can see why musicians drink while they're on tour. It makes the time go by, but there's nothing worse than waking up with a wicked hangover and facing a long day of sitting on a tour bus and wishing you were home. I hated that feeling more than just about anything.

As awful as it was, I had trouble stopping. I'd made a personality out of being a drinker and a drug user. Alcohol and rock and roll go hand in hand. I slipped into the habit without thinking about what I was doing to myself and kept at it long after it stopped being fun.

Oh shit, we're drinking *again*?

You mean we're going to do this *every night*?

I didn't crash a car or do anything stupid like that. After a while I just didn't like it as much. The older I got, the more the hangovers hurt. I got to the point where I wanted to stop, but kept doing the same thing every night. So I went on Antabuse. Antabuse is a drug that causes a violent reaction when you drink alcohol. It stops the liver from processing alcohol and the results aren't pretty. If you drink while on Antabuse, there's going to be a lot of vomiting, and I mean a *lot*.

The Antabuse worked well for me for a while, and then one night I fucked up. I was doing a gig in England. We'd been invited to play *It's a Shame About Ray* for a pair of shows put on by All Tomorrow's Parties at Shepherd's Bush Empire as part of the Don't Look Back series.

I think it was the first time I'd done something like that with *It's a Shame About Ray*. Playing an entire album in sequence is kind of a trip. It's a new experience for the band, but not for the audience.

Sometimes it can feel like the fans know the material better than you do, which is cool, but it can be a drag if you do it too often.

That night Josh Lattanzi played bass, with Bill Stevenson on drums. I loved hanging out with Bill because he didn't drink. It just wasn't part of his deal. He never needed drugs or alcohol to have fun—just a shitload of coffee. We had such a good time playing *It's a Shame About Ray* that I forgot all about the Antabuse. I was at the tail end of a two-month cycle of the drug. I had two drinks. That's all it took.

So. Much. Puke.

It was awful. I didn't have to go to the hospital, but it was a hairy situation. It's definitely not an experience I recommend.

That put me off alcohol for good. There's something about having your body physically rejecting the booze that makes you realize how toxic it is. All alcohol does is get between me and the things I want to do, and where's the fun in that?

Drugs are a bit different, especially narcotics, and it takes more than a little pill to get off the stuff.

* * *

Things on the home front weren't so great. While I was working with Bill in Hermosa Beach, I lost my wedding ring. It wasn't lost in that I'd misplaced it and it would turn up somewhere, but lost as in totally gone. I had no clue where I'd left it. I couldn't go home without a wedding ring, so I got a new one from Tiffany's that was exactly like the old one.

Elizabeth noticed right away. As soon as I walked in the door she said, "Nice ring."

Even though it was the same ring, it wasn't *the* ring. We didn't talk about how I lost the ring, but she knew I'd replaced the original.

RUMORS OF MY DEMISE

There were a lot of things we didn't talk about in those days, but money and drugs were at the top of the list.

I was touring—not as much as in the old days—but I was still gone a lot. She had her modeling gigs. We spent a lot of time in different places, and we slowly drifted apart. When we weren't working, we partied, and then it was more than partying. We had a great run of six or seven years, and then things gradually fell apart.

We were trying to keep the money coming in, but neither one of us was in demand like we used to be. We didn't talk about that, either.

One day I left to play a show in London. It wasn't a tour, just a one-off. I came home to an empty apartment. Elizabeth just packed up and left.

I haven't seen her since.

THE FLY IN THE OINTMENT

Considering my apathy toward "Mrs. Robinson," you would think I'd steer away from an album full of cover songs. I wasn't worried about a repeat of "Luka" or "Mrs. Robinson." I wasn't fishing for a hit—I should be so lucky. Besides, the songs you love are never the ones that get popular. It's always the most out-of-the-box, dashed-off, throwaway songs that become hits.

I wanted to work with Gibby for the simple reason that I love hanging out with him. It was such a lame idea—to do an album full of cover songs—I figured I'd better get Gibby to produce the record because he would make it weird and wonderful.

"I'll do it," Gibby said, "on one condition."

Uh-oh, I thought. "What's that, Gibby?"

"I get to pick the songs."

Well, I wanted it to be weird.

Gibby compiled a bunch of songs for me to choose from and we narrowed it down from there. He made me do songs I never would have chosen, like Christina Aguilera's "Beautiful" and "Dirty Robot" by Arling & Cameron, a Dutch electronic duo. Gibby flipped the script on that one by having Kate Moss sing the vocal parts, while I repeat the chorus through a vocoder so that it sounds nice and evil. I also invited Liv Tyler to sing on the record, and she does the backup vocals on Leonard Cohen's "Hey, That's No Way to Say Goodbye."

Gibby's perverse sense of humor comes through in some of the song selections. GG Allin's "Layin' Up with Linda," a punk rock honky-tonk stomper, is a good example of that. Gibby wasn't a complete sadist about his picks—he knows me, and he knows what I like. That's why we kicked off the album with "I Just Can't Take It Anymore" by Gram Parsons. We also did "Waiting Around to Die" by Townes Van Zandt, another favorite of mine. While I didn't *love* all the songs before we did them, I do now.

The music was recorded at a bunch of different studios, but we did the bulk of the vocals at Daniel Rey's place on Fourth Avenue in New York City. Daniel collaborated with the Ramones and produced three of their later albums. He also worked with Boston bands Gang Green and Murphy's Law. John Perry of the Only Ones—another one of my old favorites—plays guitar on a bunch of tracks.

Gibby was tough on me in the studio. He didn't cut me any slack just because we're friends. You can hear Gibby encouraging me with "Awesome, dude!" at the end of a couple of tracks. He grilled me on those vocals, but we had a great time doing it.

Why *Varshons*? The word comes from Keith Richards. When I was in Jamaica listening to his old cassettes, a bunch were labeled "Varshons," like "Versions" (but rhymes with "Martians"). Instead of writing down the songs and the dates, Keith just wrote "Varshons" on the label. I liked the idea of doing my own "Varshons" of other people's songs.

I mean, if it's good enough for Keith Richards . . .

* * *

RUMORS OF MY DEMISE

I never got into a lot of trouble with the police. This may sound odd considering all the illegal behavior I've engaged in, but I'm not comfortable breaking the law. I would be a terrible gangster. While some people are naturally drawn to the criminal side of the druggie lifestyle—like my friend Mark Lanegan; that guy was a straight-up pirate—I never want to get into a situation that's dangerous or extreme.

I've always been a drug user but never dealt drugs to supplement my habit. The cops generally don't want the users; it's the dealers they're after. But when the cops set their sights on me in 2010, it was because of a magazine article.

Juliana and I were playing together and she wanted to do this dumb interview for *New York* magazine. It was a bad idea because the press had not been kind to either one of us. My wife had been gone for a while and I'd let my apartment slip a little bit. It was pretty terrible, actually, so we moved the interview to a coffee shop. After the interview I let my guard down, and this journalist from the magazine ended up coming to my place to hang for a while before we went out for the evening. What is it they say about vampires? You have to invite them in?

Juliana and I had played a show together the night before and had a small get-together at my apartment afterward. The coffee table was a bit of a mess, so I didn't realize until it was too late that I'd left some empty baggies and other paraphernalia out. I tried to play it off like it wasn't a big deal and covered up the incriminating evidence with a record, but it was an uncomfortable scene.

It was no surprise when the magazine came out and the whole article was like, "Evan Dando is living in squalor!" The reporter devoted an entire paragraph to the contents of my coffee table, describing everything from charred spoons to a copy of Aleister Crowley's *The Diary of a Drug Fiend*.

EVAN DANDO

The reporter asked me about the drugs, and I answered her honestly, like I always do. In my mind the interview had taken place in the coffee shop and now we were hanging out for a bit, just two people being real with each other. I specifically asked her not to print what I'd told her. Not only did she make the whole article about my squalid little life, she included the part I asked her not to talk about (including the part where I ask her not to talk about it).

Someday I'll learn.

Reporters don't pull that shit when you're selling out shows and moving lots of records because they know the record company will tear them a new one and cut off their access to other artists on the label. But when you're not such a hot ticket anymore, they line up to kick you on your way down.

After the article ran, I started seeing undercover cops on the street. They'd hang out in front of my apartment building. They'd follow me around town. Everywhere I went, they were there. This wasn't a men-in-black situation. It was *the same two guys*. I know that sounds paranoid, but it's true. (I know this is also what you'd expect a paranoid person to say, but bear with me.) In addition to the undercover cops, my phone started making these weird clicking sounds.

The undercover cops weren't menacing-looking secret agent types. They were just ordinary-looking cops doing their job and not being all that super secretive about it. By that time, I'd developed a pretty severe heroin habit and had to go out and score every day. It's hard to be chill about a $400-a-day habit when you're being followed. I got to the point where I was almost blasé about it. Oh look, it's the cops.

How did this happen? I didn't get a heroin habit until I was almost thirty. For the longest time heroin was something I could take or leave. I'd dabble with it here and there. For a while I only smoked it because I was afraid of getting AIDS, but they had clean needles in Australia, so I'd experiment with it when I was down there. In New York it was so easy to score that I'd have Thursday night heroin parties with other musicians. I thought I could keep my habit under wraps by restricting my use, but after a while I was *really* looking forward to those Thursday nights, and I started to slip. After my wife left me and the Lemonheads went on hiatus, heroin became my full-time job.

So the cops came after me.

I thought I'd be slick and catch a ride from a friend to the ATM, but they just followed my friend's car. It wasn't like we were making evasive maneuvers. They watched me get out of the car, grab some money from an ATM, go up to the spot, and come back to the car. That's when they nabbed me.

Was "living in squalor" probable cause? What about going to an ATM? I don't know. They got me on a stop-and-frisk, which has since been deemed unconstitutional.

I'm not trying to say I wasn't guilty, because I was, but it wasn't a fair bust, and these undercover cops were such sanctimonious assholes. They'd made arresting me their mission, and once they accomplished it, they lorded it over me.

"You're gonna thank us one day," one of them said.

"So many people thank us because we get them off drugs," said the other.

I wasn't exactly feeling the gratitude.

Although I'd rather be arrested in Manhattan than anywhere else, it's no one's idea of a good time. My secret admirers handcuffed me and put me in a van. That part wasn't so bad. It was the waiting that got to me. Because it was New York, they had all these other arrests to make. So we drove around and I waited in the van while they busted people. I had no idea what they were being arrested for. They grabbed this guy. Then they grabbed that guy. It was like we were carpooling to jail.

When the cops got hungry, they went to McDonald's and stuffed their faces while we waited in the van. I gradually went from being annoyed to scared. The longer this song and dance went on, the more anxious I became. It was Friday afternoon. In order to get out of jail, I had to be put in jail. It had been hours since I was picked up and I hadn't been processed yet. I was running out of time. If I didn't get processed soon, I'd have to spend the weekend in jail while going through serious heroin withdrawal.

I didn't relish the prospect of spending the weekend in the Tombs. I kept thinking, *Fuck, how many more people do we have to bust? Can't we go to the station already?*

There was one guy in the van who had to go to the bathroom. "I gotta pee!" he yelled over and over again, but the cops didn't pay any attention to him. There were no bathroom breaks on this ride. Eventually, he got quiet, and everyone knew that he'd pissed himself. What else could he do? He couldn't hold it anymore. I felt terrible for the guy, but I had my own problems.

Finally, we pulled up to the station and they booked us. Still, the cops kept hassling me.

"Would you like a cigarette?"

I tried not to get my hopes up, but when I looked their way, they lit up their own smokes right in front of me. They thought that was hysterical. I didn't take it personally. It may have been a bad day for me and everyone else they'd arrested, but it was just another day on the job for these assholes. The fact of the matter was I would have killed for one of those cigarettes, anything to take my mind off the feeling clawing up the back of my spine and into my brain that I was going to have to spend the weekend detoxing in a prison cell.

RUMORS OF MY DEMISE

Going through withdrawal sucks. Every substance in your body turns to liquid. Your mucus, your shit, your vomit. Everything. Your nose runs and you sweat like crazy and everything hurts. There's no good place to kick heroin. I usually go to a hotel so my neighbors don't hear me scream and I can get clean sheets and towels when I need them. One time I got it into my head that it would be easier to kick in jail because the brutality of the situation would enable me to bear it better. Maybe my adrenaline would kick in and get me through it. That, of course, was crazy talk.

When the cops sat me down, they asked me all these questions about the credit card in my wallet that was in Elizabeth's name.

"That's my wife," I said, which was still technically true, but the fact that they were asking me about a bullshit credit card told me they didn't have much of a case against me.

As one hour turned to two and the worst-case scenario began to unfold in my imagination, one of the cops came and got me out of my cell.

"You're free to go."

The cop didn't say anything else. He just looked right through me.

I got out of there just in the nick of time. No trip to the Tombs for me. Instead, I went home and spent the weekend in my apartment getting extra high, like I deserved it. I felt somewhat validated that I'd been right about those undercover cops. They weren't figments of my imagination. Those fuckers were real.

I did have to go to court, though. The judge sent me to rehab. I guess getting busted ended up being a good thing after all. When I get myself in trouble, I can usually straighten up and fly right—at least for a little while.

* * *

We were on tour with the Psychedelic Furs when I got arrested at a tribal casino in Arizona. After the show, I wanted to smoke some weed, but we were all out, so I went into the crowd and bought pot with a painting I'd made. I guess "barter" is the more accurate word for the transaction. I was into making these weird little paintings—still am—and I used one as currency to buy pot from a fan at the show. I'd done this a few times before and it seemed like a great way to get high without having to pay for the drugs. I got like fifty dollars' worth of weed with my art, which seemed like a good deal for both parties.

You have to be careful with fans. Obviously, you can't be a dick, but you can't be too nice, either. They can get the wrong idea and expect stuff from you, which is annoying and strange. A fan will come up to me and say, "You should give me a T-shirt because I drove a long way to be here." What am I supposed to say to that? *I drove a long way to be here, too, so why don't you give me a T-shirt?*

I get odd requests from fans all the time. I always find it weird when people ask for things for free. Not friends, but fans. Like they want to be rewarded for their loyalty. It's hard for me to just give stuff away like that because I get emotionally attached to things, especially things I make, but sometimes I like to turn the tables on fans by offering them stuff they might want in exchange for what I need.

Like weed.

So the art-for-marijuana transaction worked out well. Me and my bass player and a friend of mine who was on tour with us were getting high in our hotel room bathroom and having a good old time. It had been a fun gig and we were feeling good. We were singing Nick Cave songs and blasting Black Sabbath and calling up friends on the phone. Our mistake was we'd left the door open.

This tribal security guy came into our room and got heavy with us about smoking weed in the hotel. He was weirdly judgmental about it. He said we needed to "act right" and all this other nonsense. As he was leaving, his demeanor changed and he seemed almost friendly.

"Don't worry," he said, "I'm not going to do anything. Just put it out."

Well, when someone with a badge tells you not to worry, you better start fucking worrying.

The guy totally lied to us, because he went straight to the Arizona police and brought them back to our room. The next thing I knew there were a dozen cops crowding around my bed, asking me all kinds of questions about drugs.

"Where did you get this?"

"Who sold it to you?"

And then, to each other, "Should we take him in?"

Fuck it, I thought, *I'm not going to remain silent.*

I told them about how the weed was a gift from a fan and that no money had changed hands, only art. Granted, that may have confused them, but I wasn't going to let me or my friends get arrested, and I wasn't letting them take me out of the room. I'd heard all about Maricopa County sheriff Joe Arpaio and his tent city jail and pervy policy of making his male inmates wear pink underwear to humiliate them. (I always wondered, do they give the women blue underwear?) I told the cops I'd take a ticket or a fine or a summons, but I wasn't going to put on the pink underwear over a couple of buds of weed.

We had to scrounge up $500 to avoid going to jail and my useless tour manager Rudy was nowhere to be found. I later found out he was in bed, ignoring my texts and phone calls because he didn't want to get involved with the Arizona cops, and I can't say I blame him.

I was explaining for the thousandth time how a fan had given me the weed in exchange for some art when the president of the casino came in and told everyone to clear out and let me sleep it off like I was on some kind of dangerous narcotic.

I thought I'd dodged a bullet, but I got a summons in the mail and had to go back to Maricopa County two more times. They called the three small buds of pot I'd bartered for a Class 6 felony. When all was said and done, I had to shell out $25,000 for legal and court fees. It was a total shakedown.

Good thing all I bought was pot. If it had been coke or dope I would have been in the pink underwear for sure.

* * *

If I could go back in time and give a bit of advice to myself, I'd say, "Evan, don't be such a dick." My biggest regret in life is not being more considerate to people. It's not that hard and it's a better way to be.

There were so many times when I was a dick for no good reason at all. Friends, family, total strangers. I wasn't trying to hurt anyone. I'm not someone who gets off on inflicting pain on others, but I would absolutely lose sight of the fact that other people have feelings, too. I hate that about myself.

The irony is that every time I act like an ass, I always feel bad about it later. I'm not blaming drugs or alcohol for my bad behavior, although that certainly plays a role, but afterward I have trouble moving on. I always beat myself up over it. I can't make myself not care.

I would never dismiss the validity of an experience—good or bad—simply because I was high. That's a hard concept to express without sounding like a spokesperson for getting high. "Hi, my name is Evan Dando and I like drugs." I caught so much shit for that in the nineties. I would talk freely about drugs, not because I was high, but because I was honest. I found that most interviewers assumed I was high anyway. Those who gave me the benefit of the doubt would ask me about the drug references in my songs. What a tiresome thing that became. Every fucking interview. Drugs, drugs, drugs. It followed me everywhere.

Now that marijuana is legal, people are going to forget what a big deal almost everyone made about weed. People used to be so heavy about drugs they declared war on them. I was just a young, sensitive kid who liked to get high. I didn't see the harm in it. I was into altered states, the whole acid thing, the potential to expand human consciousness. I was interested in all that stuff, but to say that I was just "intellectually curious" is a cop-out because I ended up a heroin addict. Obviously, there is some danger there. You have to be smart about it, or at least smarter than I was.

A lot of my drug issues stemmed from feeling out of control. Whether it was anxiety, nervousness, or depression, drugs were something that made the bad feelings go away. Even when my night terrors subsided in my twenties, I worried about them coming back. I was anxious all the time—except when I was high.

When I was younger, if I was feeling bad about myself, I'd lash out at the people around me. For instance, if I was bored, I would tell the people they were boring, which isn't nice. It's not that I was trying to create drama, but I would take things too far and be inconsiderate of other people's feelings. I was never calculating about it. I'd shoot my mouth off and then regret it later. *Why did I say that? What was I thinking?*

All my life I had this hippie positivity trip drilled into me by my parents. *Be here now. All you need is love. You can be whatever you want to be.* All that crap. I think that's part of what I was rebelling against. This mindless impulse to stay positive. After my parents' divorce, I didn't see the point in staying positive. I wanted to get fucked up and break things.

Nothing good ever comes from saying something negative about someone else, especially another musician. Of course, the press feeds into it and makes everything worse, especially if you've got a reputation for being candid, like I do. Early in my career—I think it was 1992—a reporter asked me, "What's the worst record of the year?"

"Live's *Mental Jewelry*," I said.

I didn't even think about it. I just picked a band that was wildly successful at the moment. I was punching up, so to speak, at a band who was enjoying a lot more success than the Lemonheads. It's not like my tossed-off opinion was going to hurt Live's album sales or anything like that. But in those early days as a major label artist, I was eager to show off my punk cred by being obnoxious.

In that moment I lost sight of the fact that those guys in Live are human beings who care about their art just like everyone else. When the band found out what I'd said, they were sad and angry. Of course, we ended up playing a small festival together at a college later that year and they confronted me about it.

"We really liked you," they said. They were really bummed by what I'd said about them, all because of some stupid interview.

What could I say, "I didn't mean it"? The only response to that is "Then why did you say it?" Now that I'm in my fifties, it's easy to say "It was a dumb, immature thing to do and I'm sorry."

Those words were a lot more elusive in my twenties.

It just doesn't pay to be negative about people, but especially other artists, because you will forget about the stupid shit you say, but they will remember it forever.

Another time a writer at *Melody Maker* asked me, "Who would you kill if you could?"

I said, "Bob Geldof, of course."

I meant it as a joke. Nothing against Bob Geldof—though I guess it's Sir Bob now, but he was a musician and a humanitarian and the face of Live Aid. Only a psychopath would want to kill Bob Geldof.

Turns out his wife at the time, Paula Yates, had a crush on me. Paula had a talk show called *The Big Breakfast*, where she interviewed people in a bed onstage. She had pictures of me up on the wall at home, and Bob would deface them while calling me a "fucking prick" because of my rude comments in *Melody Maker*. Paula told me all about it while we were in bed together on her TV program. Even though I never met the guy, we had this animosity between us. Bob didn't like me much, and I can't say I blame him. I'd be mad, too, if my wife was climbing into bed with someone who advocated for my death.

I've learned it doesn't cost anything to be polite, and you can ruin someone's day by being a jerk, so why not be polite all the time?

I find it's better to hold back from saying negative things to people, especially if I don't know them. That's my rule for living nowadays: don't be an asshole.

After I got signed to Atlantic, I'd actively antagonize bands I thought were lame. One time we played with Collective Soul, and when I found out they were a Christian rock band, I went satanic on them. I broke into their dressing room, found all these press photos, and wrote *666* on every one of them. Getting wasted and messing around in other people's dressing rooms was something I did a lot, like a childish version of Charlie's creepy-crawl tactic to unnerve people. It was like I was subconsciously acting out this deep-seated fear that I didn't belong in the company of these artists by committing petty acts of vandalism. I almost always got caught, and narrowly managed not to get beaten up by surly crew members on numerous occasions.

The closest I came to getting my ass kicked was at Reading. I was pissed off at Marilyn Manson for appropriating Manson's name. I felt proprietary about Charlie, which is stupid and childish and weird. "I was into Charlie first!" I was very drunk at that festival, which isn't good for my social skills.

I threw a banana at Marilyn Manson's tour bus. "Fuck you, Marilyn!" Right as I let the banana fly, the doors opened and the band emptied out of the bus. The banana smacked Marilyn Manson's tour manager right in the face. That guy went absolutely apeshit. He wanted to kill me. I had a friend who was friends with the band, and he smoothed things over for me. They ended up being very nice about it and I felt like a prick.

I don't want to be that annoying person who always causes trouble, but who am I kidding?

Deep down that's who I am. I have this almost perverse desire to be the reason that things don't go smoothly. The fly in the ointment.

* * *

A few years ago I pissed off a bunch of people at the Boston Music Awards when I was inducted into its hall of fame. I was supposed to get there early and do a long interview before the ceremony that would be filmed, but I didn't show up in time to make that happen. The organizers were pretty upset with me.

To be honest, I had mixed feelings about the whole thing. I think awards are basically scams. When you get nominated for an award, you're supposed to behave a certain way, and if you veer from the script they get annoyed because as soon as people stop caring about their award, they're out of business.

Awards aren't for the artists. They're for record companies, the organizations that give them out, and the journalists who write about them. It's a big feedback loop. The awards organization announces its nominees, the record companies act like it's a big deal, public relations teams push their contacts in the media for coverage, music critics write about the so-called winners and losers, and none of it has anything to do with art.

Then there's the whole question of what to do with the actual award if you get one. In 2008, *It's a Shame About Ray* received a Classic Album award—whatever that means—at the NME Awards in LA. It's basically a bronze statue of a middle finger. I threw it away the second I got offstage. I think someone dug it out of the trash, but I didn't want it. The episode was written about in the press as more evidence of "bizarre behavior from Evan Dando," but I guarantee that other artists aren't displaying those awards in trophy cases at home. They're just a bit more discreet about how they dispose of them.

The reason I was late for the Boston Music Awards, however, had nothing to do with a principled stance about awards shows. I was in New York waiting for someone to bring me heroin and it took longer than expected. It always takes longer than you think it will. That's the thing no one tells you: you spend more time getting the drugs than you do getting high. It's basically a full-time job.

I didn't mind the wait because I didn't want to sit down and do a long "This Is Your Life Evan Dando" type of interview. Even though some of these people had been covering my career since the beginning, something about it rubbed me the wrong way. I didn't want to feed the whole pro-Boston propaganda machine. Do we all work for the Boston Chamber of Commerce now? Can't the music speak for itself? Can't they give another award to Tom Scholz of the band Boston instead? Has anyone ever seen Tom Scholz and Black Flag's Greg Ginn in the same room at the same time? Are we absolutely certain they're not the same person?

In all seriousness, I just didn't want to do the interview, and when someone tries to make me do something I don't want to do—even if it's something I'd agreed to do—I push back in a not-very-nice way, and my "don't be an asshole" rule goes out the window.

The night wasn't a total disaster. We made it in time for the ceremony, so I didn't completely blow them off. They got wicked mad at me and it was very uncomfortable for a while. Then they gave me the award, which was kind of weird, but I played some songs afterward and it was cool. My dad came down and it was one of the last times he was able to see me perform before he got Parkinson's. After his diagnosis he wasn't able to get around that easily.

Of course, I lost the award almost immediately after they gave it to me. I have no idea where it is.

What I should have done was show up on time and be grateful. Instead, I got into a big fight with one of the organizers. It was all so stupid. They're probably still thinking, *Screw Evan Dando! Fuck that guy!* The worst thing about it is I still feel bad about it. After all these years it still bothers me.

It goes back to being polite because most of the people you're dealing with in these types of situations are just doing their jobs. Even if it's essentially meaningless, it's cool to get an award. They were just trying to do something nice for me and I reacted badly. I regret that. If I could do it over again I would, but what was it Gibby said about regret?

It's better to regret something you have done than to regret something you haven't done.

TAKE IT EASY

Here's something about Gibby I bet you didn't know: he once received a postcard in the mail from Samuel Beckett. The writer sent it off about a year before he died in 1989. This is what he had to say about the Butthole Surfers: "I don't like the music, but I'm very interested in the lyrics." A fucking fan letter from Samuel Beckett!

Gibby was there the last time I walked in my sleep. It was also one of my most violent episodes. I was living up on Tea Lane in Chilmark when Gibby and his wife, Melissa, came to visit me on the island. I gave Gibby my bedroom and moved into another room that was cluttered with junk.

I was sleeping on this silly little bed at a weird angle. It had been so long since I'd had a sleepwalking episode that I didn't give it too much thought. I should have known how triggering sleeping in a space like that can be. Over the years, I have figured a few things out. I need an open ceiling, the simpler the better, with nothing dangling down, like a light. A claustrophobic corner or something in my face is not good for me.

In the middle of the night, I got out of bed and put my hand through a window, shattering the glass. I think I was trying to walk through the window. Maybe I thought it was open or that I could step through it, like the kids in *Peter Pan*. I cut myself pretty badly, and when I came to there was blood everywhere. I went to my bedroom to wake up Gibby and show him what I'd done.

"That looks really bad," Gibby said.

"You should go to the hospital," Melissa added.

"Do we really need to?" I asked, even though the blood was dripping down my arm and getting all over the place.

"We don't," Melissa said, "but you do."

So Gibby drove me to the hospital. It was dark and foggy. One of those nights when it felt like we were the only people on the island.

"Thanks for driving me," I said.

"Well," Gibby said in that laconic way of his, "I wasn't doing anything."

On the way to the hospital, we saw this big black horse come galloping out of the fog. It was scary and beautiful. I looked over at Gibby and Gibby looked over at me. I think we both needed reassurance that the horse was real.

At the hospital they gave me something like twenty stitches. Thankfully the cuts weren't that deep and it didn't impact my guitar playing.

I don't know if sleepwalking is something you grow out of, but I haven't had an episode in years.

* * *

What's a bigger slacker move than making your fans wait ten years for a new record and dropping *another* album of covers? That's essentially what *Varshons II* is—the ultimate slacker album.

Varshons was always kind of an inside joke. With the Lemonheads' tenth studio album, I totally leaned into it. I know how it looks from the outside: You had ten years and all you can come up with is another record full of cover songs?

That's not how my brain works. I don't have anything to prove to anyone. People I've collaborated with know that I have a real passion for performing. A good song is a good song. Putting out *Varshons II* was a way to share some music I love and remind people that I was still alive.

I didn't ask Gibby to produce the album for a couple of reasons: I wanted to choose my own songs this time, and I wasn't sure he'd do it. We recorded it at Old Soul Studios in Catskill, New York. Some of the selections are no-brainers. There's a sweet little pocket of country-ish songs with John Prine's "Speed of the Sound of Loneliness" and Lucinda Williams's "Abandoned." I don't know what it says about me, but I love singing songs from the point of view of a scorned woman.

I finally covered one of the Bevis Frond's songs, "Old Man Blank," from the album Nic turned me on to all those years ago. I also got to meet Nick Saloman, and he played with the Lemonheads in London. Funny how the world works. A friend turns me on to an artist and the artist becomes a friend. I also did the songs "Things" by Paul Westerberg and "Straight to You" by Nick Cave and the Bad Seeds—two songwriters that were a big influence on me.

I closed out *Varshons II* with the Eagles' classic slacker anthem "Take It Easy." The song has become kind of a mantra for me these days. What better message is there for these troubled times when everyone is one smartass remark away from going berserk? We only get one trip on this great green world of ours, so we might as well take it easy.

I've been called a slacker all my life, but I'm actually pretty goal-oriented; it's just that things have a way of getting between me and my goals. I'm working on a new record—regardless of whether the world wants one or not. I've got a bunch of songs and have at least one more Lemonheads album in me. I'm not ready to spend the rest of my career playing anniversary shows. Once you get on the human jukebox circuit, it can be hard to get off.

*   *   *

Acting isn't all it's cracked up to be. I'm not that good at it and it's not that fun. I liked being in plays in high school. I thought I would do more of it, but once I got a sense of how tedious it is, I kind of lost interest.

Even though my acting career never took off, a few years ago I had a cameo on the show *The Goldbergs*. But the story of how I got to be on that show is stranger than anything the writers could have dreamt up.

Growing up I had these cousins down in Jenkintown, Pennsylvania, named Kremp. Four boys who all grew up together. There was a kid named Adam Goldberg who lived next door and he kind of idolized the Kremps. They were like a second family to him. When Goldberg grew up, he created a show about growing up in Pennsylvania during the 1980s, and a lot of it involved the Kremps. Some of the storylines on the show were about my cousins.

There's also a musical component to the show, and Goldberg's character is in a band called the Dropouts. The show licensed some of the Lemonheads' music and a couple songs have been on the show, which is pretty cool. Any time you can get your music on television it's a good thing.

Goldberg was at some of the family gatherings that I played at back in the day, and those memories are particularly vivid for him. The show doesn't have anything to do with me, but I'm connected to it all the same because of my relationship with my cousins. It's this weird, cool thing.

I was out in LA for the release of *Varshons II* and the producers of *The Goldbergs* had me come in for a cameo on the show. On the show, I'm kind of a derelict. I'm the guy known as Joey Wawa, who hangs out in the convenience store parking lot and buys six-packs of beer for minors.

"Five for you, one for me," he tells them. "That's the rule," which seems legit.

On the show, they had me audition for the Dropouts, and the guy who auditions after me plays one of my songs. So an actor plays a younger version of me while I play someone who hopefully isn't an older version of me.

I guess we'll have to see how that one shakes out.

*   *   *

I have one more Charlie Manson story.

In early 1995, I was Mia Kirshner's date to the Academy Awards. She'd been in the movie *Exotica* and her people flew me out to California first-class. I had all this ecstasy in my pocket and I was handing them out at the Oscars like candy.

I'm not sure how it happened, but after the ceremony we ended up sharing a limo with Quentin Tarantino. He'd just won an award for his screenplay for *Pulp Fiction* and he'd been nominated for best director. He was riding high and we went to a couple parties together. I wish I could remember what I talked about with Tarantino, but we talked a *lot*.

So fast-forward to 2019. I'm sitting in the theater watching *Once Upon a Time in Hollywood*. I was super excited to see Tarantino's take on the summer of 1969. Tarantino films have a strong moral sensibility. He puts the most despicable people in his movies—Nazis, slave owners, sadistic criminals—so that you don't feel bad about cheering on their death until it crosses the line into horror. Then he's got you.

I loved *Once Upon a Time in Hollywood*. I think it's Tarantino's best film—even better than *Pulp Fiction*. It's rare that someone with such a high profile in the arts progresses as their career goes on. I especially loved Brad Pitt's character, Cliff Booth, who was most certainly inspired by Shorty Shea. Everyone talks about how the movie is a tribute to Sharon Tate, and it is, but don't forget about Shorty Shea!

I'm sitting there in the theater, my mind blown, wondering where Tarantino is going to take this Manson Family fairy tale. Cliff is driving home and picks up a hitchhiker named Pussycat. Pussycat's character is based on Ruth Ann Moorehouse, a teenager that Charlie seduced after her father picked him up while hitchhiking and brought him home. All that Manson lore I read about as a teenager in *The Family* was coming back to me. And then I hear it. The opening notes to "Mrs. Robinson," which have been seared into my brain forever, fill the theater.

Doo doo doo doo doo . . .

It was a schizophrenic moment for me. Right as I'm getting into the story, Simon & Garfunkel ripped me right out of it. It felt like Tarantino was sitting behind me in the theater and tapping me on the shoulder.

"Sorry, Evan, don't get too comfortable in my movie . . ."

* * *

It's no secret that I don't love "Mrs. Robinson." As I've said, I never liked having the song on *It's a Shame About Ray*. We never took that song seriously. Because it was forced on us, I hated playing it at shows. Fans always asked for it, and if I didn't play it, I was an asshole for not playing the song that brought so much attention to the Lemonheads. To say I have a complicated relationship with the song would be an understatement.

The song has been on a bunch of movie soundtracks over the years, including *Wayne's World 2* in 1993, *The Other Sister* in 1999, and *The Wolf of Wall Street* in 2013, which has made it even more popular with casual music fans. The song just refuses to go away. For many years, it felt like an albatross around my neck.

But when Scorsese put the song in his movie, my feelings about it began to change. As much as that song doesn't belong on *It's a Shame About Ray*, it absolutely belongs in *The Wolf of Wall Street*. It's the perfect place for that sleazy little number. If anyone should know, it's Scorsese. I'm not going to second-guess him. If Scorsese says its good enough for one of his movies, then it's good enough for me.

What's funny is I didn't even find out about it until after the movie came out and people were telling me about it.

"Your song is in the new Scorsese film!"

I think my manager, who knew how I felt about the song, was afraid to tell me. *Just put the money in the bank and don't tell Evan . . .*

The funny thing is I'm actually enjoying playing the song for the first time in my career. I think it's because we didn't rehearse it to death. We played it with the intensity of a punk song. When I hear our version of "Mrs. Robinson" now, there's a freshness there that's pretty cool.

The history of rock and roll is littered with songs that the bands who wrote them thought were trash. The Rolling Stones thought "(I Can't Get No) Satisfaction" was a throwaway and it became the band's breakout hit, the song that changed everything. I think it happens more than people realize. The song that's meant to be a hit fizzles, while the throwaway becomes a classic. I'm not saying that our cover of "Mrs. Robinson" is a classic—it's not even our song—but we're linked to the song and probably always will be. I'm okay with that. Its success used to irk me, but doesn't anymore. I'm finally at peace with "Mrs. Robinson."

For what it's worth, I've heard that Art Garfunkel likes our cover, but Paul Simon hates it. I used to agree with Paul, but he can suck it.

MEMOIRS OF A GRUNGE RELIC

In 2013, I moved to Martha's Vineyard to get clean. I wasn't a city person, but I felt like I had to be in New York for my career. That hadn't been true for a long time. The real reason I stayed in New York for as long as I did was the easy access to drugs. It was that simple.

I loved being back on the island. The best place to take in the sunset on Martha's Vineyard is the beach at Aquinnah on the southwestern corner of the island. The end of an island is a good place for a new beginning. Back when I first started going out there it was called Gay Head, but the old names given to the land by the Wampanoag have been rightfully restored.

It's stunning out there. The clay cliffs at the end of the promontory look bloodred when the sun hits them. The legend goes that a giant rose out of the sea and swung a whale by the tail, smashing it against the cliffs and getting blood all over the rocks, giving them their distinctive reddish color.

We love our whale tales in New England. The first European expedition to Cape Cod was led by Bartholomew Gosnold. He helped colonize Virginia and was a privateer, which is basically a pirate who works for the government. Nice work if you can get it.

Gosnold had a daughter named Martha, who was named after old Bart's mother-in-law. The island was likely named after one of these two women, but I like that no one really knows for sure.

The island has about a half dozen communities that fall into one of two categories: up-island and down-island. Down-island consists of Edgartown, Oak Bluffs, and Tisbury. This doesn't make sense if you look at Martha's Vineyard on a map because these down-island communities are all on top of the island—in other words on the north side of the island, across from Cape Cod.

The distinction between up-island and down-island has a class element as well. People from the island will tell you that up-island is nicer and more exclusive. Aquinnah, Chilmark, Menemsha, and West Tisbury are all up-island, meaning the southern side. The communities down-island cater to the tourists who come to the island. That's where you'll find the bicycle rentals, T-shirt shops, and ice cream parlors. The island economy runs on tourist dollars, but the folks with million-dollar mansions up-island are isolated from all that. All the ferry terminals are located down-island, and the one that remains open all year long is in Vineyard Haven—which is just down the street from where I used to live in my trailer in the woods.

Regardless of your address here, the population is divided into three types of people: natives, washashores, and tourists. The natives were born here, and they never let you forget it. Washashores are people who drifted in from somewhere else, but live on the island year-round. The natives treat washashores like something that just got spat out of the sea. You can live here for forty years, like my father, and you'll never be more than a washashore. Tourists are just passing through. To be considered a washashore, you have to put down roots, which I was never able to do.

RUMORS OF MY DEMISE

Every time I got close to reaching washashore status, I left to go on tour for a few months, and when I came back, I was a tourist all over again.

When I first started coming to Martha's Vineyard to spend time with my dad, we struggled to reconnect. Although he was a constant presence in my life, we didn't know each other anymore. We bonded by fishing, which was something he liked to do. One thing my dad excelled at was having a good time. He'd get a case of beer and take me and Holly up to Lobsterville in Aquinnah on the Vineyard Sound. The beaches are a bit rocky and it's not on the open ocean, so it isn't as popular with tourists. We'd have the whole beach to ourselves. Or we'd go to a place called Squibnocket on the south side of the island.

"Squibnocket until you try it, Griff."

That joke never got old.

My dad took me to all his favorite fishing spots on Martha's Vineyard—Menemsha, Philbin Beach, Tashmoo. We didn't have a boat, but you don't need one on the island. We'd go out in the morning or the early evening and fish right from the shore.

I loved fishing and I was pretty good at it. When I was fifteen, I entered a fishing derby and won the junior prize for catching the second-biggest false albacore, which is a type of tuna you find in the waters around the island. They gave me a Bulova clock, which seems like a weird prize for a fishing competition. I hit my peak as a competitive fisherman early, because I never entered another derby.

As far as I know they haven't made it illegal to jump off the bridge between Vineyard Haven and Oak Bluffs. I used to love jumping off that bridge. I'd park my lobster-bisque-colored truck on the shore, walk to the middle of the bridge, and jump. I usually waited until there was no one around, but occasionally I'd give the ladies driving by in their Mercedes something to think about as I jumped into the water.

Sometimes when I was done fishing for the day, I'd strip down to my underwear for a quick swim. The water was so clean and clear that in some places you could see right through to the bottom. I went into the water most months of the year. I didn't care how cold it was. I loved how warm it felt in September, but I also liked the winter months: the cold, wet weather, the bracing wind. There's nothing like it. Better than any drug.

When I was a kid, I wanted to be an oceanographer. I don't think I knew what an oceanographer did, but the idea of being alone at the bottom of the sea was appealing to me. Gimme a one-way ticket to the octopus's garden, please.

*   *   *

It's a terrible thing to lose a guitar, but it happened to me all the time on the island. "Lose" is probably too strong a word. Nothing stayed lost out on Martha's Vineyard for long. Things had a way of eluding me, but they eventually found their way back.

I've been a guitar buyer all my life. Even when I was waiting tables and broke most of the time, I bought myself a nice guitar, a Gibson 220. It was an old learner guitar, but a nice one. I had that guitar for a good long time and left it in a taxi in Sydney. I was chatting with Elizabeth about how much it cost to put a new pickup in the Gibson and we left it behind. We were actually talking *about* the guitar, and somehow I managed to forget it.

If you're going to leave a guitar in a taxi, I suggest you do it in Madrid. The cabdrivers pride themselves on always returning the items that people leave in their cabs. I've left guitars in Madrid before, and they always find their way back to me.

I lost a guitar when a friend overdosed. He was in a band called Sorry. This was back in 1995. I left a nice Heritage guitar over at his apartment. When I heard that he'd overdosed I felt as though the guitar went with him. I wasn't going to call the family and ask for it back.

"I'm sorry for your loss, but there's a guitar involved . . ."

You just don't do that.

I had a bunch of guitars scattered around the island with more in storage and it could be difficult keeping track of them all. I'm not a hoarder—although you might think otherwise if you'd seen some of the places I've lived. I get attached to things, but I'm not sentimental about my mess. Stuff has a way of piling up—especially when you're reluctant to let it go—and sometimes I don't have a way to get rid of it all. If you try to help a hoarder clean up, they'll be like, "Don't touch that!" or "I might need that someday!" I'm not like that. I'll take all the help I can get.

Hanging out with Tiffany got me into the habit of keeping my eyes open for things that others had cast aside—especially on Martha's Vineyard. It was almost a crime to let them go to waste. We called the town dump the free store. The dumptique. You could find all kinds of valuable things at the dumptique, from expensive furniture to Brooks Brothers suits. The trickle-down economy worked on the island.

When *It's a Shame About Ray* and *Come on Feel the Lemonheads* achieved gold record status, the label had a bunch of plaques made in honor of the occasion. It's an important milestone. A gold record ensures that you get to keep making records for the label. Stop making gold records and you won't be on the label for long. I couldn't tell you where any of those gold records are today. I had one that I gave to my sister hanging in our rehearsal space out on the island, but I have no idea how it got there.

Not too long ago I lost a nice 1959 Gibson J-50. I think those are the best. I thought it had been stolen, but it turned out I left it outside. I was at the construction site where they were putting up a new residence on the spot where I destroyed that cottage in Aquinnah and I went to go see it. I was so overwhelmed by the strangeness of the situation that I left my guitar on the roof of the building site without realizing it. Then, when I couldn't find the guitar, I assumed it had been stolen.

A month later my friend found my missing Gibson at the site. It was the middle of winter, so the guitar had been snowed on and rained on and was in terrible shape. I'm still sad about it because it was my favorite guitar. First I destroyed the house, then I destroyed the guitar. Cease to exist and all that.

I try not to get too obsessive about my guitars, but I hate to see them go. Some are definitely better than others, but they're more than just tools of the trade. I especially like the old ones from the fifties. I try not to get too attached to them, but it's hard. Some of the best moments of my life have been with a guitar in my hand, sharing songs with people I love.

* * *

There was a time not that long ago when I couldn't imagine living anywhere else, but living on Martha's Vineyard has plenty of drawbacks. It's impossible to be anonymous. It's a gossipy place, which got on my nerves. Everyone knew who I was, but everyone knew everyone out there. Who I used to be didn't carry much weight. In that regard, I was no different from anyone else.

There are lots of rich people on the island, but most of them have been there a long time. It's expensive, but not over the top like the Hamptons. Not even close. There's hardly any crime and no one locks their doors. If someone rips you off, where are they going to go? Who are they going to sell it to?

It was a little too easy to lose track of things. Time, space, reality. It was quiet—sometimes a little too quiet—especially during the off-season, when time moved slower and the mainland felt farther away. I used to hop on my board and skate around the island at night. I'd think about the past, the people I'd played with, the places I'd been. I'd think about my favorite songs to play and why they matter to me. The older we get, the more the edges blur.

It's harder to stay clean in some places than others. I tend to blend in with my surroundings. When I was young, if I was hanging out with someone who was getting high, I'd get high, too. Whatever they were into, I'd be into it as well. I'd slip into their life and see what it was like. Sydney started out as a speed city because of the people I was hanging out with, but it was not my drug of choice. The way I'm wired, I'd rather mellow out than get amped up.

Eventually, Sydney turned into a heroin city. All cities are heroin cities now. Even Falmouth. That's the problem with cities. The drugs are everywhere. The bigger the city, the worse it is. In Manhattan, if you have enough money, all it takes is a phone call and you can have someone at your door in less than an hour with a laminated drug menu and anything you need.

The hardest place to stay clean is on tour. Temptation follows me on the road. I'll still have the odd drink. I like to smoke pot. I don't know if being completely sober is something I ever want to be. I'm just trying to stay away from heroin and the stuff that leads to heroin, like crack. Those are off the table, but keeping them off has been a struggle.

It's been said before, but cocaine is a terrible drug. If you do too much coke, you need a little heroin to hit the pillow and land somewhere. That was the pattern that got me in the end. First the coke, then the heroin, a balancing act that never ends. That's why cocaine is a dealer's best friend—all it does is make you want more. More booze, more pills, and more coke.

The horror of heroin is well-documented. Before I took my first hit, I knew how hard it was to kick. That doesn't mean I knew what I was getting into—I don't think anyone does—but thanks to junkie lit, I knew all about the sleazy side of the lifestyle, the relentless need and constant fear of arrest that heroin addicts face on a daily basis.

No one talks about how often you get burned. Addicts deal with the sketchiest people imaginable and it's so easy to get ripped off, especially on the road. If you travel with drugs you put the whole touring operation in jeopardy, so the dealers have you over a barrel. They rip you off and they're not even subtle about it.

You roll into town and maybe you know someone or have an idea of where to score, but if you don't, what do you do? You get in a cab and tell the driver to take you to the worst part of town.

"Can you take me to where the lowlifes hang out? That's where I want to go."

That's a bad way to go through life. The compulsion is horrible. It's satanic. Doing heroin is like a deal with the devil: you can get what you want, but you always pay a price.

Addiction teaches you things about yourself that you'd prefer not to know. It makes you more selfish. Everything becomes secondary to the drug. When I see a photograph of myself high on heroin I look . . . wrong. Others might not see it, but I'll recognize it right away. I've got a glaze over me. I look damaged, diminished. I think heroin destroys your soul.

RUMORS OF MY DEMISE

Plus, it's dangerous. Before I quit for good, I was in the Hollywood Hills at the home of a famous actor who was married to an even more famous actor. I went to his house to watch some movies in his home theater. I had some heroin and I left it out. He asked if he could have some. I was in the next room and without thinking about it, I said, "Go for it." He thought it was coke and snorted a big line. He slumped to the floor and was completely out. We had to call an ambulance, and thankfully they were able to bring him back, but I almost killed the guy. I probably would have gone to jail.

I don't want that in my life anymore, which is why I had to leave Martha's Vineyard and start over in another hemisphere.

*   *   *

No one expected the Lemonheads to get as big as we did. We were just dumb kids getting off on making noise, but all these unexpected things kept happening. Our first show at the Rat was incredible. Our London debut was an event. We were legitimately popular over there. The Lemonheads were on *Top of the Pops* four times. Our faces were on the sides of buses. We were regulars at Glastonbury and Reading and on TV all the time. *Come on Feel the Lemonheads* came in at number five in the UK.

Our expectations were low. The gulf between what we thought was going to happen and what actually happened was huge. It was a slow climb up the ladder rather than this meteoric rush, like what happened with Nirvana, but when the opportunity to make a little money and have a lot of fun was presented to us, we went for it. That lasted longer than anyone expected and just kept getting bigger and bigger and bigger.

Did we know we were going to be famous?

No. That answer never changed, but people kept asking us. I think that's because the gap between how we were depicted and what the band was actually like was pretty significant. Even some of our fans bought into our "image," the cover boy bullshit.

We never got all the way to the top. When people talk about us, if they talk about us at all, they always mention us in terms of Nirvana and Pearl Jam, even though we didn't sound like either band or were nowhere as big. We were lucky enough to breathe a few gulps of that rarefied air and think, *So this is what it's like at the top*, before drifting back down to earth. After *Car Button Cloth* came out in 1996 and Atlantic dropped us, I don't think I ever became bitter. But success has never tasted as sweet as it did the first time around.

The funny thing is I never wanted to be famous. In my own way I always kind of was. I had an exceptional childhood. Most kids didn't have long blond hair. Most kids didn't have a mom who was a model. Most kids didn't run off every other summer to go surfing in France. That was all kind of exotic for a kid from Boston and was its own type of celebrity.

At the end of the day, I think fame is about luck, and the Lemonheads were very lucky. It's tempting to look at my career as a progression—from punk rock kid bashing away on a drum kit to an indie rock singer-songwriter strumming on a guitar. But to me it seems like a series of happy accidents.

Then there's the dark side of celebrity. People mobbing hotel lobbies and surrounding tour buses. Groupies popping up at the most inappropriate times. When the Lemonheads were kind of a big deal in England there were so many people trying to get to us: reporters, fans, shakedown artists, weirdos. There were people whose only job was to keep them away from us. Anytime we were getting ready to perform we'd have to hide out in little rooms. We could hear them through the walls, trying to find us. *Where are they? Where are the Lemonheads?*

There was nothing we could say or do or be that would be enough for them. They wanted more. It was all so strange and disorienting. No one knows what they're getting into when a record becomes popular, even though the pitfalls are well-known. Still, it's a surprise when things get ugly and the people who sang your praises on the way up become the enemy on the way down.

I think I was different from a lot of people because I tried to make the most of the rock star thing. I told myself that if I was going to be a rock star, I wasn't going to let it become my job. I would be true to myself and enjoy it to the fullest. And because I was in my early twenties, being true to myself meant doing lots of drugs and partying all the time. Everyone did it, but you were supposed to act like you didn't.

Well, I didn't get that memo. I took the opposite approach and tried to have fun. Did I cross the line a few times?

Maybe I treated fame like a game, like a big experiment. What are you supposed to do when you're being interviewed by the English press and they're asking all these rude questions and calling you names like Dippy Dando?

It got to a point where it didn't matter what I said, they were going to write what they wanted to write. That was a dangerous realization, because I had to say *something*.

The press was always trying to paint me as this weird throwback to the sixties or something. I just let them go with it. It was all kind of funny at first, but then became less so as what people wrote about me took on a life of its own. It didn't matter if I paid attention to it or not, because the rest of the media did and they'd construct this narrative around me. The end result was that no one took us seriously.

I knew from helping out with those early Taang! mailings that any coverage, good or bad, could help get you on the radio. I'm just glad our moment in the sun came and went before the internet turned everything completely toxic. My advice to songwriters today is simple: Don't share personal details with the press. Keep that shit under wraps and save it for your art. The people who are paying attention will get it.

It's no longer uncommon for people to be famous for being famous, but I think all fame is like that. Fame brought me into the orbit of all kinds of people I never would have met otherwise. I got to play with just about every musician I ever loved. I got to play with Iggy Pop, and he gave me some career advice.

"Be careful. I was stabbed twice out there."

Good to know.

I got to know one of my earliest heroes, Jonathan Richman, because his wife was a big Lemonheads fan. I met Jonathan one evening in San Francisco and he invited me to come see him in New York. I brought my mom, who is also a fan, and he played songs for us all night, anything we wanted to hear. Do you think Jonathan Richman would have serenaded my mother if the Lemonheads weren't "famous"?

Probably maybe.

I'm not famous anymore, but the elder-statesman era of the Lemonheads has been good for us. We have opportunities to go on the road and play for our fans. We've had some rough spots along the way—sorry, Jawbreaker—but I still enjoy touring because I love to play music. There's nothing better than jamming with some friends. It's kind of egotistical to say that you don't have a big ego, but I don't know many singer-songwriters from my era who will fill in on drums when their friends go on tour, which I did a few years ago with the Frogs.

People are surprised when they realize how many records the Lemonheads have put out, how many songs we've written. That's what happens when your most popular song is a cover.

Every time we turned around, Taang! was pressing up a new version of one of our records in a different color. Then, when CDs caught on, Curtis slapped our first two records together and sold it as *Create Your Friends*.

There's an old saying in Hollywood: the person who gives you your first big break is entitled to rip you off.

I don't care how the music gets out there, whether it's a corporation or someone in their basement. As long as people can hear the music, I'm happy. If someone else comes along who can do a better job, sign me up. You can call me a sellout, you can call me a fool, but at least I'm not a hypocrite.

* * *

I never learned how to play a piano properly. I can play a little bit, but I don't know what I'm doing. I always thought it would be cool to learn how to play the violin, but I don't have the finesse for that. It's just too hard to push through the noise. Every time I try to play the violin I just want to stop.

I don't know how to read music, either. I learned the basics a long time ago, but I let it go. I was never able to read music and play at the same time; that was always beyond me. I mostly played by ear and from memory, just feeling my way around the guitar. When I first started writing songs in the eighties I used tapes, and that's still what I prefer to use today. I don't like using my phone or any digital device because it picks up every horrible noise and the recording sounds slushy. Plus, it's a lot easier to lose a phone than a tape recorder. I've lost as many phones as I have guitars. Probably more.

A tape is finite. You have a limited amount of space to work with. I like the constraint of a cassette. Tapes are fragile. They're so easily damaged. You have to take care of them. When someone gives you a tape to listen to, what do you do with it? You put it in your breast pocket, close to your heart. I think cassette tapes are one of the few things my generation got right.

When I'm sitting at home and I want to record something, I use a Sony 5000 tape recorder. They have two heads and aren't too big. They're portable and have a leather carrying case that's handy for when I'm traveling.

I love listening to old tapes I've made of jam sessions, parties, or just hanging out with my friends. Digital is disposable, but a tape is a document.

I've never stopped playing the drums—just ask my neighbors. Drumming remains an integral part of my songwriting process. I'll write down the drum parts to a song to provide a little guidance for where I want the song to go. If the song is going to go places, the beat has to be right.

I play on a vintage sixties drum kit that used to be owned by the late, great Charlie Watts. He gave it to Marlon on his tenth birthday and Marlon gave it to me. I've had it for about fifteen years, maybe more. I'm supposed to give it back at some point, but I don't want to. I like having the heartbeat of the Rolling Stones close to me.

Once I lock into something I like I'll record it. Then I'll play along to the tape and just feel things out, see where it wants to go, discover what's out there. Maybe a melody will come out of it or even a bass line. I'll start singing, and something like the skeleton of a song will emerge.

It's like fishing. Most of the time you're fiddling with your gear, casting out your line and reeling it back in, but every so often you get something. You feel a slight tug and the next thing you know you're wrestling this big wriggling fish out of the water.

I think a lot of songwriting comes from curiosity. How did I do that? Where did it come from? Have I heard this before? Where can I take it?

When I'm playing fanatically, I start to make up my own sounds on the guitar. That's another way a song might start for me. I make up chords, and something will register.

This feels like something . . .

Every guitar is different. Where you put your hands is often dictated by the shape and even the structure of the instrument, how wide the neck is, where your hands feel comfortable. That's why it can seem like the guitar is writing the song, because your hands want to go to different places on different pieces.

The lyrics are almost always the final piece of the puzzle. For me, they usually come after I've got the riff. Lyrics provide a song with its final shape. They give the song a place to go. Don't ask me where lyrics come from because I don't know. No one does. Sometimes all you need is a good title and you're off. That's what my friend Dan Treacy of Television Personalities used to say.

One of my earliest songs was called "Deep Bottom Cove." It's about two boys who go out on a boat on a beautiful summer morning and drown in the ocean, but I had no idea that's what I was writing about when the song came to me.

There are no hard-and-fast rules to any of this. The first song that I wrote on my own was about something that happened to me, so the lyrics came first. Because the idea for the song came out of a very specific feeling, I had the words before I had anything else. I had this riff I'd been kicking around and I slapped the words and the lyrics together and it worked. You just put the pieces together and do your best.

I'm probably the worst person to give songwriting advice because my songs are kind of unconventional. I'm notoriously ambivalent about choruses. But I do know this: the songs that take a long time to write are never as good as those that come out all at once.

I've benefited from having some great collaborators. The most important aspect of collaboration is desire. If you're unsure about working with someone or go into it half-heartedly, it's not going to work. But when you find someone you click with, it's magic. That doesn't happen very often.

The biggest obstacle to a good collaboration is time. It's like any relationship. You're going to have ups and downs with varying degrees of intensity. You may go through a phase when you hit it off with someone, but inevitably you're going to fall out of it. It's not anyone's fault. That's just the way it goes.

In my experience, it's hard to find somebody to collaborate with. For instance, Juliana and I click musically, even though personality-wise we aren't a match. Once you get that spark, you've got to ride it out for as long as you can because it can end abruptly. Those moments don't last and—like so many things—you don't realize what you have until it's gone.

Also, no one knows how to write a song. Here's another fishing analogy. If you sit around with a fishing pole long enough, you will eventually catch something. Same with songwriting. It doesn't come from you. It comes from somewhere else. You just have to open up the shop and be there for it. You hope to catch a fish every time you cast your line, but only a fool expects to. If you can apply that mentality to songwriting, you'll spare yourself plenty of heartache.

I think anyone can write a song. As Lou Barlow says, "It's not magic." He says that if you hang around other songwriters, eventually you will write songs just from seeing it done. I believe that's true. Songs don't emerge fully formed any more than paintings, novels, or films do. It takes time to gather all the pieces. Then it's a matter of putting them together in the right way. Watching that process demystifies it, but it's still a process, a series of events that takes place over time.

I think everyone has that creative spark inside them, but most people don't seek it out or expand their enjoyment of it. They don't look to the past to experience the things that others have created. They don't look at paintings. They don't read books. There's so much great art literally at our fingertips.

The beautiful thing about art is you don't have to be any good at making it to enjoy it. You can just go for it. There's value in your limitations. Look at Lou Reed and the rest of the musicians in the Velvet Underground—they didn't know what they were doing, but that didn't stop them from making something new. The Stooges are another good example. There was nothing complicated about what they were trying to do, but they came at it fresh and pure—simplicity being a virtue and all that. How many bands followed the Stooges' example? How much great art did they inspire?

Just understanding the parts and knowing how they fit together is 90 percent of songwriting. There's more to it than that, of course. You have to want to do it. No one writes a song by accident. You have to seek it out. Most people go their whole lives without feeling the urge to write a song. That inclination is rare, and if you have it, you should pursue it.

EVAN DANDO

A lot of songwriters try to make the process sound more mysterious than it is by refusing to talk about it. I don't go along with that. I love it when songwriters open up about their process, but more often than not they'll steer conversations away from the actual writing of songs. "Oh, you want to talk about *that*?" they'll say, as if you've brought up an unpleasant memory or a bad experience.

I think wherever songs come from, whatever that place is, it's closer than you think. You can access it all kinds of ways: dreaming, reading, taking drugs, staying up late, being alone, immersing yourself in beauty. How many songs have been inspired by a glance from someone that gets your motor running?

There will always be something ineffable about it. I think that's cool. That kind of mystery is interesting to me and always will be. I like people who keep their antenna up, alert for inspiration—even if it comes from an altered state.

My parents were passionate about music and my dad had an inclination to play. It was only a matter of time before I picked up a guitar. I never saw him play the drums, but when I sat down behind the kit it felt natural to me.

Sometimes before shows I'll take my guitar and play a couple songs for the people lined up outside. The point isn't to draw a crowd. The point is to connect with some fans on a very real level. No bullshit. Just play my songs for a few people who don't care what I look like or what I'm wearing. These impromptu performances help me remember why I'm doing what I'm doing.

I love making music. Once I've got some songs that are ready to go, the next step is to get into a studio environment and make some demos. That part can be a challenge for me. Not the recording itself, but the logistics: booking the room, getting the players, showing up on time. I'm essentially the same person I was at Commonwealth:

I love the creativity, but once it starts to feel like homework, my brain turns on me.

For a long time the demo tapes for the *It's a Shame About Ray* sessions were lost. They were just gone. It was a great moment when I found someone in New York who had a copy. The demos were a revelation. They were so simple. Just acoustic 4-track recordings that I did with Juliana in Allston after I got back from Australia.

There's one song where she comes in to sing backup. You can hear the door slam as she enters the studio, but she doesn't miss her mark, she gets the vocal in right on time. It's a funny moment I'll always remember and it's there on tape. If the demo was done on Pro Tools they would have edited it out like it never happened, but I keep that memory close to my heart.

That demo is part of the thirtieth anniversary reissue of *It's a Shame About Ray*, which I'm happy about because it was one of those rare moments when I knew we'd landed something special.

EPILOGUE

This is not a redemption story.

Addicts don't get better. They're either using or they aren't. That's it. There's no middle ground. Nothing gets easier. There's always another tour. Winter always comes. Life is full of struggles. But the thing that drives me, more than the feeling of pushing off on my skateboard or reeling in a big fish, is music.

Making it. Listening to it. Playing it for other people. It's a blessing and a privilege. At this stage of my career, I can appreciate how rare it is to put out a gold record, and rarer even still that all these years later people still want to hear those songs. I am grateful for that because I like playing them. Whether it's a Lemonheads song or someone else's, I love playing music for people.

I've spent my entire life asking myself, "Why not?" Why not turn the Lemonheads into a collective? Why not make a record with Gibby? Why not put out a record with nothing but cover songs? Why not do it again ten years later?

When you ask yourself "Why?" it can shut you down real quick. It puts you in the fast lane to second-guessing yourself because now you have to justify your decisions. Why write a song?

EPILOGUE

I'm not sure anyone knows the answer to that question, but the question "Why *not* write a song?" is an invitation to pick up a guitar. Suddenly, instead of thinking about it, I'm doing it.

I know I can't escape my past. I've turned into the grunge relic I was always afraid I'd become, but playing music never gets old and I'll never stop doing it. Whether it's writing a new song, playing an old one, or bashing out a beat on Charlie Watts's drum kit I still haven't gotten around to returning, I'm happiest when I'm playing.

Getting off of drugs allows me to reconnect with the things I'm passionate about. The way reading a good book makes me feel. Spending time with people I care about, like my mom and sister. Making music. Those connections are so important.

They're everything.

I've still got problems I haven't solved. Issues with my family. Issues with myself. Thankfully, I don't sleepwalk anymore. I made it through that period relatively unscathed.

Everything I've ever wished for has come true, which makes me one of the luckiest people alive. I'm still living that dream, even if the dream isn't always what it's cracked up to be. I'm no more or less anxious about the world or my place in it than when I was a kid, but I sleep easier now because I'm more at peace with myself. Music comforted me as a kid when my parents got divorced and continues to do so today. All I have to do is put on a record and there it is.

I'm moving on, looking ahead. I left Martha's Vineyard after my father passed away. The night after he died, I drove out to Black Point Beach with my girlfriend Antonia. I had a light saltwater rod with a ten-pound test and tied on a Boone needlefish jig. Black Point

EPILOGUE

isn't a fishing spot—it's a place to bask and chill—but I always bring a rod. On the fifth cast I started getting bored, and as I slowed my retrieve to a little faster than a second hand, the way my dad taught me, I said out loud, "Is this right, Pop?"

Sure enough a fish slammed my lure.

I shouted, "God, the Holy Spirit, and Jesus H. Christ!"—just like my dad.

Godspeed.

Sometime after that, I had to fly out to LA to play a gig for some folks who had given me $300,000 for a percentage of my publishing. It was at a cemetery, but I don't remember playing. Massive amounts of edibles on top of my usual speedball jag fucked me good and proper. Thank goodness Antonia filmed it so I could watch myself giggling through songs, forgetting the lyrics, stopping in the middle. That was what convinced me to go to rehab. This time because I wanted to.

Now I'm making a new life for myself in Brazil with Antonia. We're thinking about buying a house together down here and I'm making new music. There are still plenty of things that don't go my way, but I get through them. Something happens that shakes me up and makes me take a closer look at life. I've been through plenty of fucked-up situations, but I'm still here. It's easy to blame other people for stuff that happens, but at the end of the day it's up to me to make the best of it.

I'm not that different from how I was when I was a teenager, but I'm not as impulsive as I used to be. I sit with things. I reflect. I still do all the things I used to do: play music, write songs, get high, go fishing. I may have traded hemispheres, but wherever I go you'll find me playing guitar or cruising around on my skateboard,

EPILOGUE

taking it easy. Maybe that makes me out of step with the rest of the world, but I've always found that a comfortable place to be. I'm a foreigner from Boston on a journey through Kansas. It's a rush.

—Evan Griffith Dando
São Paulo, Brazil
May 2025

ABOUT THE AUTHOR

Evan Dando is a singer and songwriter who has been the front man for the alt-rock band the Lemonheads since 1986. He currently resides in South America when he's not on tour.

D.O.A.
LEMONHEADS

WITH

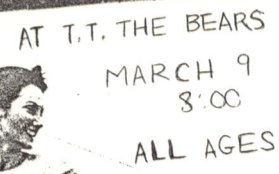

AT T.T. THE BEARS
MARCH 9
8:00
ALL AGES

G.T.O.

WHRB BENEFIT!
Cleveland's **PAGANS**
LEMONHEADS
BULLET LAVOLTA
TT'S—SUNDAY
10 MAY 2 PM
ALL AGES